YESTERDAY:
A HISTORICAL VIEW
OF OAK PARK, ILLINOIS

Vol. I Prairie Days to World War I

by

Jean Guarino

ISBN 0-9703661 – 0 – 8

Library of Congress Control Number 00 – 092165

Copyright 2000 by Jean Guarino

Published by Oak Ridge Press
          1004 N. Oak Park Ave.
          Oak Park, IL 60302

Printed by Offset Press, Inc.
          Oak Park, Illinois 60302

Typography by J. Alan White Inc.
          Oak Park, Illinois 60304

All photographs in this book, unless otherwise noted, are from the archives of The Historical Society of Oak Park & River Forest, which retains the copyright to its images.

To avoid confusion the reader should be aware that Oak Park had several earlier names including Kettlestrings Grove and Oak Ridge. Also, both Forest Park and River Forest were known as Harlem prior to 1880.

In listing specific addresses on east-west streets I have adhered to an earlier numbering system that was used until about 1915. Under this system the street numbers ran east from Harlem Avenue to Austin Blvd. For example, the Steiner building located on the northeast corner of Harlem Avenue and Lake Street at what today is 1144 Lake Street, was originally 101 Lake Street. This system was later reversed to run in the opposite direction, going east from Austin Blvd. west to Harlem Avenue.

Also, numbering on north-south streets has changed through the years, varying a block or two over time. For instance, the original address of the Ernest Hemingway birthplace home was 439 N. Oak Park Avenue. The current address is 339 N. Oak Park. Whenever possible, I have included old and new addresses to assist readers in understanding locations referred to in the text.

Community Bank of Oak Park River Forest is proud to underwrite this insightful and comprehensive work by Jean Guarino. It is the first of two volumes that will document the rich and varied history of our Village and its residents.

Community Bank's mission is to direct its resources to help improve the quality of where we do business. Our support of this publication reflects the Bank's continuing effort to sponsor local projects that enhance the understanding and growth of our community and the people that reside here.

We hope you enjoy reading about Oak Park, its families and the fabric of life they have created for all who live and work here.

Sincerely,

Martin J. Noll

President

PREFACE

Shortly after my first book, *Oak Park: A Pictorial History,* was published in 1988 Carol Goddard, then editor of the *Oak Leaves,* suggested that I write a biweekly history column for Pioneer Press. Although neither of us was aware of it at the time, her invitation marked the beginning of a fascinating journey back in time for me.

Over the past twelve years I have learned the stories of those individuals who were here before us: Native Americans, pioneers, soldiers, suffragettes, developers, entrepreneurs, farmers, educators, artisans, philanthropists, architects, ministers, editors, tradesmen, bankers, writers and even a few rogues and rascals. Their accomplishments, and the way they lived their lives, have been passed down to us in the many public and private papers, books, newspapers, reminiscences and other historical data available at both the Oak Park Public Library and The Historical Society of Oak Park and River Forest. Working with this material I have tried to separate fact from hazy recollection and truth from legend and lore. It has not always been easy.

Sifting through this primary material has been invaluable in helping me understand Oak Park in a larger context as one of the most unique communities in northeastern Illinois. At the beginning of the last century Oak Park stood apart from other Chicago suburbs as a community that was intellectually progressive with one of the best high schools in the country and boasting a rich cultural and social life. And, even at that time, the village was also known for its diverse architectural mix of imposing Queen Anne, Italianate and Prairie Style homes.

My objective in writing this book is to provide present and future generations of school children, newcomers to the community and others unfamiliar with our heritage with a compact, anecdotal and, I hope, entertaining account of all that has gone before. It is not intended to be a definitive history. My objective in volume two, which will cover World War I to the present, will be the same.

This book could never have been completed without the assistance of others. I am especially indebted to Frank Lipo, Executive Director of The Historical Society of Oak Park and River Forest for his unrelenting attention to detail in reviewing my manuscript. Frank's considerable knowledge of local history enabled him to clarify facts that tended to be fuzzy, redirect my focus when I wandered, recognize omissions and inconsistencies and, in general, fine tune the entire manuscript. Any errors that remain are my own.

My appreciation also extends to the staff of both the audio visual department and the reference desk of the Oak Park Public Library for their assistance; to Martin Noll, President of Community Bank of Oak Park and River Forest for his encouragement and help and to Tom Nelson of Offset Press who has guided me through the publishing process—and made it an enjoyable learning experience.

Most of all, I am grateful to my husband Victor for his unwavering support throughout this project. Whenever I became discouraged or mired in minutiae he was able to look at the problem with a fresh perspective and offer positive suggestions that were, invariably, right on the mark.

TABLE OF CONTENTS

CHAPTER IV
VIGNETTES OF VILLAGE LIFE
PAGE 92

CHAPTER V
VILLAGE LANDMARKS: PAST AND PRESENT
PAGE 116

CHAPTER I

SETTLING THE LAND

Dwight Perkins' 1903 photo of presettlement oak tree located in what is now Thatcher Woods between North and Chicago Avenues.

Potawatomi Villages Flourished Along the Des Plaines River

While Illinois was still part of the Northwest Territory and before the State was admitted to the Union in 1818, this region was an unsurveyed and unspoiled land of plenty that was home to several tribes of Native Americans who lived by hunting the bears, deer and small game they found in abundance in the forests and woodlands along the Des Plaines River.

But by the time Joseph Kettlestrings purchased his quarter section of land in 1837 in what is now Oak Park many tribes such as the Sauk and Fox had already been forcibly removed from Illinois to land west of the Mississippi after the terms of the 1833 Treaty of Chicago which ended the Black Hawk War. Still others, including the Ottawa, Chippewa and Potawatomi, had ceded their land to the federal government and were preparing to move west across the Mississippi.

The Des Plaines, a tributary of the Illinois River, had been christened the Aux Plaines or "river of the plaines" in 1673 by the French explorers Father Jacques Marquette and Louis Joliet. Just as the entire region was crisscrossed with ancient Indian trails, the banks of the Des Plaines were also dotted with villages, burial mounds and chipping stations where these hunters shaped and sharpened their arrows and other stone blades.

The Indians were originally attracted to this area because of its high ground. Thousands of years ago the region north to Wilmette, west to LaGrange and south to Blue Island was covered by a glacial layer of ice geologists called "Lake Chicago." When the ice melted the terrain of the region had evolved into a low marshland interspersed with a series of high sandbars or ridges that were created from the gravelly sediment of ground up rocks and boulders.

The Indians naturally chose trails along these high points. Ogden Avenue, which later became the first planked road leading west from Chicago, was their southerly trail. St. Charles Road was another heavily traveled trail and, as early as 1836, it extended as far as Stacy's Corner in what is now Glen Ellyn. The Des Plaines River intersected both trails and fording this body of water that

Turn of the Des Plaines River north of North Avenue, near site of Native American village and chipping station.

overflowed its banks every spring, proved a formidable task for both Indians and settlers. In contrast to these higher trails, the Indian route we know as Lake Street today was low, swampy and impassable for much of the year. This trail is thought to have been originally a narrow footpath used by both Native Americans, and later settlers on their way west from Fort Dearborn. But another theory is that it was first traveled by James Watson Webb, an officer stationed at Fort Dearborn in 1822.

Memories of the Fort Dearborn massacre of 1812 were still fresh in the minds of settlers living in isolated homesteads west of the Des Plaines River when, ten years later, rumors began to spread that another Indian uprising was imminent. According to legend, Webb volunteered to make the perilous journey in midwinter from the Fort to the garrison on the Rock River at Dixon to warn the soldiers and settlers. The route he took was straight west down what is now Lake Street.

Early Burial Grounds

In the Oak Park area the high ground or sandbar known as the Oak Park Spit originated at North and Ridgeland Avenues in Galewood, ran diagonally through Taylor Park and ended in a ridge in Forest Home Cemetery in Forest Park, just north of Roosevelt Road. (This historic cemetery is the site of the homestead of Ferdinand Haase, founder of Forest Park.)

The ancient ridge or hill in Forest Home was marked by a large circular mound or hill with a flat summit about a hundred feet wide that most likely served as an open-air assembly room in which tribal meetings were held. In 1900 Lena Haase, Ferdinand Haase's daughter-in-law, gave a talk to the River Forest Women's Club in which she provided greater details about this meeting space.

"The summit was girdled by a beaten track or ring in which ponies were exercised. On the edge of the ring were circular indentations which marked the locations of the teepees, it being apparent that the huts had been erected over these holes," she said. "On Mr. Haase's arrival these pits still contained stones and ashes indicating the location of the campfires. The hill also contained larger pits or caches in which were stored grain for the winter."

In our area the sites of three Indian villages have been identified: a settlement and chipping station a half-mile north of North Avenue is what is now Evans Field; a village directly east of the Des Plaines River and south of Lake Street at Thatcher Avenue in River Forest and the village and burial mounds found along the river in Forest Home Cemetery. Few traces remain of the first two villages. But in 1941 a seven-foot granite monument depicting an Indian on horseback was erected to mark the site of the single Indian mound that was left undisturbed in Forest Home Cemetery. No one knows who or how many bodies are buried in this mound. The plaque on this historic gravesite reads in part: "This is the site of a village and burial ground of the Potawatomie Indians from ancient times to 1835, when they were exiled to lands beyond the Mississippi."

The first person with legal ties to the land that is now Forest Home Cemetery was Leon Bourassa, a French trapper who held the original title for the land signed by President Martin Van Buren in 1839. When the tribes were forced from their land Bourassa and his Potawatomi wife, Margaret, stayed behind to farm and trap along the Des Plaines River and to care for the graves of her ancestors. In 1851 Bourassa sold his holdings to

Ferdinand Haase, a young man recently arrived from Germany who purchased the land with an inheritance he had received. Haase purchased additional land and his holdings eventually included all the land bounded on the east and west by First Avenue and Des Plaines Avenue and on the north and south by Roosevelt Road and what is today the Eisenhower Expressway.

Haase Unearths Signs of Earlier Life

Ferdinand Haase found the open prairie ideal for raising cattle. And, although his land was the highest elevation west of Chicago, the surrounding area was so low and swampy that in the winter he was able to ice skate to and from Chicago. In the summer Haase's prairie was covered with a growth of wild

Ferdinand Haase

sunflowers so high that even when riding horseback through them, only a rider's head could be seen bobbing up and down.

When Ferdinand Haase first attempted to till the soil on his land he made several discoveries. One of the most startling were the tusk and bones of a huge mastodon found about 150 yards east of the Des Plaines River in a gravel bed about ten feet below the surface.

In 1869 Haase, with the help of Charles Kennicott, a young River Forest archeologist (not to be confused with Robert Kennicott, first director of the Chicago Academy of Sciences), identified several burial mounds on his property. These mounds were not opened until 1900 when they were found to contain a number of human skeletons and many artifacts and silver ornaments.

Lena Haase described what the Haase family found when these mounds were leveled. "Four score of graves have in the course of local improvements been unearthed and their contents exposed to human eye and hand," she said. "There were five mounds in number, irregular in shape and about thirty feet in diameter. Each mound contained about ten bodies surrounded by the individual's personal property. This consisted of arms, knives, wampum, kettles, crosses, arm bands, beads and other ornaments made of silver, undoubtedly brought here by the white man, for which he received valuable furs in return."

It was not until 1969 that the silver pieces were cleaned and examined by Dr. James Van Stone, curator of anthropology at the Field Museum who determined they had been made in Canada between 1750 and 1810 and used by the French Voyageurs to trade with the Indians for beaver skins. He considered them to be the finest collection of Indian trade goods ever found in the Great Lakes. (The Haase family gave these silver pieces, Indian artifacts and mastodon remains to the Forest Park Public Library when the cemetery changed ownership in 1969.)

The picturesque setting of Ferdinand Haase's land that spanned both sides of the Des Plaines River prompted many of his

Ferdinand Haase's French-Creole style home.

German friends to encourage him to open a picnic grove. In 1856 Haase's Park became a popular recreational attraction. Haase also converted his spacious French-Creole style home into a guesthouse for visitors. And, to make it easier for people to reach his picnic grounds, he struck a deal with the Galena & Chicago Union Railroad. In exchange for carloads of gravel needed for construction, the railroad built a spur line from the main tracks directly to Haase's Park. Special picnic cars—just flat cars, with rough board seats across—transported thousands of picnickers seeking fellowship with their countrymen and to escape the sweltering heat of the city to Haase's grove.

Haase offered visitors a number of diversions including a steam excursion boat called the *White Swan,* small rowboats or "swan" boats popular with courting couples, fishing, bowling and swimming. He also sold his fresh farm produce.

However, by 1864 attendance at Haase's Park began to drop when Chicago's 110-acre Lake Park opened on the city's lakefront. (After President Lincoln's assassination this recreational space was renamed Lincoln Park to honor his memory.) Perhaps it was just as well. Liquor had always been sold in Haase's grove with the result that rowdyism and vandalism had become a serious problem. Haase was forced to build a jail on the premises to placate his neighbors who complained that their summer Sabbaths were being disrupted by unruly crowds. (For some time after the land was converted to a cemetery the jail was used as a burial vault.)

In 1872 a group of prominent Oak Park leaders including Henry Austin, James Scoville and O. W. Herrick proposed establishment of a nonsectarian cemetery on his land that would serve English-speaking, middle-class residents of the area. Ferdinand Haase agreed and was named president of the cemetery corporation, which was granted a perpetual charter by the State of Illinois in 1876. The Haase family operated the cemetery until 1969.

Kettlestrings Grove was Center of Oak Park's First Main Street

In 1837 a land sale took place in what is now Oak Park that, by current monetary standards, was insignificant. Yet that real estate transaction—and the subsequent subdivision and sale of smaller parcels of the original 172.78 acre tract—had a tremendous impact on the growth and development of Oak Park.

The buyer was Joseph Kettlestrings, the first settler to live permanently in Oak Ridge (the original name of the village) and the seller was the federal government which offered settlers like Kettlestrings the opportunity to purchase large tracts of land at bargain prices under the Public Lands Sale Act of 1820. And no one had to tell the ambitious young Yorkshireman that the $215.98 or approximately $1.25 an acre he paid for this quarter section of virgin prairie and woodlands was, indeed, money well spent.

Joseph and Betty Kettlestrings' quarter section of land purchased in 1837, often referred to as Kettlestrings Grove, is now the center of present day Oak Park.

The deed or certificate to the quarter section that came to be known as Kettlestrings Grove by other pioneer families was signed in Washington, D. C. by President Martin Van Buren on March 20, 1837. Kettlestrings' tract was bounded by what is today Chicago Avenue, Oak Park Avenue, the Metra tracks and Harlem Avenue

According to his son Walter, Joseph Kettlestrings did not stop with this initial purchase of land but later bought 160 acres north of North Avenue, running west to the Des Plaines River, plus 40 acres north of Kettlestrings Grove and another 40 acres to the south. But, with an eye for future development, he enclosed his original 172 acres with a rail fence. The Land Sale Act opened the land for pre-emption and allowed settlers to live on it as squatters until it was offered for sale. Although Kettlestrings did not have title to his land until 1837 he took advantage of the pre-emption clause two years earlier. In 1835 he built a small and drafty log cabin on Lake Street just east of Harlem Avenue for his growing family and so became Oak Park's first permanent settler.

Joseph Kettlestrings was born in Newton, Yorkshire, England in 1808. In 1828 he married Betty Willis, daughter of a Methodist minister, and, in 1832, the couple and their two young children migrated to America determined to purchase their own parcel of land. A neighbor, George Bickerdike, had made the same journey in 1830 and wrote glowing accounts home about both Chicago and the heavily timbered land he found along the Des Plaines River just ten miles west of Fort Dearborn. It was here Bickerdike and another Yorkshireman, Mark Noble, set up a saw mill along the Des Plaines River just north of today's Lake Street that provided sawn lumber used in the cabins that were being built around Fort Dearborn and in the bridges spanning the Chicago River.

Joseph and Betty Kettlestrings arrived in Baltimore in 1832 after an arduous eleven-week sea voyage and set out immediately in a covered wagon for the "frontier outpost" of Chicago. But rumors of an Indian uprising in this area forced them to spend the winter in Cincinnati where their third child was born.

When the Kettlestrings finally reached Chicago in the spring of 1833 they found it bore little resemblance to their friend Bickerdike's idyllic description. Instead they were dismayed to find it was little more than a dismal collection of unpainted frame homes set in a sea of mud, bogs and sloughs and lashed by unceasing rains. It was hard to believe the sun ever shone here and the Kettlestrings didn't wait to see. Instead they pushed on further west nearly ten miles until they came to the first dry land they had seen in weeks, a broad-topped ridge in a forest of oaks.

Here the family rested atop the hill in what is today Scoville Park at Oak Park Avenue and Lake Street where the World War I Memorial now stands. The forest of majestic oak and beech trees that existed at that time on the site reminded them of the English forest they had left behind and they knew this was the end of their journey.

Kettlestrings claims his quarter section of woodlands and oak prairie

In his later years Joseph Kettlestrings acknowledged that the reason he claimed the quarter section that came to be known as Kettlestrings Grove was because it was the only dry land between Chicago and the Des Plaines river. But he did not settle on it immediately. Instead Kettlestrings moved his family into a log cabin near Bickerdike and Noble's saw mill and spent the next two years working for his friends. Betty Kettlestrings' chores were more numerous. In addition to caring for her growing brood that eventually included eleven children, she was also expected to "board the hands" or cook for between 20 and 30 mill hands at any given time. Her son Walter recalled later that a typical meal was a beef stew with plenty of potatoes and other vegetables served in great pans.

OAK PARK'S FIRST HOTEL
Drawing made from the recollections of Mrs. P. J. Kester of 1860. The building pictured was the Oak Ridge hotel, the first house built in this neighborhood by the first settler, Joseph Kettlestrings. It was on the south side of Lake street, about 100 feet east of Harlem, according to Mrs. Kester. The floor of the front porch was even with the ground and was used by those who passed that way as a shelter in summer and winter. The long rambling stables of the caravansary was across Lake street. It was destroyed by fire in 1866.

6

But in 1835 Joseph Kettlestrings, a cabinetmaker and carpenter by trade, returned to his claim and built a small frame house from walnut logs sawn at the mill. The house was built in spring and, after withstanding the summer's heat, the clapboards began to warp and paper and rags had to be stuffed in the cracks before winter arrived.

But, however flawed it may have been, Joseph Kettlestrings' house was one of the very few structures between Chicago and the scattered settlements west of the Des Plaines River and so he offered hospitality to all travelers who stopped at his door. There were no sleeping rooms but visitors were welcome to spread their blankets on the floor in front of the blazing logs and partake of Betty Kettlestrings' board.

But as the number of visitors increased, Kettlestrings built a small addition, renamed his home the Oak Ridge Hotel and put a price on his hospitality. He charged travelers fifty cents for supper, breakfast and lodging. Although his home was often referred to as a "tavern" no alcohol was ever sold. Kettlestrings, a strict Methodist, was vehemently against both the sale and consumption of liquor and in his later years joined Henry Austin in banning it from the community.

By 1843 there were a few more houses scattered in Kettlestrings Grove. There were also Indians and rattlesnakes, about which Dora Kettlestrings later recalled, "we knew not which we feared most." Probably the rattlesnakes for Betty Kettlestrings once killed one in her kitchen.

At this point schools had yet to be established in Oak Ridge. As a result, Kettlestrings rented his farm and moved to Chicago for the next 12 years so his children could be educated. The city was rapidly expanding its boundaries and Kettlestrings was able to obtain city contracts grading streets in these newly annexed areas.

But while the children did receive a rudimentary education in the city it was also a time of great sorrow. Three of the Kettlestrings children died of scarlet fever and four-year-old Dora Kettlestrings was left deaf in one ear when an epidemic of that disease swept the city.

Subdivision of Kettlestrings Grove spurs growth of Oak Ridge

When the Kettlestrings family returned to Oak Park in 1854, Joseph Kettlestrings retired from business and began selling his land to "good people who were against saloons and for good schools and churches." Several individuals who had purchased Lake Street property from him years earlier had either opened saloons themselves or sold the land to others who purchased it for the purpose of building a saloon. Kettlestrings was determined to keep the community "dry" and so inserted a clause into every deed of sale that bound the buyer never to sell intoxicating liquor on the premises.

Joseph Kettlestrings reputation for honesty was sterling and he never profited by another man's misfortune. Whenever Kettlestrings sold a lot and the buyer was unable to meet the payment, he took the property back and returned whatever sum had been paid, less interest. The resourceful Kettlestrings also accepted goods and services as payment for his land.

In 1859 Albert Schneider, a recent immigrant to Oak Ridge from Germany, wanted to buy five acres owned by Kettlestrings north of Chicago Avenue. The young man was cash poor but could provide a service that

The house Joseph Ketterstrings built in the 1850s at Lake Street and what is now Grove Avenue. When Grove was made a through street, the house was moved to Scoville just north of Lake Street. It was demolished in 1935 and the girls' gymnasium at the high school was built on the site.

7

was much in demand. Schneider was a cobbler by trade and, over a period of years, paid Kettlestrings $100 a year in boots and shoes for his family.

When he began selling his land Joseph Kettlestrings also sold his farm and drafty frame house and built a new home in the center of what is now Grove Avenue, facing Lake Street. When Grove was graded as a through street this house was moved to Scoville Avenue, just north of Lake Street. It was not demolished until 1935 when it stood in the path of an expansion of Oak Park and River Forest High School.

The tiny community of Oak Ridge began to grow throughout the 1850s and 1860s as a result of the sale and subsequent subdivision of Kettlestrings Grove. The small enclave on Lake Street between Oak Park Avenue and Harlem Avenue contained several dozen stores and large comfortable homes owned by businessmen, bankers, teachers and storekeepers with names like Austin, Gale, Bolles, Herrick, Niles, Dunlop and Scoville.

But one very essential thing the community still did not have in 1854 was a school. The only place where children in both Oak Ridge and surrounding communities could obtain even a rudimentary education was in a primitive frame structure built in 1850 on Lathrop Avenue in what is now River Forest. This was the first school built with public money from the sale of land set aside for that purpose in Proviso Township.

To ensure that children living in Oak Ridge could be educated without leaving the community Joseph Kettlestrings donated a lot at Lake Street and Forest Avenue. In 1854 the first school and meeting hall was built on this site with the understanding that both the land and the small frame building would revert back to him once a permanent school was established.

Although Joseph Kettlestrings was a charter member of the First Methodist Church in Oak Ridge he generously allowed other denominations to use his meeting hall (renamed Temperance Hall when Henry Austin purchased the property) until they were able to build their own churches. In later years Mrs. Carlos Ward recalled a typical Sunday service in the 1870s. "It was then that the entire population of our little country village came together at the old Temperance Hall, before Oak Park boasted any other place of worship. It was there that Mr. Blackmer led the singing and Mrs. Blackmer brought real music out of the wheezy little organ—and when as sometimes happened—Mrs. Pitkin took her place (she was sweet Lily Morey then in her white dress and blue sash), nobody blamed Mr. Pitkin for hovering very near to turn the pages of the old hymn book."

In 1873 Joseph Kettlestrings donated land on the northeast corner of Lake Street and Forest Avenue for the First Methodist Church. When the church was destroyed by fire in 1923 a new and much larger structure was built at 324 N. Oak Park Avenue.

Joseph Kettlestrings died in 1883 and Betty Kettlestrings died two years later in 1885. Their surviving children married the offspring of other early settlers with familiar names such as Dunlop and Herrick.

River Forest Pioneer Ashbel Steele Master of Many Trades

Ashbel Steele, River Forest's first permanent settler, possessed both the resourcefulness and tenacity that earlier pioneers lacked. In 1836 when he moved to "the beautiful woodland skirting the shores of the river of the plains" and built a substantial house for his growing family he found both a log cabin and a barn in ruins on his property. These were remnants left by earlier settlers or squatters living on land they did not own and who were either unable or unwilling to endure the loneliness of the frontier.

But Steele, a Yankee of English descent, was made of sturdier stuff. He was a mason and builder by trade but versatile enough to be able to provide other homesteaders who followed him with basic services. At various times he served as Cook County coroner and sheriff, innkeeper, postmaster and storekeeper.

Records show that Ashbel Steele may have purchased his 117-acre tract in present day River Forest in 1830 while still living in Rochester, New York. 40 acres of his holdings were on the west side of the Des Plaines River while the largest parcel was bounded by Thatcher Avenue and the river on the east and west and the Metra tracks and Madison Street on the north and south. However, Steele did not build his fine red brick house on this site until 1836, three years after his arrival in Chicago.

Julius Ashbel Steele was born in Derby (New Haven), Connecticut about 1794. His first wife died in 1823 giving birth to their son, Julius Augustus in Rochester, New York. In 1827 Steele married Harriet Dawley. On their wedding trip to New York the couple bought the substantial mahogany furniture and piano they would use to furnish their home in River Forest. The Steeles had two sons and seven daughters. Only one daughter died in childhood, a remarkable record given the prevalence of cholera and other diseases that took their toll on settlers.

In 1833 Harriet and Ashbel Steele made their long-planned move to Chicago. Steele arranged to have his wife, three children and household goods travel by boat, the safest and easiest means of transportation, while he made the trip overland by horseback.

Remains of Ashbel Steele's home, located in present-day Thatcher Woods, shortly before it was demolished in 1914.

Steele had planned to arrive far in advance of his family but, because of a combination of favorable winds that speeded the boat and unmarked trails in the dense forest that slowed his pace, they arrived the same day. As Steele approached Fort Dearborn he was amazed to see the boat carrying his family just lowering sail and dropping anchor.

Elected Cook County Coroner

For the next three years the Steeles lived in Chicago. Ashbel (he dropped the "Julius" when he arrived in Chicago.) bought land and built the first brick house in Chicago on the present site of Marshall Field's store. Steele quickly became a man of importance. In 1834 he was a member of a vigilance committee to guard against a cholera epidemic which threatened Chicago. That same year he was elected coroner of the newly formed Cook County and served four years.

It was during his tenure as coroner that Steele built a substantial house for his growing family on the land he had purchased along the Des Plaines River years earlier. The house, plus outbuildings that included a woodshed, brick smokehouse, tool house, barn, chicken house and pig pens, were located just south of the Metra tracks and approximately fifty feet west of Thatcher Avenue. Steele positioned his whitewashed clapboard and brick house to face the river with its back to Thatcher Avenue. However, the entrance gate was on Thatcher with a long curving road that led to the front door.

One of the attractions of this location was its proximity to the steam sawmill on the east side of the Des Plaines River, a quarter mile north of Lake Street, that Steele had purchased with a partner, Theophilius Smith, a lawyer who also owned substantial land along the Des Plaines in River Forest. Smith later became a Justice of the Supreme Court of Illinois and was the first president of the Galena & Chicago Union Railroad.

This mill was the same mill that had been built around 1830 by George Bickerdike and Mark Noble. It was a profitable business venture for Steele and Smith as demand for lumber was constantly increasing as new settlers arrived in Chicago daily.

Bickerdike Mill, established in 1830 on the east bank of the Des Plaines River north of Lake Street, provided sawn lumber for the homes of early settlers.

The single photograph of the mill that has survived shows a complex of buildings including the two-story mill and several smaller buildings that housed the workers. We know it survived until after the Civil War when returning Veterans referred to it as an "eyesore." A limestone footing north of Lake Street at the base of the bluff where the river turns south is all that remains of the mill today. The foundation was covered with fill after the buildings were demolished.

When the house was complete Steele planted an orchard that included a large variety of apple, plum, pear, mulberry and peach trees. Long rows of currant and gooseberry bushes and wild grapevines also produced a vast quantity of fruit. There was also a beautiful grove of walnut trees and an abundant vegetable garden tended by Harriet Steele.

While the Steele children were growing up they always enjoyed "the gayest of good times." All of the sisters played the piano, Emma Steele the guitar, Ashbel John the flute, and several of their friends, the violin. When the girls were of marrying age, hospitality was extended to the eligible young men in Chicago and there was always singing, music and dancing. In the summer, parties were held on the wide front porch that had a smooth level floor ideal for dancing. The pergola and porch columns that extended the full length of the house were made of bark covered tree trunks. Over this a rustic frame of wild grapevines spread a charming leafy cover.

The girls attended Miss Dearborn's Academy in Chicago where they studied music, dancing, French, embroidery and painting. The boys went to Bryant and Stratton's Business College in the city.

Steele's favorite diversion was hunting, a sport he shared with his oldest daughter, Frances. Once, when she was bitten by a rattlesnake while hunting with her father, he immediately slashed the bite and then sucked out the poison.

On another occasion he shot a panther in the children's playhouse. "The scream that the animal gave in the early dawn struck terror into our hearts, but with one bullet, well-aimed, my father killed the animal," recalled Steele's daughter Clara.

In 1840 Ashbel Steele was elected the first Sheriff of Cook County on the Whig ticket. He retained his home in River Forest during his tenure but moved his family to Chicago where they lived in the residence provided for the sheriff on the northeast corner of Clark and Randolph Streets.

Although he was one of the most prominent men of that era, Ashbel Steele's likeness was never captured by a camera or on canvas. But, according to eyewitnesses, he was said to be a slender, fair-haired man who had a sense of humor and was known to be kindly and generous—until crossed. For example, on Election Day in 1841 Sheriff Steele arrested a man for starting a fight in a Chicago polling place. A mob, headed by a judge of the Illinois Supreme Court, went to the jail where the judge ordered Steele to release the man. Steele replied that any attempt by the judge to exercise his authority outside his court would not be recognized and, if any man attacked the jail, he would be killed. The crowd dispersed.

Steele also had a strong sense of duty and in 1848 when cholera struck the camp of workmen building the Galena and Chicago Union Railroad, he nursed the stricken laborers using homemade arrowroot pudding and brandy as remedies.

Montezuma Hall is early shopping center

By 1846 Steele had moved his family back to River Forest. At the same time he moved his business out of his home when he built Montezuma Hall on the southeast corner of Lake Street and Thatcher Avenue. This building served as an inn, tavern, post office and general store and stagecoach stop. On the front of the building was a painted sign of General Winfield Scott, a hero of the War of 1812. Scott, famed for having two horses shot out from under him in battle, was shown in the picture on a white charger.

Steele's store and inn were tended by his older children. Open cracker barrels of maple sugar, flour, pepper and other household essentials tempted customers. They were sold by weight and wrapped in brown paper. Bits of tallow candles sunk into blocks were set out on the counter to light the way for guests spending the night at Steele's inn. Copies of the latest Chicago newspapers were available and one night's lodging cost 12 1/2 cents.

Supper and breakfast were served for an additional twenty-five cents. Rum, wine, gin and whiskey were also available at Steele's inn to wash the dust off the rasped throats of passengers who had spent the day in a Frink and Walker stagecoach being jolted over Lake Street which, at that time, was a

Ashbel Steele, River Forest's first permanent settler, made the bricks for Harlem School in 1859. The building is still used by River Forest Elementary School District 90.

planked road and the main artery between Chicago and Elgin.

When the driver sounded a loud blast on his horn as the stage came lumbering into town it was a signal not only that visitors had come to this sparsely populated region, but more important, that the mail had arrived. And settlers from surrounding hamlets came to Montezuma Hall to receive and send their mail and to hear the latest news.

There were no stamps or envelopes. The writer placed his message on one side of a large sheet of paper, folded it into a neat oblong with the blank side out on which he wrote the address and left a corner blank where Steele, as postmaster, would write the required postage due. Twenty-five cents was the price for the average letter to the east, but a single man had to pay an additional charge. The cost of sending a local letter was one cent.

Although Ashbel Steele was a jack of all trades, his primary business was that of builder and he is responsible for many of the early buildings in River Forest. One of his last projects was the landmark Harlem school at Lake Street and Park Avenue built in 1859 of the same red brick Steele had used on his house years earlier. It was the largest school building of its time between Chicago and Elgin and served several surrounding communities including Maywood and Forest Park. Today this building houses the administrative office for River Forest Elementary School District 90.

Ashbel Steele died in 1861 and his wife Harriet survived him until 1895. One of their sons, George Steele, lived in the family home for more than 60 years until his death in 1914. Three years later his heirs sold the homesite to the Forest Preserve District of Cook County for $68,898.35. The District demolished the house and buried the rubble on site and divided the parcel into Thomas Jefferson Woods and the Grand Army of the Republic Woods. At the same time, Washington Blvd. was paved between Thatcher and First Avenue.

Ashbel Steele never plowed or grazed his 117 acres (except for his neighbor's pigs, which he allowed to be turned loose on his property.) As a result, these two Forest Preserve holdings are a showcase of native flowers and grasses that have disappeared from other parts of Illinois.

Elizabeth Porter Furbeck Recalls Challenges of Prairie Life

One of the most vivid recollections of pioneer life on the prairie west of Chicago was given by Elizabeth Porter Furbeck on May 25, 1898 when she presented a paper to the Society of the Pioneers of Chicago. The then-62-year-old Furbeck recounted the hardscrabble life of the Porter family as her father, Augustin Porter, struggled without success to establish a homestead in several small settlements west of the Des Plaines River. It was not until Porter moved his family to Harlem (River Forest) in 1844 that he finally prospered as a farmer. Later, when Proviso Township was formed in 1857, he served as its first assessor and justice of the peace.

Elizabeth Porter Furbeck in later years.

Augustin Porter came to Illinois in 1835, walking most of the way from Cicero County, New York. After laying claim to a quarter section in Babcock's Grove (Lombard) where his sister and her husband had already settled along the Du Page River, Porter returned to New York to fetch his wife and children.

In 1836 this land had yet to be surveyed and so could not be legally sold. But a man could claim a quarter section or 160 acres and, if he lived on it, could purchase the land when it was offered for sale at the government price of $1.25 an acre.

The Porter family traveled to their new home through Lake Huron and Lake Michigan against both strong headwinds and dead calm. Elizabeth was a fretful baby and the captain told her mother that, if she did not stop the child's crying, he would throw her overboard. "When I think of it I pity my mother and have no apology for my bad behavior," she observed tartly. "At the present time what woman would think it possible to travel so far in such a way with so young a child?"

At Babcock's Grove Augustin Porter built a sawmill next to an existing log house. But, because of the constantly fluctuating levels of the river, it was not a success. After seven years of struggle Porter was unable to pay for his claim and so was forced to move his family back to Chicago.

"It was a bright November morning in 1843 when we left the house on the Du Page River to move to Chicago, with two loads of family and furniture," said Elizabeth. "After passing the last house on the road we were overtaken by what we now call a Dakota blizzard. The tired horses were blinded by the storm and we could make no progress. Night came and there were no lights to guide our path and we nearly perished. Many people and animals were frozen in the storm. It was the beginning of a very severe winter."

The Porters spent that winter in Chicago and the following spring Augustin Porter bought another parcel of land in the vicinity of what is now Lyons. "A yoke of oxen and two cows were all that we had to begin another farm with. Nothing could be raised without a fence so the first thing we did was to split logs and drew them from the woods with an ox team. But when we had been on that place about a year a tornado swept the countryside. Nearly every house and fence was blown down but, strange to say, our house escaped except that the west side was blown in."

Still, Porter decided it was time for another fresh start and, in the spring of 1844, moved his family to Harlem. He built an addition on an existing log shanty and began to farm, this time with greater success. Elizabeth recalled those early self-reliant years: "The first years we were here mother used to spin, color and weave the clothing worn by the family; all hosiery was home knit and soap and candles were also made at home." It was about this time that other pioneers from the east, lured with the promise of rich farmland at bargain prices began arriving from the east to stake their claim. Prairie schooners, as their white covered wagons were called, could be seen daily heading west along the mud trail that was Lake Street.

And the Potawatomie still returned occasionally to visit their ancestral land. "The white man's fences and wheat fields were no obstruction. They only had to lift off two or three rails and their ponies would jump over. They were followed by men, women and children with often a papoose strapped to the mother's back and finally, by the pack of horses without riders," she remembered. "My mother said she knew they were friendly but felt safer when the last one had passed. She kept us in the house and let us look at the procession through the window."

"If you have never lived on the natural untrodden prairie, you can hardly imagine the beauty of the wild flowers, as each month from early spring to late fall brings flowers of different kinds and colors in the greatest profusion. I love the prairie as the sailor loves the sea."

Although the term "family values" had yet to be coined, the Porter family was the embodiment of it. "How to govern the children and what shall we do with them, had not occurred to parents at that time. The home was considered a mutual institution, and all members must do what they could to help maintain it," said Elizabeth.

There was no church in the vicinity for the family to attend, but when Sunday came it was observed. "We were not compelled but, as I recall, there seemed to be a sanctified atmosphere. We were told it was God's holy Sabbath and, the example of our parents made us believe it and ever since to remember it."

The wild animals of Elizabeth's childhood were the timid deer, rabbits, gophers and prairie wolves that would come in the night and take the little pigs from the pen. "The tall sandhill cranes, wild geese in large flocks, whose migration was our thermometer, wild ducks, prairie chickens and pigeons were also very numerous," she added.

"I love the prairie as the sailor loves the sea."

In 1845, the summer after Augustin Porter moved his family to Harlem, 9-year-old Elizabeth Porter began her education . "My parents did not want to send me. I heard of the school and persuaded them to let me go. They thought the long walk would be too much for me," she said. The school she most likely attended was in the home of Ashbel Steele and her teacher was Steele's 14-year-old daughter Elizabeth. The first school in Harlem built with funds from the sale of public lands was not constructed until 1850.

The Porter house, built in 1860 at Central and Bonnie Brae in River Forest. Augustin Porter was Justice of the Peace and the small annex in the rear was referred to as "Porter's Court House."

14

It was most likely on her long walks to school that Elizabeth fell in love with the prairie and, years later, was able to give a strikingly detailed picture of everything that flourished on it.

"If you have never lived on the natural untrodden prairie, you can hardly imagine the beauty of the wild flowers, as each month from early spring to late fall brings flowers of different kinds and colors in the greatest profusion. I love the prairie as the sailor loves the sea."

Pioneer youngsters followed the example of the Indians and had no fear of burning the prairie. And, far from being harmed, the native flowers and prairie grasses only grew in greater profusion after being burned. "When the wind was not too strong we made our own fireworks by setting the high grass and weeds on fire. And we carried an armful of hazel brush to beat it out if it was liable to do harm," she said.

"As you stand upon the green flowery carpet, with the blue dome of heaven above, not a sound to break the silence and nothing to obstruct the vision of the horizon all around, where else in the whole universe can you feel so alone with God?"

The Creator was on the minds of many settlers when death struck without warning. There was no undertaker, no embalming and no ice. But there was usually a carpenter who could make a coffin and burial took place as soon as the coffin was completed. "And we knew that so far as they could hear of it, everyone who could, came willingly and rendered all possible assistance," recalled Elizabeth. "The fraternal feeling between the pioneers was of great comfort to the bereaved."

Before the Civil War the area was divided into political precincts. When these precincts were, in turn, divided into townships in 1857 Porter proposed the name of Cicero Township for the area that included Oak Ridge because he came from Cicero, New York. The region to the west that included present day River Forest was designated Proviso Township at his suggestion because the Wilmot Proviso was being hotly contested in Congress at that time. This proviso or bill to prohibit slavery in new territories was tacked onto President Polk's request to Congress for funds to buy more territory from Mexico.

Augustin Porter, who was considered by his neighbors to be "an intelligent and enterprising gentleman," was made assessor of Proviso Township and was also named Justice of the Peace of River Forest. He held court in a small building he added at the rear of the fine brick house he built for his family at the corner of Railroad Avenue and John Street (now Central and Bonnie Brae in River Forest.) which his neighbors referred to as "Porter's Court House." His tasks as Justice of the Peace included officiating at marriage ceremonies in which members of his family often participated as witnesses.

Pioneer Schools

Education in both Oak Park and River Forest was a haphazard affair until the 1850s when funding for separate school districts was made available from the sale of township land set aside for this purpose.

In 1850 the sale of school lands provided funds for the construction of River Forest's first district school, a small frame building just twelve feet square and located on Lathrop Avenue between the railroad and Lake Street. It was replaced the following year by a larger building that was later moved across the street to 7571 Lake Street. Between 1859 and 1861 Frances Willard, later a suffragette and founder of the Women's Christian Temperance Union, taught at this school.

Willard accepted the position against the wishes of her family and even the advice of the county superintendent who told her that this was the least desirable of any school on his list. It was, he said, in an isolated spot on the prairie and attended almost exclusively by the children of foreigners.

In her book, *Glimpses of Fifty Years,* Willard described her school as being dirty beyond description with muddied floors and a latticework of cobwebs. Also, the roof leaked and her desk was wet. But that was the positive side.

Willard was a replacement for the previous teacher, Henrietta Ferguson, who quit suddenly when one of her more unruly students came to school with a shotgun, which he pointed at her. This disruption was not an isolated incident. The new academic year in this pioneer school usually began peacefully. But the tranquility was shattered after the harvest when the older boys who had been kept out of school to help bring in the crops rejoined their classmates. These loutish farm lads, chafing at being forced to attend school, took special pleasure in harassing their usually inexperienced teachers.

In 1859 Harlem School, River Forest's first brick school was built at Lake Street and Park Avenue with Ashbel Steele acting as contractor.

Directly north of the school was a large clearing where Indians came from their reservation in the Mont Clare area of Chicago to sell their beads, baskets and moccasins to the settlers. Wild strawberries, raspberries and hazelnuts also grew in profusion amid the prairie grass in this field and were gathered by the students during recess. And gum did not come out of a Wrigley wrapper but rather from the rosinweed that also grew in abundance in the field.

Central School at Lake Street and Forest Avenue was built in 1859. It housed all 12 grades until 1891 when the first high school was built at Lake Street and East Avenue to relieve overcrowding.

Central School

1859 also marked the construction of Central School, a three-story brick building at Lake Street and Forest Avenue in Oak Park that housed all twelve grades. This, too, was the first school built with funds from the sale of a section of township land set aside for this purpose. The section was divided into 230 lots and sold for $100 an acre. All the lots were sold but many were later foreclosed and, after all legal bills had been paid, a total of $88,000 was available for establishing the school district.

Central School replaced the village's first school, the small frame building directly across the street built in 1854 by Joseph Kettlestrings as a makeshift school. O. W. Herrick, a popular young bachelor who later married Dora Kettlestrings, came from New York to be the first principal of the new school.

16

Class of 1880 in front of Central School. Man in back row with broom was most likely John Powell who served as janitor for 46 years.

Students who attended Central School had James Scoville to thank for their spacious playground. The lot selected for the school was large enough for just the footprint of the building and taxpayers balked at paying for "frills" such as a playground. However, Scoville had more foresight and purchased the lot behind the school for $800. He held onto this property and, as the enrollment soared in just a few years, sold it to the school trustees for exactly what he had paid.

In 1876, John Powell was hired as janitor for Central School, a job he held for the next 46 years. Among Powell's chores was to screw large iron bolts into the railing of the stairs leading to the second floor because it had been weakened by the many students who insisted upon sliding down it.

Warren Wilkie, who was hired to serve as the third principal of Central School in 1868, was given a one-year contract with a salary of $1,800. "Mr. Wilkie's services being appreciated, he was retained by the board from year to year and in 1873 his salary was raised to $2,000," recalled Horace Humphrey who

attended the school with his three brothers and sisters. Humphrey remembered the school as a no-nonsense temple of learning where expectations were high.

"A boy starting to demonstrate a theorem on the blackboard: 'The rule is...' 'I don't care what the rule is,' would be Mr. Wilkie's sharp reply. 'How do you do it?' And we did learn after the Nineteenth Century fashion. We could name and point out on the map all the counties of Illinois. We could name all the States of the Union and their capitals. We recited the multiplication table in chorus and were thoroughly convinced that the nominative case covers the verb."

"In mathematics we could converse brilliantly in language bristling with X and Z and were familiar with many cheerful facts about the square of the hypotenuse. In English we used the standard reading books until we knew every piece almost by heart. And we spoke pieces, too. Spartacus to the Gladiators, Mark Antony's funeral oration, Thanatopsis, The Feast of Belshazzar and a lot more of the classics with now and then

1895 high school graduation.

a dialogue like the quarrel between Brutus and Cassius."

"And we composed. The orthodox formula for introducing the subject was like this: 'The horse is a very useful animal. There are many different kinds of horses,' etc. These cast iron compositions were a source of great trial to Mr. Wilkie and he tried faithfully to induce a freer style and a less hackneyed form."

But in matters of discipline, Mr. Wilkie was a believer in the old method of "Spare the rod and spoil the child." The boy who whispered or otherwise violated the rules knew what was coming if he was caught, particularly if it was one of the days when the master had an aching tooth or disordered liver.

"Those were the days when he went round the room on a whaling expedition, using strap, black board pointer, ruler or whatever instrument was most convenient. On such days, several of us would go home like locomotive engines with tender behinds. But it was all in a day's work. These eruptions caused no lasting feelings of resentment on the part of either of us or our parents. Friendliness of feeling continued unabated on both sides."

Students who completed all twelve years of Central School's strict

"Those were the days when he went round the room on a whaling expedition, using strap, black board pointer, ruler or whatever instrument was most convenient. On such days, several of us would go home like locomotive engines with tender behinds. But it was all in a day's work. These eruptions caused no lasting feelings of resentment on the part of either of us or our parents. Friendliness of feeling continued unabated on both sides."

18

regimen had reason to be proud when they graduated. The *Oak Park Vindicator* recounted the impressive ceremony honoring the thirteen graduates of the Class of 1887. "The young ladies in spotless white decorated with flowers, ribbons and roses, looked the ideal graduating Miss. Their essays were of high character and showed clear, original

$160,000

==OF==

High School Bonds

are desired by the Oak Park and River Forest Township High School Board. A public meeting, to which ladies and gentlemen of Oak Park and River Forest are cordially invited, will be held at the Colonial Club of Oak Park, corner of Elmwood Avenue and Lake Street, to consider this question

To=night, Saturday, Jan. 7, 1905, at 8 o'clock

This referendum to purchase land from James Scoville for $33,500 to build a larger high school on Ontario between East and Scoville passed by a vote of 397 to 214.

thought clothed in terse fine language. They were read with expression and effect and were well received by the audience, each one being heartily applauded for her effort."

"The orations of the young gentlemen showed the results of the years of study, application and work and were creditable alike to scholar and school. The music, both vocal and instrumental, was very fine and suitable to the occasion."

"President Bassett of the board presented the diplomas to the class with appropriate remarks to each. At the conclusion the class was presented with a bountiful supply of floral offerings, books, prizes and souvenirs and thus closed a most successful and happy school life for the graduating class of 1887."

Central School continued to serve all twelve grades until 1891 when the first high school was built on the southwest corner of Lake Street and East Avenue to relieve overcrowding. By 1899 there was a great deal of discussion on the need to create a separate high school district with its own taxing power. School District #1 (Cicero Township) and District #8 (Proviso Township) each held an election on April 8, 1899 to vote on the question of establishing a township high school that would include both villages. The proposition carried by a large majority in both districts. This was the beginning of Oak Park and River Forest High School.

In 1923, historic Central School was razed to make way for Lowell School which, too, was demolished in 1972. Today a stone commemorating the location as the site of both Lowell and Central Schools marks the location of both schools. 100 Forest Place, a residential and retail rental development completed in 1986, now occupies the site.

Edwin Gale's Memories of a Youth Spent on the Prairie

Oak Park's earliest leaders such as Joseph Kettlestrings, Henry Austin and James Scoville were all astute businessmen with reputations for great integrity, vision and generosity. Edwin O. Gale, who built an impressive Gothic Revival house for his wife and six sons on the corner of Lake Street and Kenilworth in 1865, was gifted with these same qualities. But Gale was also a poet, author and inveterate man of letters.

Edwin Gale wrote *Falling Leaves,* a collection of poems. And in 1903 he published *Reminiscences of Early Chicago* in which he recalled his arrival in Chicago via the Erie Canal in 1835, a boyhood spent in a large house on Randolph Street where his mother amazed visiting Indians playing the "bird in the box" as they called her piano, and his boyhood adventures attending Fort Dearborn school.

Edwin's parents, Abram and Sarah Gale, were among the first merchants serving Chicago's early settlers. Abram opened a meat market near the corner of Lake and South Water Streets while Sarah, who had brought a stock of millinery goods with her from the east, was the proprietor of the New York Millinery Store at Lake and Wells Streets. Hats proved to be a more popular commodity than meat so Abram closed his shop and concentrated on helping his wife.

During the first public land sale in Chicago in 1837 Abram Gale paid $200 for 320 acres on the ridge or highest spot on the edge of glacial Lake Chicago running from what is today Grand Avenue, southwest to Lake Street. At that time much of Chicago was a swamp that was a breeding ground for deadly diseases and Abram was determined to buy a tract on higher ground. The area he purchased, known today as the Chicago community of Galewood, is bounded by North Avenue, Armitage Avenue, Austin Blvd. and Oak Park Avenue.

Abram Gale built a farmhouse on his newly acquired land where his growing family spent their summer vacation. They did

Residence of Abram Gale in Galewood in 1883.

not move there permanently for another twenty years when all the children had finished their schooling.

In 1872 when the Chicago & Union Pacific Railroad ran a stretch of tracks along the north edge of his property, Abram Gale decided the time was right to begin subdividing a portion of it for residential development. The Western Brick and Tile Manufacturing Company also opened a plant in Galewood a few years later because the clay to be found in the area was of a superior quality. Today the Brickyard Shopping Center on Grand Avenue occupies the site of this manufacturing plant and quarry.

The southwestern portion of Galewood on North Avenue between Oak Park Avenue and Ridgeland, was leased to the Westward Ho Golf Club in 1899. This area remained a golf course until 1927 when the clubhouse burned and the Gale family decided to subdivide this land for residential development.

Galewood, one of the many small communities within Jefferson Township, became a part of Chicago when the Township was annexed to the city in 1889.

As a young man Edwin Gale traveled frequently between his parent's house in the city and their country home in Galewood. In 1898 he recalled those journeys: "And now, after more than half a century has elapsed, those beautiful summer mornings when I was permitted to go to the farm return to me with marvelous freshness. Again am I riding out of town behind 'Old Charley' on Lake or Randolph Streets, winding among the modest homes of the west side scattered through the tall grass and sturdy rosinweed, cutting across vacant blocks toward the stone quarry at what is now Western Avenue (at that time the western edge of the city) when, if in season, I stop to gather strawberries there growing in their perfection."

"After satiating my appetite I am again headed for Whiskey Point (Grand Avenue)

Galewood, Spring 1904: view of cottage in foreground and store in background is looking northwest from Gale residence.

over the most perfect of Nature's boulevards, the prairie road which is spread out before me like a long roll of black velvet. Those of us who, in our youth, enjoyed the privilege of riding on those prairie roads have treasures stored up that are incompatible with a densely populated country, and that an advanced civilization can never bestow."

However, Edwin Gale balanced this idyllic picture of the prairie with a more realistic description of the area submerged by melting snow and heavy rains in the fall and early spring. "When the rains descending filled the ground with moisture and every depression became a slough without a ditch anywhere to carry off the accumulated floods, when the wheels sank to the hubs and the hearts of the drivers sank correspondingly, when blows and coaxing were unavailing to start the exhausted horses, we had the other picture also drawn true to nature. All that could be seen was a cheerless lake without a house from the Ridge to the engulfed city."

When elections were held in those early days one voting place was selected in each township and males over 21 years of age had to find their way to the appointed place which was usually a tavern. "There are but a very few who remember how we used to obtain from railroad officials permission to have the only morning train stop on the prairie at Rollo Pearsoll's Four Mile House," recalled Gale.

"From there we tramped across Pearsoll's muddy field to his tavern. There, in a dingy room filled with the smoke from ancient pipes, we would exercise our high prerogative of American citizens, which carried with it the necessity of walking two miles through the mud to the horse cars at Western Avenue."

The prairie west of Chicago was the natural habitat of numerous animals that were increasingly threatened by the many new settlements and homesteads that were beginning to dot the landscape. Gale recounts the fate of a lone wolf that encroached on his family's farm. "One Sabbath morning about 1844 a large gray timber wolf startled by the Beaubien and Robinson boys in the Des Plaines timber three miles from here, found its way to the farm followed by shouting men and yelping dogs. The hired man and I were in the barn but hearing them, I took but a moment to join in the chase with a fresh dog and two bareback riders."

"The poor worried animal headed for the river timber again. My dog, a large powerful fellow, seized him as he was crossing the smooth ice west of the grove, worried him until the other dogs arrived and, although the wolf was a savage one fighting for his life, the odds in number too great. Several dogs felt his fangs and, to avoid useless suffering, a pistol shot from Alexander Beaubien put him out of his misery. The tip of his tail was given to the youngest in the company, and no brave ever felt prouder than I did with this evidence of my prowess."

Finally, as an adult Edwin Gale recognized that the departure of the wolves and other wild creatures from their native habitat was the sad, but inevitable, result of expansion and settlement of the region. "After becoming a citizen of Oak Park I frequently saw as the afternoon train passed where Austin is now, a prairie wolf but a short distance south of the track, a sad solitary connecting link between the fast fading past and the brightly dawning future, forming a striking picture of the rapid changes that are constantly occurring in the marvelous march of the middle west."

The Schneider Family Settles Oak Park's North Prairie

In terms of measurement the shortest distance between two points is a straight line—except when that distance is Marion Street, a meandering north-south thoroughfare in Oak Park that grew haphazardly over a period of years as the village's commercial center expanded. Today Marion jogs slightly to the west at three intersections: Lake Street, Chicago Avenue and Augusta Blvd.

Albert Schneider, Sr., plied his trade as a cobbler even in his later years.

Although the nucleus of Oak Park's business community began on Lake Street, it eventually expanded both north and south of Lake on Marion Street. However, Marion Street north of Chicago Avenue was still an unbroken prairie in 1859 when Albert Schneider, a cobbler who had recently immigrated to Oak Park from Germany, purchased a large tract of land from Joseph Kettlestrings. Schneider's parcel was bounded by Lake Street and Augusta on the north and south and Harlem Avenue and 150 feet east of Marion Street on the east and west.

At that time much of the land Joseph Kettlestrings was selling was being purchased by developers such as Milton Niles, E. A. Cummings and James Scoville who began subdividing these large tracts into suburban lots. But Albert Schneider was not interested in making a profit on the land he purchased.

The intent of this farsighted young man in buying such a large parcel was to establish a kind of family compound where all his children and their families would be able to live near each other. Schneider also wanted to guarantee that there would be land available as needed for future family business ventures.

In 1860 Albert Schneider married Dorothy Karsten who had come to Oak Ridge from Germany when she was a child. He built a little cottage set on the back of the lot on the northeast corner of Lake and Marion Streets where the couple lived and Albert plied his trade making boots and shoes. The couple eventually had eleven children. Seven reached maturity and, with their families, they all lived near one another as adults in homes clustered around Schneider Street, a one-block street between Harlem Avenue and Marion Street just north of Chicago Avenue.

Growing up on the prairie in the 1870s offered little in the way of amusements for the Schneider children except "cutting up around the streets." The boys thought it was a huge joke to change signs on the stores and, as the village's only policeman made his rounds only once a night, there was no one to interrupt their pranks.

In those days the only drainage was the "big ditch" that ran along Harlem Avenue from North Avenue to Madison Street. When the Des Plaines River overflowed each spring the fish came up in the ditches and, when the water receded, they were trapped. The children thought it good sport to run across the road with a bucket and scoop up a mess of pike, bass or perch.

One evening in October 1871 no one in Oak Ridge found it necessary to light candles or kerosene lamps at dusk as the flames from the Chicago fire lit up the night sky. Every man and boy was wild to see the ruined city for themselves. But Chicago was an eight-mile walk and train fare was hard to come by. However, this did not present a problem for Albert Schneider. He made a pair of boots for the engineer on the North Western train who then allowed the cobbler and his 9-year-old son Albert to ride into the city on the cowcatcher of his engine. According to young Albert, the devastation they saw was so complete he wished he had not come and for months he suffered from nightmares recalling some of the things he had seen.

Albert Schneider was a deeply religious man and one of the founders of St. John's Lutheran Church at Belleforte and Augusta Blvd. As a young boy he carried with him from Germany a large Bible with a wooden cover given to him by his grandfather.

"At home we were all to be at the breakfast and supper table when Dad read a prayer from that Bible. He carried it with him to and from his shop and used it to his very last day," recalled his daughter Dorothea.

In 1880, as his sons approached manhood, Albert Schneider built a large two-story building on the Lake Street frontage of his lot on the corner of Lake and Marion Streets. The first floor served as a general store run by his children while the second floor was used as living quarters. In later years Schneider divided the center-entry store to accommodate new business ventures launched by his sons. Albert, Jr. opened the village's first floral shop in one half of the building while his brother Frank's barber shop occupied the other half. Both businesses were successful and the sons attributed their prosperity to the help their father was able to give them.

In later years Frank Schneider recalled that, in those days shaving was the mainstay of the profession. But a good barber also had to be proficient in trimming mustaches, Vandyke beards and goatees. Every man had his own shaving mug and woe to the barber who tried to use a substitute.

But in 1912 the Schneider store was razed after a group of local businessmen purchased this choice corner lot and commissioned architect Henry G. Fiddelke to build a small, perfectly-proportioned building to house the State Bank of Oak Park on the site.

Schneider's Grocery on the northeast corner of Lake Street and Marion.

24

Young Albert Schneider began cultivating plants and flowers at an early age on his father's land north of Chicago Avenue. In 1884 Albert married Minnie Wendt and the couple set up housekeeping on the second floor of Senne Undertaking, then located on Lake Street near Harlem Avenue.

The young entrepreneur could not afford the train fare into Chicago, so three times a week he carried his boxes of cut flowers to Garfield Park, where the horse cars began, to take his products to Chicago retailers.

By 1889 Schneider's business was so successful he built a large greenhouse and a three-story home facing Harlem Avenue on the five acres his father owned north of Chicago Avenue and surrounded the entire property with a white picket fence. Minnie and Albert's children walked to Central School and played together on Schneider Street with their various Schneider cousins, just as their parents had done before them in the little house behind Schneider's grocery on Lake Street.

Albert Schneider's business was so successful he opened stores on Marion Street, Lake Street and Concordia Cemetery plus a retail outlet at the Harlem Avenue greenhouse. But one winter night the hailstones that rained down upon his greenhouse, shattering almost every pane of glass, almost put him out of business. Schneider knew he had to take quick action to prevent his plants from freezing. So he filled the holes with paper and fired his furnace so hard he was able to survive until spring when the broken panes were replaced.

As Albert Schneider's business flourished he was able to indulge his passion for horses. In 1900 he built stables behind the greenhouse for both the horses he used for deliveries and the fine carriage horses he displayed at the Oak Park Horse Show, an important social event held every September. Schneider regularly captured blue ribbons for both his horses and the elaborate flower-bedecked floats they pulled.

In later years Philander Barclay recalled, "Remember how Albert Schneider, Jr. paid $800 to have a florist wagon built to order for the Horse Show parade? And, on top of that, another $500 for a team of fine gray mares to pull it? I'll say Albert made a hit with the spectators along the curbsides."

Albert Schneider, Jr., and his family in front of their home on Schneider Street, north of Chicago Avenue, in 1898. Greenhouses facing Harlem Avenue are in the background.

The Lost Village of Edgewater

Today few people realize that, at the turn of the century, Chicago Avenue ended at Thatcher Avenue while Division Street extended west to the Des Plaines River. Today, of course, the reverse is true. More important, Division Street also marked one of the boundaries of the "lost village" of Edgewater, a small enclave of homes clustered on the east side of the Des Plaines that existed from approximately the turn of the century to the early 1930s.

The aptly named community of Edgewater was reached by a road that extended from Division Street through the land that now belongs to the Forest Preserve District of Cook County. It was bounded on the east and northeast by the Soo Line Railroad, on the west by the river and on the south by Division Street.

Today all that remains of these "lost" homes are photographs taken by Philander Barclay who recognized the importance of preserving on film our links with the past. Some of Barclay's most dramatic photographs are pictures of homes almost completely submerged in floodwater that regularly spilled over the banks of the Des Plaines River every spring.

Flooding from the Des Plaines River inundates homes in the community of Edgewater.

Although the exact date these homes were built in Edgewater is unclear, we do know the names of many of the families who lived in the community thanks to the recollections of residents such as Hazel Ney, a granddaughter of Mr. and Mrs. John Schneider. The Schneiders build their home in Edgewater around 1905 and raised thirteen children in it until 1921 when flooding finally drove them out.

According to Mrs. Ney, Edgewater was a location at which the Soo Line trains stopped to take on water. She recalled that her grandmother cooked for the railroad workers when they came to repair the tracks in the spring. One of Mrs. Schneider's favorite recipes was cherry soup with dumplings. The cherries came from the acres of cherry orchards that could be found on the west side of the river. There was also a canning factory that processed the fruit adjacent to the orchard.

Albert Trebass, who was also raised in Edgewater, recalled that the area around Chicago Avenue at Thatcher was flooded much of the year with water deep enough to float a boat. When Albert and his brother rode across it they had to get up on the horses' back to keep their feet from getting wet.

In those days Thatcher Woods was a nesting place for a variety of animals that provided both food and sport. Trebass and his brothers spent many hours fishing along the banks of the Des Plaines. His recollections of his childhood make the area sound like a legendary Eden: "Fish were both plentiful and so close to the surface that they could be scooped up in a net. And there were wild ducks. They came by the hundreds sitting so close you couldn't get a finger between them. Wild pigeons there were, too, lighting in such droves they broke the branches from the oak trees they settled in."

Prairie chickens were plentiful and good meat, but farmers did not have the time for hunting, so an Irishman named Frank Mooney devised a way to trap them. "We got so many that even with our six children, we could not eat them all," said Trebass. So his father salted them down in a 50-gallon barrel like pork. That way they would keep a year and, soaked in fresh clabber, (sour thick milk) would come out like new killed meat.

Charles Spear, another River Forester who spent his boyhood in Thatcher Woods, caught many fish in the river which he cooked and ate on the spot. "There, floundering in shallow pools after the spring floods receded, we caught many pickerel which, split, cleaned and their flaky white meat broiled in a fashion never quite as appetizing since, also brought untold satisfaction to our continually empty stomachs," he recalled.

As early as 1907 famed architect Dwight Perkins recognized that, as Chicago continued to expand, there was an urgent need to create an Outer Belt Park System that would provide open recreational space for future generations. As a leader in the formation of the Forest Preserve District of Cook County, he lobbied suburban municipalities to set aside large tracts of undeveloped land before developers could purchase them.

Thatcher Woods, "too low and seasonally submerged" to sustain any more development, yet rich with a variety of native wildflowers, seemed a natural site for recreational use. On May 3, 1917 the Forest Preserve District of Cook County acquired title to all of Thatcher Woods, including the homes in the community of Edgewater.

Little was done with the site until the 1930s when, in the midst of the Depression, WPA workers were used to make a series of repairs and improvements to the Forest Preserve land.

Division Street was closed west of Thatcher, the houses were demolished and trees planted where they had once stood. The native vegetation was allowed to reclaim the land and the community known as Edgewater ceased to exist.

27

Bird's eye view of Oak Park, River Forest and Forest Park in 1873 drawn by itinerant German artist.

CHAPTER II

FROM COUNTRY HAMLET TO CITY SUBURB

Frank Schneider leaning against Pagers barber shop at 107 Lake Street.

Long Battle Freed Village From Boss McCaffery

When Chicago was incorporated in 1837 the remainder of Cook County was divided into large areas called precincts which bore no resemblance to the small neighborhood entities we call precincts today. These precincts offered little in the way of services for the increasing number of settlers who were clearing the land for farms.

But by 1857 the Illinois legislature had consolidated these precincts into townships and established the township form of government. Oak Ridge, along with Austin, Ridgeland, Cicero and several smaller communities all became part of Cicero Township, named for Cicero, New York where many settlers had migrated from.

Cicero Township was governed by an elected five-man board. Each trustee had a specific job: clerk, tax assessor, commissioner of highways, justice of the peace and overseer of the poor. But one of these men held the additional, and very influential, post of supervisor. This job, in the wrong hands, could be extremely lucrative to the individual holding it at the expense of the taxpayer. At various times prior to 1867 this position was held by James Scoville, Henry Austin and Milton Niles, all Oak Ridge men of unquestioned integrity.

However, in 1867 John McCaffery, a Machiavellian politician from Brighton (now a community on the southwest side of Chicago), was elected supervisor. Three of his cronies were also elected while Oak Park's representation dwindled to just one man.

That same year the Illinois legislature passed a new charter for Cicero Township that expanded the board of trustees from five to seven men. Further, the charter gave these men authority to borrow money for local improvements on the town's credit and without waiting to collect the special assessments levied to pay for them.

"This most vicious provision cost the Township of Cicero about $500,000 of which Oak Ridge had to pay its quota," said John Lewis, an early village historian who chronicled McCaffery's regime. "For a number of years John McCaffery was the dominating spirit of the board and the virtual dictator of local improvements. And the specifications for these improvements read like a fairy tale."

Villagers also seethed over the exorbitant fees paid the trustees. The charter provided that they were entitled to receive $3 for each day's attendance at meetings and limited compensation to no more than $156 a year per trustee. But, in reality, each man including McCaffery, received lump sums of $1,200 (not a huge sum today but very substantial in that era.)

ANNEXATION!!

..Shall we...

Annex Austin?
—OR—
Austin and Oak Park?
—OR—
THE WHOLE TOWN?
How will either affect the Schools and the Saloons?

MASONIC HALL, BERWYN,
Saturday, April 1, 1899, 8 p. m.

Come and hear what JOHN LEWIS and O. D. ALLEN of Oak Park have to say.

Mr. E. S. OSGOOD, President of the Board of Education of District No. I, will discuss the schools.

What shall we do about the SALOON QUESTION if annexation carries?

What about our Schools?

McCaffery ousted by irate voters

These and other abuses finally roused voters in all the communities governed by Cicero Township to vote McCaffery out of office in the election of 1873. Although several Oak Park men were elected, they did not have a majority and so found themselves continually engaged in battle with trustees from other communities such as Cicero who resisted their attempts to curb gambling, drunkenness, corruption and other vices that flourished unchecked in these communities.

In 1893 a delegation of citizens presented the board with a petition with 1,690 signatures asking that the Hawthorne racetrack "be suppressed and that there be no renewal of saloon licenses in the town and that the ordinance granting licenses to sell liquor be repealed." After listening to a number of impassioned speeches, the board referred the matter to the committee of the whole who, after due deliberation and, to absolutely no one's surprise, rejected them.

The majority trustees often used subterfuge to outwit the minority board members. In the small hours of December 20, 1898 they passed four "midnight ordinances" that granted additional rights to several small railroads that served the township and provided for a five-cent fare to Austin—with an additional three-cent fare west of Austin—a distinct slap at Oak Park residents who commuted daily to the Loop.

All of the trustees but one were present at the meeting where a vote was to be taken on these laws. The absentee was one Peter MacDonald who was confined to bed because of an accident. When the board took a short recess, the three Oak Park trustees, concluding that the only way to defeat the ordinances was by preventing a quorum of the board, left the Town Hall in Austin and went to the home of Jesse Baldwin in Oak Park.

At midnight after checking the town hall and finding it deserted, the Oak Park trustees assumed that the meeting had been ad-

---

NOTICE!

THERE WILL BE A

MASS MEETING

Held at 133 Lake St.

Friday Eve., Dec. 13, 1901

at 8 o'clock, in the interest of the

People's Independent Ticket

for Officers of the new Village of Oak Park.

The several candidates will address the meeting and speeches will be made by A. B. MELVILLE and other prominent citizens. Come out in force and bring your friends.

Remember, 8 P. M., Friday, at 133 Lake Street, Oak Park.

6th Precinct,	ALLEN S. RAY, Candidate for President.	
5th "	GEO. M. AMBROSE, Candidate for Clerk.	
1st "	FRANK B. MACOMBER,	
2d "	CORNELIUS P. DUNGAN,	Candidates
3d "	WALTER S. HOLDEN,	for
4th "	C. R. McHUGH,	Trustees.
7th "	R. R. CUTHBERTSON,	
8th "	EVELYN P. SPERRY,	

V. G. BARFIELD,
Secretary.

J. I. JONES,
Chairman Campaign Com.

journed and so went home, satisfied that they had saved their constituents from an outrageous fare increase. However, in their absence the majority trustees drove to Peter McDonald's house and persuaded the injured man to accompany them to the Cicero Town Hall. They reconvened around 2 a.m. and passed the ordinances.

The *Oak Park Times* noted this sad state of affairs. "Oak Park trustees are continually outvoted on everything from issuing a liquor license to Cicero saloonkeepers and lucrative contracts to cronies of Cicero trustees to auditing outrageous inflated bills. And the anger of voters counted as nothing to these politicians."

But the anger and frustration of Oak Park residents had its limits. As early as 1880 villagers had lobbied for a separate government. But at that time no law existed under which a home rule government could be set up. However, in 1891 the legislature passed an act allowing for the separation of incorporated towns. According to this law, none of the individual towns could vote themselves out of the township. Rather the entire township had to vote on the question.

Unfortunately many communities such as Austin were jealous of Oak Park's greater share of wealth and influence. As a result, the village's first attempt to break away in an 1895 election was defeated with most of the "nays" coming from Austin. Oak Parkers returned the favor four years later by mustering a vote large enough to have Austin annexed to Chicago, even though most Austinites opposed the move. At the same time Oak Park citizens finally were able to vote themselves out of the township.

But it was a short-lived victory. Austin residents challenged the vote in the Illinois Supreme Court which upheld their annexation to Chicago but also negated the Act of 1891 which left Oak Park back at square one as the unwilling chattel of Cicero Township.

But by then there was no turning back. A committee was appointed to draw up an amendment to the Cities and Villages Act that would permit separation. The law was passed and went into effect on July 1, 1901. Oak Park residents lost no time in organizing a township-wide election in November to decide whether the village should remain a part of Cicero Township. The result was an overwhelming vote in favor of allowing Oak Park to separate from Cicero Township and establish a self-governing municipality. In December the first slate of eight officials was elected and the first formal session of the new Oak Park board of trustees was held on January 2, 1902 in Scoville Institute.

Lake Street Was Business Center From Earliest Days

Oak Park's central business center known today as Downtown Oak Park, has always been a work in progress. As early as the 1830s when Joseph and Betty Kettlestrings offered hospitality in their cabin to travelers, the two-block Lake Street business district bounded by Harlem and Forest Avenues has always served the commercial needs of the public.

Beginning in the late 1850s a scattering of frame buildings began to appear on Lake Street when Kettlestrings began subdividing his quarter section into lots. One of the earliest businesses was Steiner's grocery and dry goods store on the northeast corner of Lake Street and Harlem Avenue. It was established in 1856 by a Mr. Furbeck, who sold it two years later to Mrs. Catherine Pattock, who ran it alone until she married William Steiner.

Lake Street did not really develop as a vibrant commercial area until after the Civil War. After being mustered out of the Union Army many Veterans such as Delos Hull, Dr.

"Oak Park is located eight miles west of the Chicago River with an abundant elevation. It is a bower of beauty. It is the home of luxury and refinement. Here education flourishes and religion and temperance triumph. There is no place for anything that savors of discord or disorder. Saloons are excluded. Animals are not allowed to roam and a hog or cow is never seen on the street. The streets are always cleanly kept. One feels relaxation and comfort within its borders and along its shaded walks. Gaily dressed children romp and the air is vocal with the music of their sweet voices. Churches, schools and society halls meet the eye at every turn."

Orin Peake, E. A. Cummings, Anson Hemingway, William Beye, Christian Schlund and Charles Bolles to name but a few, moved to the village and opened businesses that provided much-needed services. These men were joined by other entrepreneurs who also recognized that the village had all the attributes that would act as a magnet to families seeking to escape the dirt and congestion of the city.

The Chicago Fire in 1871 was another catalyst for both economic and residential growth in the village as many Chicagoans decided to relocate in Oak Park. As a result, between 1870 and 1890, Oak Park gradually evolved from a small country village to a thriving suburb. The population which was approximately 500 in 1870 more than doubled in the year after the fire, and is given as 4,589 in the 1890 school census.

William Halley, editor of the *Oak Park Vindicator* and self-proclaimed cheerleader for the community, summarized some of the reasons Oak Park was an attractive choice for both families and new businesses in his 1898 book, *Pictorial Oak Park*.

"Oak Park is located eight miles west of the Chicago River with an abundant elevation. It is a bower of beauty. It is the home of luxury and refinement. Here education flourishes and religion and temperance triumph. There is no place for anything that savors of discord or disorder. Saloons are excluded. Animals are not allowed to roam and a hog or cow is never seen on the street. The streets are always cleanly kept. One feels relaxation and comfort within its borders and along its shaded walks. Gaily dressed children romp and the air is vocal with the music of their sweet voices.

Steiner's Grocery and Dry Goods on the northeast corner of Lake Street and Harlem Avenue was established in 1856.

Churches, schools and society halls meet the eye at every turn."

Lake Street merchants offered shoppers few amenities

Most of the early merchants who built two-story frame buildings along Lake Street lived above the store with their families. Since Lake Street was still an unpaved road all of these buildings had wooden sidewalks in front to prevent pedestrians from sinking into a quagmire of mud as they did their shopping.

But, as the *Oak Park Reporter* noted, these sidewalks were poor affairs. "The boards soon rot, or become loose while the nails creep up to catch and tear the ladies' dresses." And in the spring when the mud was deepest, pedestrians had to carry wooden boards on which to step to get across the street.

Still, when the Cicero Township Board attempted to grade and gravel the street villagers denounced the improvement as unnecessary and something that would destroy the rural simplicity of the village. However, by the 1880s, Lake Street was not only graded and graveled but, during the dry summer months, it was also regularly sprinkled to minimize the dust.

Once darkness descended on Lake Street the only source of illumination was the moon and pedestrians had to rely on kerosene lanterns to light their way. Children carrying these lanterns were dispatched by their mothers to the train depot on Marion Street to light the way home for their fathers returning from the city. During the 1870s oil streetlights were installed, but only at intersections. Children followed the men in charge of changing the carbon fillers in these lamps. They used the discarded charcoal as chalk to mark the wooden sidewalks for games such as Sky Blue and hopscotch.

But when Oak Parkers were given the opportunity to illuminate their streets with electricity many initially opposed the idea. In 1897 a large meeting was held in Steiner's Hall to protest the electric light poles that were in the process of being installed on village streets by the Cicero Gas, Water and Electric Light Co. at a cost of $85 for each light per year.

"Dr. W. C. Gray offered a series of resolutions which pointed out the evil effects of the poles and called for the appointment of a

Looking west on Lake Street from Marion Street.

committee to consult with officers of the electric company and request the removal of the unsightly poles," said the *Vindicator*.

"W. H. Wood responded with a well tempered address in which he took issue with some of Dr. Gray's statements. He offered a modification of the resolution but this was voted down and Dr. Gray's resolutions were carried. It is understood that a conference will be held Monday between the committee and the company. In the interim, work will cease, the town authorities having notified the company to stop putting up the poles."

Some of the early businesses established on Lake Street included Kaltenbach hardware and tin shop at 117-19 Lake Street, William Johnston's blacksmith and carriage making shop at 121-3 Lake Street, and the Holley Block, at 125-27 Lake Street, a substantial building erected in 1870 by Nathan Holley. This building housed several important businesses including Father Robbins harness shop in the basement, the Hotel Leonard, Berlin Grocery and the meeting rooms for the Women's Christian Temperance Union.

In 1878 George Nordenholdt opened Oak Park's first bakery at 138 Lake and in 1869 Frank Pebbles who later gained national recognition as a portrait painter, had a paint and decorating store at 144 Lake. Also after the Civil War Dr. Orin Peake opened the village's first drug store and doctor's office at 206 Lake Street. In 1886 Dr. Peake opened a registry in his store and asked all residents to record their name and address in it. This was the basis for the first village directory which was published in 1886 and every year thereafter. In 1871 O. W. Herrick, who had earlier served as Oak Park's first school principal, opened a general store and post office next to Dr. Peake's and began to compete with Steiner's grocery a block away.

Lake Street Business District Expands

Until 1880, Marion Street was just a one-block thoroughfare running from the North Western tracks to Lake Street. But it also had its share of businesses as the commercial center of the village expanded. Or, as one early settler noted, "In those days after the Civil War Oak Park was a regular country vil-

Looking south on Marion Street from Lake Street.

lage, sprawling like a spiderwort bloom over the plain, its tentacles shooting out in all directions but the slim-bodied center already settling down in the Lake-Marion district."

The Post Office Block at 105 Marion housed both the post office and Postmaster Delos Hull's coal business. In 1895 the Chicago Telephone Company installed the first phone in the village with one operator in charge in Lovett's Drug Store which was located on the southeast corner of Lake and Marion. Hoard's Block, a substantial three-story brick building built in 1876 by Elijah Hoard was across the street on the southwest corner. Hoard's Hall served as the village's social center in those early days. The first floor consisted of several storefronts while the large rooms on the upper floors were used for dances, socials, recitals and concerts.

In a 1921 issue of *The Oak Parker,* Mrs Carlos Ward took a look back at the Lake Street business district through the eyes of a young girl. "It is not hard to imagine myself again as a school girl strolling down Lake Street with no web of electric wires overhead, no pavement to disturb the richness of the natural soil. Those were indeed happy days when Mr. Herrick dealt out sugar and jokes together over the counter of his grocery store, when, if there was a call for a bottle of camphor or a pound of copperas (used in water purification and to treat anemia), Dr. Peake measured it out to us at his drug store."

"In those days, too, we used to board the trains for the city from the station at Marion Street. When we needed a spool of thread or a yard of calico we went down to Lake Street and bought it of Mrs. Steiner who not infrequently berated us for neglecting her and visiting the city stores in an ambitious search for more pretentious finery than she kept on sale for our convenience."

In the 1860s many of Oak Park's most prominent citizens such as Charles Bolles, Edwin Gale, James Scoville, Rueben Whaples and Joseph Kettlestrings built handsome Italianate and Greek Revival homes on Lake Street east of the business district. One of the most outstanding was Henry Austin, Sr.'s estate at Lake Street and Forest Avenue, which was designed by John Blair, the landscape architect who planned Garfield Park. (At that time Blair's home and nursery were on the site of what is now the Frank Lloyd Wright Home and Studio at Chicago and Forest Avenues.)

Henry Austin's estate was set apart from nearby homes and businesses on Lake Street by a picturesque split rail fence. In later years Albert Schneider, Jr. recalled the one feature on the Austin property that left a lasting impression on him as a young boy: "You know those wooden Indians that used to stand in front of cigar stores? Well, Henry Austin had a lot of them set around in his woods. I suppose that was to make it look wilder."

Nathan Holley also developed a city block of substantial houses on a densely wooded tract of oaks he purchased from Joseph Kettlestrings bounded by Ontario, Harlem Avenue, Lake and Marion Streets. By the 1950s all of these homes had been razed to make way for the Holley Court parking lot.

(An interesting business aside: In 1875 C. A. Pillsbury came to Chicago with samples of his new "Pillsbury's Best" flour. Nathan Holley's son, Lyman Giddings Holley, purchased the first carload of this flour, which he sold in small lots to customers. In 1885 he became the exclusive agent for the Pillsbury Company in Chicago.)

Early Black Residents

As early as the 1880s there were many African American families living in Oak Park. Although some Blacks had purchased lots and built their homes north of Augusta Boulevard in northwest Oak Park, the majority lived in small cottages on William Street, the one block east-west enclave between Harlem Avenue and Marion Street. (This thoroughfare was known as Hoard's Alley in the 1870s. It was renamed Westgate in 1931 when it was developed as a commercial area.)

Most had migrated from the south in search of a better life. Those Blacks who settled in Oak Park found jobs were numerous, yet offered little chance for advancement. Black women worked as maids, cooks, laundresses, nursemaids or house servants while higher paying clerical positions were closed to them. Black men found jobs as coachmen and domestic servants in private homes. They also worked as baggage handlers, porters and laborers shoveling coal on the

Black delivery man navigates ruts on unpaved Lake Street in 1880s.

North Western engines, but they could never become engineers.

But although these early Black Oak Parkers worked at menial jobs, they were still undeniably better off here than they had been in the rural south, where they had usually been exploited by the sharecropping system. A capable laundress or cook in Oak Park or River Forest could command $1.50 per day, plus carfare and a meal. This was more money than she might earn for an entire week picking cotton in Mississippi.

In the 1890s Black villagers held prayer meetings in Central School. These services were scheduled for Thursday evening because that was when most domestic had their one "night off."

But by 1905 the newly-built Mt. Carmel Colored Baptist Church became the social and spiritual focal point for Oak Park's Black community. The Church was located at what is now 1138 Westgate. It was built on a lot that was given to the congregation by a former Black maid of Elijah Hoard, an early settler whose house was on the corner of Marion Street and Westgate. The gift of the lot had been Hoard's reward to her for long and faithful service. The congregation also received financial help from many Oak Park families including a $500 gift from John Farson.

Congregation of the Mount Carmel Colored Baptist Church in front of their church on William Street (now Westgate).

38

Center of Commerce Shifts to Oak Park Avenue at Turn of Century

By 1900 the aging wooden stores on Lake Street between Harlem Avenue and Marion Street that had served the needs of early settlers were badly dilapidated. The Oak Park Improvement Association attempted to persuade owners of these decrepit buildings to replace them with modern structures.

"It hardly seems possible that the architectural beauty of the new buildings on the Avenue and the old wooden business blocks on Lake Street can be the expression of the same municipal life and spirit. Yet they exist side-by-side," noted the *Oak Leaves*.

"Oak Park Avenue is growing to be very attractive. In fact, the increasing attractiveness of the Avenue as a business center must soon begin to draw trade away from Lake Street and to injure the value of Lake Street property unless steps be taken to put the Lake Street business section on a par with the Avenue."

In 1893 Normand Patton designed the handsome Romanesque and Queen Anne building at 116 N. Oak Park Avenue for the Cicero Water, Gas and Electric Light Company who used the space for both offices and as a showroom for their appliances. (This building was placed on the National Register of Historic Places in 1981.)

As a good-will gesture the company reserved the upper floor for public meetings. In 1894 the *Oak Park Reporter* noted, "The Oak Park Council, No. 18, Royal League, held its first meeting in the new hall of the Cicero Gas Company building. Avenue Hall is a very pretty lodge room, handsomely carpeted and furnished, with a seating capacity of about 75."

By 1899 Charles Burton Scoville, son of James Scoville, had completed the Scoville building on the southeast corner of Lake and Oak Park Avenue. This three-story complex of retail and apartments was inspired by the design of the town hall in Frankfort, Germany and boasted a unique tile roof, steep Flemish gables and projecting bays.

Still another indication of the growing importance of Oak Park's east end was construction of the community's first separate high school building on the southwest corner of Lake Street and East Avenue in 1891. This three-story brick building was intended to relieve overcrowding at Central School at Lake Street and Forest Avenue which, at that time, housed all twelve grades.

In 1902 E. E. Roberts designed Oak Park's new Municipal Hall one block east at Lake and Euclid. Roberts was also the architect for the Masonic Block built four years later at 167 N. Oak Park Avenue, on the southwest corner of Lake Street and Oak Park Avenue. The building was designed for retail on the ground floor with the upper floors reserved for Masonic lodges and

Cicero Gas, Light and Water Co. building at 116 N. Oak Park Avenue was used by the utility both as offices and a show room for their appliances. It was built in 1893.

The Scoville Building, completed in 1899 on the southeast corner of Lake Street and Oak Park Avenue, was inspired by the design of the Frankfort Town Hall in Germany.

offices. The Masonic Block was better known to several generations of Villagers as "Gilmore's" when the family-owned business of Wm. Y. Gilmore & Sons occupied the entire first floor from the 1920s until 1976 when the store closed. Through the years the building was remodeled so often that its original design became unrecognizable. It was restored in 1984 by Industrial Fire & Casualty Co.

Oak Park Avenue's position as a center of commerce was further solidified in December, 1899 when Willis Herrick, son of O. W.

The newly completed Municipal Building on Lake Street at Euclid Avenue in 1904.

Herrick, the Village's first school principal, opened Avenue State Bank in a storefront at 126 N. Oak Park Avenue. Charles Bolles, Herrick's successor as president, later built the Greek Revival building at 104 N. Oak Park Avenue. A year later the federal government purchased the corner lot on Oak Park Avenue and Lake Street for a new post office, replacing the cramped facility on Marion Street.

By 1900 Oak Park's population was almost 9,353 according to the school census. Within the next ten years when the population doubled to 20,911 residents, many people began to be concerned about the lack of open space. With the exception of uncultivated prairie that was fast being developed, there was no open land available for parks.

Homeowners such as Anson Hemingway were continually lobbying officials to purchase land for recreational use. "Is it not time that our village select a choice piece of ground and improve it in a manner that will make us worthy of the name 'Oak Park'?" he demanded.

Hemingway's first choice was Scoville Place, the historic site on the northwest corner of Oak Park Avenue and Lake Street where James Scoville had built his American Gothic home atop the rise. Scoville and his wife had long since moved to California for her health and the house had been used for a variety of purposes including a finishing school for girls and temporary home of the Oak Park Club.

In 1910 villagers were jolted by the news that Charles Burton Scoville had leased the family estate to Dunlop & Co., a real estate firm that proposed building both an office building and a hotel on the homesite. Reaction by residents was immediate and acrimonious. An *Oak Leaves* editorial sum-

This new post office built in 1902 on the northeast corner of Oak Park Avenue and Lake Street was the village's first federal building.

marized the general mood: "Everyone who has the beauty of Oak Park at heart will be pained by the news that a business building is to be erected on Scoville Place. We have all come to regard this site as sacred ground dedicated to the future glory of the community, a public breathing place to be held forever inviolate as a public square."

"It is a harbinger of what we may expect to befall this beautiful site if the people of Oak Park do not wake up and take this ground over for public use. We have been asleep long enough on the playground and park question. If we continue to drowse we shall deserve to lose this and every other op-portunity for the acquisition of public ground."

Oak Park voters heeded this advice and in 1912 approved creation of a park district administered by an elected board of five commissioners. Charles Scoville reconsidered the project and, in what is probably the greatest real estate bargain in village history, he agreed to sell both Scoville Place and the "old cricket ground" or what we know today as Ridgeland Common, to the newly created Park District for $135,637.

Quick's Maneuvers Slowed Early River Forest Commerce

River Forest's Lake Street commercial corridor between Harlem Avenue and Lathrop has grown at a phenomenal pace in recent years. But for the reluctance of Henry Quick and his son John Henry, curmudgeonly co-owners of most of this land for almost half a century, business development along this main thoroughfare might have occurred more than a century ago.

The Quicks arrived here in the 1850s from Harlem, New York and proceeded to buy most of the land on the southeast end of River Forest and the north end of Forest Park. They also named the old section road that bordered their land "Harlem" in honor of their home town. The Quicks built an elegant Gothic house on Lake Street about a block west of Harlem Avenue. It was set in a grove of beautiful ash trees and had a bowling green, harness and carriage rooms, stables and servant's quarters.

Henry Quick donated a tract of land on the corner of Lake Street and Bonnie Brae, across the street from his house, on which to build Christ Episcopal Church. But, unlike James Scoville, who gave land in Oak Park for the First Congregational Church with no strings attached, Quick expected a return on his investment.

He applied for, and received, tax-exempt status on not just the land donated for the church, but on all of his considerable real estate holdings. Quick's rationale was that because he participated in the church service each week by reading a chapter of the Bible from the pulpit, he was part of the church body and, therefore, his property qualified as church property. This blatant tax dodge earned him the enmity of other homeowners that lasted for many years.

In 1856 the elder Quick allowed his son John Henry to divide the acreage by establishing the Quick Farm in what is now Forest Park and by building a boardinghouse known as "The Barracks" on what is now Oak Street west of Bonnie Brae. This large two-story building was used by both early settlers and the men who worked in the machine shops of the Chicago and North Western railroad which was located in Harlem.

As the only landlords for miles around, father and son were able to exercise complete control over the unincorporated area that did not become a municipality until 1880. According to William Halley, editor of the *Oak Park Vindicator*, "In 1856 there was no municipal control and Mr. Quick had his

Reproduction of 1874 woodcut of the home of Henry Quick on Lake Street, a block west of Harlem Avenue (now River Forest).

Reproduction of 1874 woodcut of Christ Episcopal Church built by Henry Quick at the corner of Lake Street and Bonnie Brae Street in Harlem (now River Forest).

way in everything. He named the streets, laid out the blocks and built the sidewalks."

Henry Quick was also influential enough to have Noyesville, the small post office located on the west bank of the Des Plaines River that served settlers in both Cicero and Proviso Townships, transferred to Harlem House, a hotel he built on Railroad Avenue (Central), opposite the Harlem train depot. And, as the largest landowner in the area Quick felt he was entitled to name the entire town Harlem. But that was one of the few things in which he did not get his way. There was already a post office in Winnebago County with that name and the citizens did not intend to give it up.

Henry Quick died in 1872 and his son became sole owner of the family's extensive properties. According to William Halley, "It was hard to do business with the elder Quick, but it became a great deal harder to have transactions with his son who was a lawyer." The residents became discouraged. The post office and train depot were moved

to Oak Park and even the congregation of Christ Church became dissatisfied with the autocratic way in which the church was managed. They withdrew and organized Grace Episcopal Church in Oak Park in 1879.

"John Henry Quick retired from the scene after his house burned in 1875," Halley added. "He took up residence in Chicago but comes out every Sunday to read prayers in the old church which he still keeps open, aided by a few old and faithful adherents."

Amos Squire Pack was another early River Forest settler who had a more positive impact on the community. Although he was a member of Quick's church he tried not to get involved in the feud. Pack had been postmaster when the post office was located on the Des Plaines. He also ran a general store on the north side of Lake Street just west of Bonnie Brae. But he is best known as being one of three men appointed by a judge of Cook County to conduct the 1880 election at which River Forest voters decided to incor-

43

porate as an independent municipality separate from Harlem (later Forest Park.)

Other early River Forest businesses located on Lake Street included John Williams confectionery and tobacco store, the Vorass feed store and Heeler's grocery store on the southeast corner of Lake and Williams Street. Elizabeth Porter Furbeck remembered Heeler's as an emporium "where crackers came packed in barrels, codfish in some semblance of its original form, tobacco was weighed out loose, coarse brown paper was thought good enough to wrap around the articles you bought and, if it was a cold day, you had to wait for your molasses."

John Grandland opened River Forest's first hardware store at what is today 7575 Lake Street in 1895. "The store was complete with kegs of nails, pocket knives, straight edge razors, wash boards and tubs and all those supplies that make an old time hardware store fascinating," recalled his daughter Elizabeth in later years.

"Dad had rigged up an electric alarm system run off a dry cell that would set off a buzzer in the cottage next door where we lived whenever someone came in the door. Mother would quick put aside whatever she was doing and rush over to the store to wait on the customer," she added.

Behind the store Grandland built a shop where he operated his sheet metal and tinsmith business. In addition to the work area, the building also housed Maude, the family horse, a wagon and hayloft. And, when this building was complete, he threw a big party to celebrate. "The floors were waxed, colored paper streamers were strung across the rafters and the guests danced and ate until the wee hours of the morning. The food had been prepared by mother and served from the cottage next door," said Elizabeth. "But on Monday morning it was all business. The wax had been removed from the floor, the streamers taken down and the men were ready for work."

As a child Elizabeth liked to go to the "office" with her father on Sunday mornings to help him work on his books. "Usually I made things from metal pieces in the scrap bins," she recalled. "But the most enjoyable part of those Sundays was when Dad took Maude out of her stall, tossed a blanket over her back, put a halter on her and let me ride her around the big field west of Lathrop."

How Henry Austin Tamed Chicago's Western Prairie

In 1858 Henry Austin, a young and extremely enterprising hardware salesman from Skaneateles, New York arrived in Chicago. And, given the pumps and jackscrews he was selling, Austin's arrival could not have been better timed.

In the late 1850s Chicago's boundaries extended only as far west as what is today Western Avenue—or the western edge of Chicago. Much of the wind-swept prairie west of the city was a muddy slough. Roads were impassable most of the year and the few houses that dotted the landscape were built by pioneers who settled outside the city limits to avoid paying taxes. But although these settlers managed to keep clear of the tax collector, there wasn't much they could do avoid the flooding that left their homes under eight or ten feet of water every spring.

In 1857 the Cicero Township Board had passed a law requiring that all buildings had to be raised to keep them out of water. This was an opportunity not to be missed by Henry Austin, a manufacturer's representative for the Gould Hardware Company. He began a thriving business selling pumps to farmers to drain their fields and jackscrews that were used to raise buildings above the water level. Hardware was a natural sideline but soon became the largest part of Austin's business during the building boom in both Chicago and Oak Park after the 1871 Chicago Fire.

In 1860 Austin built a distinctive gabled house on Lake Street on a large parcel he had purchased from Joseph Kettlestrings. In his daily commute between Chicago and Oak Park he had ample opportunity to evaluate property along the way. In 1866, just five years before the Chicago Fire would create a demand for new housing away from the city, Austin purchased the 280-acre farm of Henry DeKoven and began subdividing it into six residential subdivisions. The tract was bounded by what is now Central Avenue, Austin Blvd., the North Western tracks and Augusta Blvd.

There were few trees on this prairie tract so Austin directed his gardener, George Ingle, who worked on his Oak Park estate, to plant thousands of saplings throughout his subdi-

Bird's eye view from the top of Cicero Town Hall in Austin.

45

visions. "Most of the streets are wide with double driveways and parks in the center which are planted with evergreens and nut-bearing trees, while the streets are lined with elms," reported a visitor.

Ironically, part of Henry DeKoven's land included the Six Mile House, a tavern located six miles west of the city that was a popular stopping point for both farmers and passengers on the Frink and Walker stage coach that rumbled over the Lake Street turnpike heading west to Galena. Henry Austin was a staunch supporter of the temperance movement and, as a state legislator, successfully lobbied for passage of the Illinois Temperance bill.

Henry Austin was joined by several other developers who purchased surrounding tracts until the new community of "Austinville" included a territory one-mile square, bounded on the north by Augusta Boulevard; Laramie Avenue on the east; Madison Street to the south and Austin Boulevard on the west. In just two years over 200 fine homes were built by businessmen who wanted to give their families the advantages of country living. One of the daily commuters to the city contrasted the dust and smoke of the city with the pure air in Austin, which was "as clear and fragrant as the sweet clover which grew near the station. The gates of white picket fences opened to paths that led to old-fashioned gardens and pleasant homes."

But however idyllic Austinites considered their community, it did not stop Oak Park residents, whose homesites were ten feet higher above sea level, to disparagingly refer to their neighbors as "swamp angels." Writing in the *Oak Leaves* years later Edwin Wanzer recalled, "We resented this attitude because our houses were almost as high as theirs, being built on cedar posts five or six feet off the ground. And besides, if we happened to have a hard freeze in flood time, you could sit on your front porch, put on your skates and skate to Elgin and return. Could Oak Park boast of such a skating rink? I think not."

Austin's philanthropy

Wanzer also recounted one of Henry Austin's many acts of philanthropy that made him such a beloved figure and prompted residents to name the town in his honor. A young musician named G. A. Hastreiter organized the Austin Cornet Band. The group, consisting of many musically-inclined young men, became so popular they were given free use of a room in the Cicero Town Hall to practice and were much in demand to perform. However, the musicians all worked for small salaries and could not afford instruments.

So they turned to Henry Austin for help. "He not only endorsed our plan but gave us a town lot which we sold for $200," said Wanzer. "In this way we were able to purchase two E-flat cornets, two B-flat cornets, two alto horns, one tenor, one baritone, a tuba, a bass and a snare drum. We were now fully equipped thanks to Mr. Austin."

Cicero Town Hall, Lake Street and Central Avenue.

In 1868 Henry Austin donated a four acre tract to Cicero Township for a park and a Town Hall. With the construction of the Town Hall at Central Avenue and Lake Street in 1871, Austin became the seat of Cicero government until 1899 when the community was annexed to Chicago. Henry Austin served briefly as township supervisor, and in that role he was responsible for the widening of Madison Street, Lake Street and Chicago Avenue, as well as for the layout out of nine north-south streets, among them Central and Austin.

In 1866 Henry Austin donated 30 acres of land to the U. S. Brass and Clock Company of New Haven, Connecticut and persuaded its directors to build a three-story plant at the intersection of Waller Avenue and Lake Street. Nearly one hundred new homes were built nearby to house the workers. But just two years later fire destroyed most of the clock works and prompted the relocation of many workers to Connecticut. This calamity forced the community to look to its future as a residential suburb. Although a shoe factory operated for a time in the shell of the clock works, Austin failed to attract any other large businesses.

Because the light manufacturing initially attracted working men and their families to the community the residential architecture of Austin is an eclectic blend of modest cottages and elegant residences. The community soon became a sylvan retreat for well-to-do Chicago businessmen including Seth Warner, George Philbrick and architect

The Oaks Clubhouse.

Frederick Schock who designed many of the homes in the area.

In 1880 Schock also organized the exclusive Oaks Club. A clubhouse was built by members at Lake Street and Waller Avenue on the site of the former clock factory. Although the Club was a male bastion, its drawing rooms were used for socials and concerts by popular musical societies of the era including the Handel Oratorio Society, Beethoven Club and Rubinstein Club.

The main business district in early Austin was on Park Avenue (Parkside). Nissen Brothers, one of Oak Park's most popular grocers, opened a branch on Park Avenue. Dick Traill's Drug Store, where the community's first telephone was installed, was another important establishment.

But the center of the tightly knit community in the 1880s and 1890s was the North Western Station at Central Avenue. The lit-

tle frame building became a meeting place for commuters who swapped stories as they waited for the train to take them to their jobs in the city. Because there was a clear view across the broad expanse of prairie from Austin to Oak Park, many commuters used to wait until they saw the train pull out

Parkside Avenue Business District.

of Oak Park before starting for the Austin depot.

"Those were the days when everybody in Austin knew everybody else and there was a fine spirit of mutual helpfulness," said Joseph Kampp whose father opened the community's first undertaking parlor in 1890. "There were so few of us that we had to be neighborly. We had our own fire department, composed of volunteers. When a fire occurred we turned out and worked as desperately as if we had received a dollar an hour, but we got not a cent."

But, according to Kampp, this feeling of camaraderie did not extend to Oak Park. "Austin wanted an extension of the city streetcar lines and Oak Park did not," he recalled. "A midnight ordinance was passed by the Cicero Town Board permitting the electric streetcar lines to extend to Austin. This made Oak Park mad, and when the annexation issue came up Oak Park got back at Austin by voting the community into the city."

47

'Ridge land' Prairie East of Oak Park Subdivided In 1870s

Before the Chicago Fire in 1871 Oak Park was already a prosperous and rapidly growing community with a population of about 500. In stark contrast, the prairie to the east of East Avenue (the Village's eastern boundary) was still largely undeveloped and the landscape broken by only the occasional farmhouse. However, the area was served by the Galena and Chicago Union Railroad which ran from the city as far west as Oak Park.

In the late 1860s five farsighted businessmen formed a venture capital company that purchased large tracts of land east of Oak Park for residential development. They named the area Ridgeland because much of

Unidentified family poses proudly in front of their new home at 738 (now 538) North Lombard Street in Ridgeland.

the land was on a ridge, with the summit at the intersection of Chicago and East Avenues that gradually descended to a low point at Washington Blvd. Everyone agreed that it was only a matter of time before this prairie would also be settled. In 1871 the *Oak Park Vindicator* noted: "Farmers were cutting hay on the open squares of Ridgeland this week, blocks that will some day be covered with handsome residences."

The men responsible for the development of Ridgeland were James Scoville, president of the Prairie State Bank; Joel D. Harvey, general agent for the West Chicago Land Co.; Josiah Lombard, president of First Security Trust Co.; William Ogden, first mayor of Chicago and his brother Mahlon Ogden. Today streets in the community still bear the names of Scoville, Harvey and Lombard. Ogden Street was originally named for the Ogden brothers, both Chicagoans, but that thoroughfare was later renamed Elmwood.

In 1871 "developed" land in Oak Park was selling for $1,000 an acre and barely three years later demand had driven that price to $3,000. But an acre of prairie east of Oak Ridge could be had for just $700. There was good reason why these tracts were so much more affordable. George Butters, a Chicago businessman who owned W. A. Butters & Co. Auction House, was among the first to move to Ridgeland, building a substantial house on the southwest corner of Ridgeland and Ontario Streets.

Butters described what it was like to be among the first to live in Ridgeland. "You find yourself without a store in the immediate neighborhood. Water is had from shallow wells dug fifteen feet deep. The supply is fair but the water hard and strong in the quality of lime. For laundry you depend upon water gathered in your cistern. Dependent also on the out buildings and the good old wash tub for the Saturday night bath. No sewers and the surface drains were not dependable for relief when most needed. No community church or school. All these and more are obstacles which must be overcome by you with the united efforts of your neighbors."

Self-Imposed Tax

Butters and other resourceful homeowners were determined that they, too, would have the same basic amenities enjoyed by the residents of Oak Park. They accomplished this through self-imposed taxation by forming "associations" that issued stock for the purpose of building or acquiring all the basics, including stores, a fire station, a community hall, sewers and much more. An example of their determination was the way they attracted merchants to their community.

Residents of Oak Park were able to shop for groceries and other household goods in the many shops clustered on Lake Street near Harlem Avenue. But obtaining these necessities was a lot trickier for residents of Ridgeland. Unless a household kept a horse it was a long walk to the stores in Oak Park. And carrying the heavy baskets of food home was a daunting task for most women. To add to their woes, Oak Park merchants were very independent and looked down upon Ridgeland as a "mudhole" that was too great a distance from their shops to warrant a delivery.

To fill this void some fathers and sons who were engaged in business in Chicago carried a shopping list to the city each day and returned home in the evening laden with bundles. But in 1878 the men of Ridgeland finally rebelled against these domestic chores. They formed a corporation selling stock at $10 a share to raise money to establish a co-operative store in Ridgeland. A board of directors was elected, by-laws written and a committee appointed to attempt to interest an experienced grocer and dry goods merchant to open a store in Ridgeland.

The growth and obvious prosperity of the families living in Ridgeland finally attracted the interest of Oak Park merchants who had previously scorned their trade. Mr. E. W. Phelps suggested a plan that the co-op board found acceptable. He began by making two deliveries a week to Ridgeland and later opened a store in the community on the northeast corner of Lake and Ridgeland. Phelps ran his store until 1881 when he sold it to Samuel Carmen.

Lone Democrat

Carmen had the distinction of being the only Democrat in Ridgeland. In the 1884 election Ridgeland voters overwhelmingly supported the Republican candidate for president, James G. Blaine. When Democrat Grover Cleveland was elected he appointed William Steiner postmaster in Oak Park and moved the post office to Marion Street. This move increased the distance of the post office to Ridgeland to over a mile and so entitled the community to a postal facility of its own

Sam Carmen, who was a supporter of Mr. Cleveland, was appointed postmaster for Ridgeland. His grocery store was equipped with a case of letterboxes and also served the community as a post office. Although some Republicans grumbled behind Carmen's back, they had suffered the inconvenience of not having their own post office and were happy to overlook the fact that it was run by a Democrat.

But politics were put aside when Ridgeland residents decided to form a literary club. The charter meeting was held at Sam Carmen's house on Cuyler Avenue and hosted by his daughter. "A meeting of young people was held at the home of Ella Carmen Tuesday evening at which a new literary and social club was formed. The new organization will meet once a week and the members will manage to enjoy themselves," reported the *Vindicator.*

E. A. Cummings Driving Force Behind Community Life

One of Ridgeland's most influential home-owners was young Edmund Cummings, a veteran of the Civil War who boarded with Edward Robbins on Elmwood Avenue while his new house at 163 N. Lombard was under construction. After settling his family in their new home, Cummings turned his attention to business. He formed his own real estate firm, E. A. Cummings and Co. in 1869 in Chicago. The business was so successful Cummings eventually engaged Frank

Lloyd Wright to build a small and exquisite Prairie Style building on the northwest corner of Harlem Avenue and Lake Street, which he used as a local office. Cummings also organized the Cicero and Proviso Street Railway, an electric streetcar line that eventually became the West Town Bus Company.

In 1876 Cummings was elected president of the Ridgeland Improvement Association by his neighbors. All residents were automatically members of the Association, which had no fees or dues. However, when money was needed for a particular purpose the hat was passed and the response was always generous.

For example, funds for a social hall were raised by a notice at the train depot where residents wrote in the amount they wished to pledge for the building next to their names. The money raised was used to remodel the second floor of Francis Dorn's commercial building at Lake and Ridgeland and to pay him $10 a month to rent this space. But, ten years later, the close-knit community had outgrown this space and residents decided to build a separate hall to be used exclusively for meetings and socials.

A stock company, The Ridgeland Hall Association, was formed and $10,000 raised by issuing stock. The Association purchased a lot on the north side of Lake Street between Ridgeland and Cuyler Avenues where they built a grand two story brick building that

Lake and Ridgeland Business District in about 1890. Ridgeland Hall is at the far end of the block.

was completed in 1890. The rent on the two stores on the ground floor of The Ridgeland Hall paid for the maintenance of the building. The hall was decorated by prominent Chicago artists and included a stage, dressing rooms and coatrooms. Natural lighting was provided by numerous skylights, an unusual architectural embellishment for that time.

The new hall quickly became the center of social life for both villages. In a social note in 1891 the *Vindicator* noted: "Invitations are out for the social dance to be given by the Ridgeland Club Tuesday evening at Ridgeland Hall and the young people anticipate an elegant time. The tickets are $1.50 and the Electric Railway Co. will run a special car for the occasion leaving the corner of Marion and Lake Streets at 8 p.m. and returning after the ball."

When it came to sports the gentlemanly game of cricket was favored by Ridgeland's young men who competed with neighboring teams on a cricket field that occupied the entire block on Lake Street between Ridgeland and Elmwood (now Ridgeland Common). Although he was an enthusiastic player, George Butters admitted that "the game requires great patience and skill, and generally occupying a whole day in playing a game, it never could hold a crowd of baseball enthusiasts."

tended around the depot and along the tracks.

Initially the small depot was only a "flag station," which meant that anyone wishing to take a train would have to signal for the train to stop by swinging a lantern as the train approached. The engineer would then signify by his whistle that he would stop, whereupon that person would extinguish the lantern and put it under the platform to be retrieved upon his return and used to light his way home.

About fifteen years after the depot was built residents began to comment upon its shabby appearance. Additional funds were collected to beautify the building and grounds. A caretaker was hired to maintain the grass and elaborate plantings, which were a great attraction to passengers on passing trains. The name "Ridgeland" was prominently displayed in letters two feet high made of crushed stone and cement and finished with a coat of white paint. "The citizens took great pride in stepping from the train and lingering a moment that their friends may look in envy," said George Butters.

Cicero Politics

It did not take long for residents of Ridgeland who had invested heavily in their community to realize the importance of hav-

Train Depot

One of the first things the property owners did after grading the streets and planting rows of trees on both sides of those streets was to build a four-room depot on the railroad's right of way between Ridgeland Avenue and Elmwood. Two of the rooms were waiting rooms. There was also a freight room, a ticket office and a platform that ex-

Four-room Ridgeland train depot gave the community its own identity.

51

ing their viewpoint represented on the Cicero Township Board. In 1874 James Scoville was chosen to fill a vacancy on the board and, from that time forward, property owners took an active interest in township politics and the community was always well represented on the Board.

"A meeting was held at Ridgeland Hall last Saturday which was attended by a score of interested citizens," reported the *Vindicator.* "Contemplated public improvements were among the subjects discussed as well as the importance of turning out for the approaching town elections. Remarks were made by several gentlemen and arrangements made for getting out and distributing circulars urging voters to attend the caucuses and polls on Election Day."

George Butters, a member of Ridgeland's newly formed School Board and his friend Edmund Cummings were two men who took their civic duties seriously. In the spring of 1879 the School Board advertised for proposals for a site on which to build the community's first school. Three bids were received and it was decided to call an election and let the voters choose among the proposed sites.

It was Butters' job as secretary to post notices ten days in advance of the meeting at which the vote would be taken. The meeting adjourned late and Butters decided that if he were to get the notices written before midnight to meet the ten-day requirement, he needed help. The one man who could be relied on in any emergency was Edmund Cummings. He had retired for the night, but responded promptly to Butters' knock on the door.

On reaching Mr. Butters' house the two men wrote out in long-hand three copies of the notice as required. When finished, each notice was three feet long. Then they hurried to Central School and tacked each notice to a tree. Fred Hacker, Oak Park's first policeman, was passing on his rounds and asked what they were doing. Butters and Cummings, in turn, asked him what time it was. Hacker responded that it was "five minutes of twelve," which made him a good witness that the notices were posted within the required time.

Development of the South Prairie

The large tract of land south of Madison Street known as the "South Prairie" was one of the last areas in Oak Park to be developed. (The only other large tract of undeveloped land in the village was north of Division Street and that would not be subdivided until the 1920s.) In 1891 the Cicero and Proviso Street Railway, a system of electric street cars, began offering limited service on Madison Street, making it possible for people to built a spacious house on a large lot and commute to their jobs downtown.

These sturdy little trolleys, each equipped with a cowcatcher on the front, proved so popular that by 1894 the Railway completed a new power house at Lake Street and Harvey Avenue and extended service on Chicago Avenue, Lake Street and Roosevelt Road as far west as Des Plaines Avenue.

Throughout the 1890s houses began to go up so quickly that the *Oak Park Reporter* introduced a weekly real estate column detailing who was building a new house, where and for how much. "Many prominent 'cityites' have secured lots and homes in the new Maple Avenue and Wisconsin Avenue subdivisions south of Madison Street. The elegant residence of Mrs. F. P. Buell on Maple Avenue is rapidly approaching completion and will be an ornament in that section of town," was a typical entry.

Many people living in other areas of the village took a proprietary interest in the vacant lots on the South Prairie and objected strenuously to outsiders picnicking on what they considered "their land." "Sunday picnic parties from the city are making a nuisance at the corner of Wisconsin and Madison to the discomfort of the peaceful residents in that vicinity," the *Reporter* humphed. "The grounds are private and they have no right to use them for picnics. Officers should order the intruders off."

As early as 1893 residents of south Oak Park enjoyed what is lacking in that part of town today: a well-stocked hardware store. "There is no more interesting business corner in Oak Park than what is known as 'The Centre' on the corner of Madison Street and Oak Park Avenue," noted the *Reporter* that year.

Three years earlier when N. M. Freer built The Centre which consisted of a large building with stores on the first floor and apartments on the second, he was ridiculed for establishing a business in such a sparsely set-

Oak Park Avenue north from Madison Street in 1903.

tled neighborhood and the building was dubbed "Freer's Folly.

The Wood Building on the southeast corner of Madison Street and Oak Park Avenue, built around 1890, was one of the first businesses on the South Prairie. It served as "the center" a hardware and general store.

"But the laugh is on the other side now," said the *Reporter*. "In September 1891 Messrs. Wood and Ballard, the well-known builders, took possession of the premises. Ballard withdrew to work for Patton and Fisher and M. E. Wood succeeded to the business. He put in a complete stock of builder's hardware, furnaces, stoves, tinware, etc. and pushed vigorously for business. And business came. It was not long until The Centre became one of the busiest places in the village. Besides gaining a heavy trade with contractors, he sold 52 new furnaces between May 1892 and February 1893. He keeps seven tinners at work and is still hardly able to keep up with orders."

In the first decade of the 1900s construction of the Wisconsin Central Railroad, a surface line that ran along Harrison Street, was another incentive for builders like Thomas Hulbert and Seward Gunderson to sub-

divide large tracts of the South Prairie and build comfortable family homes that middle class families could afford. By 1906 Hulbert had built 200 homes and between 1906 and 1920 Seward Gunderson constructed more than 600 homes for prices ranging from $4,000 to $12,000. They were built in two tracts bounded by Roosevelt Road, Madison Street, Harlem Avenue and Ridgeland Avenue.

Although Gunderson was a tract builder his homes have none of the cookie cutter sameness that characterize so many of the affordable homes found in contemporary subdivisions. He offered 42 distinctive models with 15 separate floor plans and all homes, regardless of size and cost, included five stained glass windows, oak floors, six closets, bay windows and a solid oak built-in sideboard in the dining room.

Seward Gunderson is credited with pioneering modern construction techniques such as steel beam supports, concrete block foundations and large front porches on stone piers. He is also responsible for raising the kitchen sink to today's height after watching a maid bending over a low sink that was the standard at the time. He realized what a strain it put on her back and adjusted the height of sinks in all his homes accordingly.

For many years Seward Gunderson lived in one of his own homes. His neighbors were so satisfied with the quality of their homes they gave the builder a banquet to show their appreciation. Gunderson homeowners

These Are a Few of Our Oak Park Homes
Gunderson Station, Met. "L" (5c fare), on Elmwood, 64th and Gunderson Aves., between Madison and Harrison Sts.
Have Others Six to ten rooms—*ready now*—or will build to suit you—*ready next Spring*
Prices Right   Cash or Terms
S. T. GUNDERSON & SONS, *Home Builders*
810 Chamber of Commerce   Branch Office on Premises

also enjoyed a sense of camaraderie with their neighbors that we might envy today.

An example was the midnight street carnival attended by more than 500 Gundersn homeowners in 1911 to welcome home from their honeymoon Benton Honens and his bride. Honens was a popular druggist whose store at 6347 Harrison was the social center for that part of town.

"When it was learned that the couple would arrive at the Gunderson Avenue station at about midnight the following night an impromptu committee resolved: "We should give him a welcome and let her know that Benton is some personage in this beautiful village," reported the *Oak Leaves.*

"There was wild cheering at this and in a short time the South Oak Park Band had been engaged, decorating committees appointed, scouts detailed and a sign painter employed. All day Thursday the committee was busy. It was decreed that carnival should reign on the south side from 11 p.m. to 1 a.m. on Thursday night. The Honens' new house at 839 Elmwood was practically concealed by scores of signs tacked to the outside walls and porches."

"Such was the temper of the people at 11:45 o'clock when Mr. Honen and his unsuspecting bride stepped from the station. The band struck up 'Hail to the Chief' and about 500 neighbors cheered. The grand marshal directed that a parade be formed and the honored ones were placed at the head and the march began."

But while the south end of the village had a well-deserved reputation for neighborliness many residents also complained about what they perceived as the insensitivity of village officials and lack of services for their tax dollars. Barely eight years after Oak Park was incorporated as a village in 1902 these disgruntled residents were circulating petitions that favored annexation to Chicago.

The drive was led by George Tough and Captain Arthur Rehm with the support of the South Side League, an umbrella group of all the improvement clubs in the area. In 1910 and 1911 the question of annexation appeared on the ballot and both times it was defeated.

•

Fred Blase serving customers in his first grocery store at 134 N. Ridgeland Avenue in 1892.

CHAPTER III

MEMORABLE OAK PARKERS

Dignitaries on platform for cornerstone ceremony for the new Municipal Building at Lake Street and Euclid Avenue represented a veritable "Who's Who" in the village in 1903.

James W. Scoville

The history of Oak Park would be much different today if young James Wilmarth Scoville, walking from Chicago to Beloit College in Wisconsin, had not stopped to rest under a grand old oak tree atop the ridge at what is now Oak Park Avenue and Lake Street more than a hundred and fifty years ago.

James Wilmarth Scoville was born in 1825 in Pompey, New York. After the death of his mother five years later Scoville, along with his four brothers and sisters, went to live with their grandmother. The young man attended Oneida Conference Academy during the day and made shoes in the evening to cover his expenses. He later enrolled at Manlius Academy, also in New York, where he swept floors and split wood at 25 cents a cord to earn enough to pay for tuition for two years. At the school he endured the snubs of the young scions of wealthy families who taunted him because of his frugality.

As a young boy Scoville seldom attended religious services because there were no churches nearby. Instead, on Sundays he would go to some quiet hilltop and spend hours with his favorite books memorizing long passages of his favorite poems. He joined the Presbyterian Church while at Manlius and planned to become a minister. But a trip to Chicago in 1848 changed those plans forever.

Hearing that much learning could be had for little money at Beloit College, Scoville set out to walk the ninety miles from Chicago to the small Wisconsin town. According to the oft-told tale, the young man stopped the first day of his walk under the shade of a majestic oak atop Kettlestrings' ridge. Although Scoville continued on to Beloit where he spent the winter, he never forgot that idyllic spot where he had paused to rest.

Scoville returned to New York in 1850 and for the next five years worked as a clerk for a number of contractors who were hired to enlarge the Erie Canal. There he learned both office techniques and how to deal with laborers. In 1853 he married Mary Huggins

Residence of James Scoville, Oak Park Avenue and Lake Street about 1900.

and three years later the young couple moved to Chicago where Scoville worked as a cashier for P. W. Gates, a company that manufactured iron products. The following year Scoville achieved his dream when he bought the large lot at the northwest corner of Lake Street and Oak Park Avenue on which the well-remembered oak stood. There he built a spacious house on the ridge where he had rested as a young man (now the site of the World War I monument).

James Scoville organized and was the first president of Prairie State Bank and his fortune increased though "never through rash ventures." In 1868 he embarked on a new venture as a real estate entrepreneur by forming a company with several other far-sighted businessmen that purchased large tracts of land in the separate town of "Ridgeland" which was not incorporated into the village until 1902.

Every morning before most of his neighbors were stirring, Scoville could be found consulting with the foreman and workers who were laying out the streets, putting in sewers, laying sidewalks and planting trees in the new community. Then he was off to the city for a day at the Bank and later, back to Oak Park in late afternoon to see what the workers had accomplished.

The full-length portrait of a rather dour-looking James Scoville that hangs in the Oak Park Public Library does not do justice to the man some viewed as stiff and unapproachable. "On the contrary, he was a very delightful person with a friendly feeling toward people and a sense of humor that saved him from conceit and stuffiness," said May

This life-sized portrait of James Scoville, painted by Oak Park artist Frank Pebbles in 1890, hangs in the Oak Park Public Library.

Estelle Cook in her book, *Little Old Oak Park.*

"Besides, he had a genuine love of learning and literature which gave him a stimulating breadth of mind. Many mornings he would entertain commuters at the train station by reciting line after line of the 'Lady of the Lake' or some other classic in a half-humorous way which showed his consciousness that his audience considered it queer for a businessman to know so much poetry."

As his fortune grew James Scoville became well known for his generous contributions to every civic, cultural and religious cause. In 1859 he proposed that the school board buy the land around Central School at

In 1878 Scoville's water reservoir at Oak Park Avenue and North Boulevard began supplying water to most Oak Park homes. In 1888 he sold this private water system to the Cicero Gas, Water and Electric Light Co.

Lake and Forest Avenue so the children would have a place to play. At a heated meeting several citizens objected to the higher taxes the purchase of this land would entail.

"Mr. Scoville took out his pencil and, after a little figuring, announced that the gentlemen's taxes would be increased by 35 cents a year," reported *The Oak Park Vindicator.* Still the proposal was defeated. So Scoville purchased the lot himself for $800, held the property until a later board recognized the need for a recreational area, and then sold it to them for what he had paid.

In 1871 Scoville donated the lot at Kenilworth and Lake Street to the newly-formed First Congregational Church for construction of a handsome Gothic edifice with a soaring spire. In 1916 the interior of the church was gutted by fire when the spire was struck by lightning. The structure was rebuilt with a lower Romanesque tower and today is the home of First United Church.

Providing the village with a supply of pure water was one of James Scoville's greatest contributions. In 1878 he dug a reservoir on property he owned on North Blvd. between Oak Park Avenue and Euclid Avenue. Then a sixty-eight foot water tower was erected on Oak Park Avenue with offices and the engine house east of it. Water mains were laid under almost half of Oak Park's streets and homeowners lost no time in laying pipes to connect with these mains. In 1888 Scoville sold this privately owned system to the Cicero Gas, Water and Electric Light Co. It was not until 1908 that Oak Park reached an agreement with Chicago to receive Lake Michigan water.

Of all of James Scoville's gifts to the community, Scoville Institute was his most cherished project. In 1883 he invited thirteen friends representing every church and civic group in the village to form a board of trustees for the new library which he endowed with $115,000 for both the lot at Lake Street and Grove Avenue and the three-story Romanesque building designed by Normand Patton.

Scoville Institute, located on the site of the present library, was completed in 1888 and served as the cultural center for the village until 1961 when it was demolished and the present building erected. Note that the words "Scoville Institute" have been carved in the lintel above the library's entrance as a way of perpetuating the memory of James Scoville for future generations.

Fortunately for us the close-knit Scovilles were inveterate letter writers. Both parents wrote to their only child, Charles Burton (Bertie) Scoville, while he was away at school, husband and wife wrote one another when they were separated for only a few days and Bertie corresponded with his parents even when he was living just a few blocks away.

The Historical Society of Oak Park and River Forest is the custodian of these letters that offer not only glimpses into the private lives of the family, but also chronicle daily happenings in the village. The letters James Scoville wrote to his son while the young man attended St. Johnsbury School in Vermont in 1874 all begin "My dear son," and are written in a flowing script on the letterhead of the Prairie State Bank.

"Your Sunday letter came to hand and received a hearty welcome as do all letters from the Same Source. We were glad to learn that the carpet reached you in safety and that, notwithstanding it is a little short under the bed and in the stove corner, it has added to the cheerfulness of your room."

"We are now having very pleasant weather. Mother was in yesterday but today is at Mr. Wallis' studio having her portrait painted. The Church is fast approaching completion (First Congregational) and it now looks as though we should dedicate it in November. I will send you a program as soon as they are out. It is getting so late that I fear we shall not go out east this fall but we have not given up entirely. Affectionately, your Father."

James and Mary Scoville did not live out all of their days in Oak Park. In the late 1880s they moved to California because of failing health. He died in 1893. After the Scovilles left Oak Park their Queen Anne house was used as a finishing school for girls and, for a short time, as the first home of the Oak Park Club. In 1912 the Park District of Oak Park purchased the Scoville estate and shortly after that the house was razed.

The Two Henry Austins.

Henry Warren Austin, Sr. is perhaps best known as the man who kept Oak Park dry for more than a hundred years. But he should also be remembered as one of the village's most successful businessmen, a generous benefactor to worthy causes and as the founder of the neighboring community of Austin.

As a young man Henry Austin, Sr. was described as having a striking resemblance to General Ulysses S. Grant and when he went to Washington on business he was often mistaken for the Union General.

Henry Austin, Sr., was born in Skaneateles, New York in 1828. He became a traveling salesman for an iron pump manufacturer located in Seneca Falls, New York. In 1858 the 30-year-old Austin was named manager of a Chicago branch that manufactured both the pumps needed to drain the city's swampy fields and jack-screws that were used to raise buildings above the water level.

Two years later Henry Austin purchased seven acres from his friend Joseph Kettlestrings in a prime area bounded by Lake, Marion, and Ontario Streets and Forest Avenue and built a distinctive gabled house for his wife Martha at a cost of $1,500. The Austin's three children, Henry Jr., Sophie and Hannah were all born in this house. And it was in the house one sad Christmas Eve that 8-year-old Hannah died. She was buried in an above-ground crypt in Forest Home Cemetery because her grieving parents could not bear to put her in the ground.

The Austin estate was enclosed with a rustic wooden fence made from oaks growing near the Des Plaines River. This fence, which had to be replaced every seven or eight years, became a landmark for villagers.

Henry Austin, Sr., who bore a remarkable resemblance to Gen. Ulysses S. Grant.

A large portion of the original Henry Austin, Sr., estate, 217 Lake Street, is now Austin Gardens.

The grounds were laid out by John Blair who landscaped Garfield Park, and included woods, landscaped lawns and vegetable and flower gardens that were all connected by winding trails that curved through the property.

The Austins were staunch supporters of the Women's Christian Temperance Union and Frances Willard, an ardent advocate of temperance, was a frequent guest in their home. Henry Austin converted a small building on the southeast corner of his estate, that had been built by Joseph Kettlestrings and used earlier as both a school and church, into Temperance Hall, a focal point for the temperance movement. He hired two fresco artists to paint a drop curtain for the hall depicting a beautiful woman pouring water into a jug of wine, the idea being temperance.

As a state legislator Henry Austin, Sr. introduced the Illinois Temperance bill into the General Assembly. It became law in 1872 A year or two earlier Austin had reached an agreement with the Cicero Town Board that, if they would issue no more liquor licenses in the community, he would be responsible for ridding Oak Park of its three existing saloons.

Henry Austin had no trouble buying the first two taverns but the owner of the Farmer's Home, a popular saloon located next to Albert Schneider's grocery at Lake and Marion Streets, refused to name a price. One day Austin stopped by and asked how much he would take for his place. The man named an exorbitantly high figure. According to legend, Austin pulled the amount required out of his pocket and handed it to the startled owner. "This place is now mine!" declared Austin as he immediately began to pour the liquor into the street. However, Henry Austin was a cautious and astute businessman and a more realistic scenario is that both parties signed a legal contract before he began disposing of the liquor.

(The absence of taverns was not a particular hardship for villagers who liked to bend their elbows because just across Harlem Avenue in Forest Park a total of 52 saloons flourished. It was no wonder that Harlem Avenue was considered by abstemious villagers as the dividing line between damnation and salvation!)

Henry Austin, Sr. died in his Oak Park home on December 24, 1889.

Henry Austin, Jr.

Henry Austin, Jr. was born in 1864, and spent his entire life, in that same gabled house his father had built. He graduated Phi Beta Kappa from Williams College. During his college years young Harry Austin was a member of Alpha Delta Phi, and for years after he graduated he hosted a party every summer for up to 400 Alpha Delts at his home. The grounds were lit with lanterns and after dinner the guests would meander through the woods singing Alpha Delt songs.

Nena Badenoch, who attended one of those parties, recalled the excitement of a June evening in 1910 when she was a guest. "As we stepped on the porch the heavy front door was opened by an aproned maid who ushered us in to lay aside our wraps and then into the parlor where Mr. and Mrs. Austin were greeting their guests. The buzz of voices was merry. When we were assembled the Austins led us from the house across the broad lawn to the great barn, up the outer stairs to the hayloft now aglow with the soft lights of Japanese lanterns strung the length of the hall. In the corner two fiddlers and a harpist were tuning up while a drummer lightly tapped his drums."

"Each couple was given a ticket for a ride through the park in Austin's Stanley Steamer. 'Now hold onto your girl,' Harry Austin directed as he pushed his car into gear. 'We go pretty fast.' Off he started and swung around the first curve at the breakneck speed of 10 mph. The girls screamed and the boys guffawed and held them tight as they rushed over the curving path which snaked through the park. Finally Harry swung into the straight road that led along the dining room side of the house and the girls stepped out on the running board with a flounce of skirts and much laughter. Our escorts guided us into the dining room for a 'lap supper' and the gracious welcome of Mrs. Austin who, forever after that, remained for me the 'First Lady' of Oak Park."

Banking begins in Oak Park

Banking in Oak Park began in 1886 when Joseph and Simpson Dunlop built a three-story building on the northwest corner of

Marion Street and North Blvd. to house their newly-established Dunlop Brother's Bank. The cashier of this private bank was Arthur Draper. A few years later Draper decided to organize a new bank in the village and began gathering subscriptions toward the $50,000 needed to receive a charter from the state. Henry Austin, Jr. made the largest pledge in the amount of $2,500.

When the money for the new Oak Park State Bank had been raised the first meeting of stockholders was held at Hoard's Hall. "Of course, Mr. Draper was named cashier and he was also a director. I was only 28 years of age, but it was considered a safe proposition to make me president with the directors all older and more experienced men," recalled Henry Austin, Jr.

Today only a fraction of a bank's assets are in actual currency. But in 1892 when the young bank president met the state auditor in the new bank building still under construction all assets were in cash. The two men sat down amid the vats of mortar and construction material and Henry Austin, Jr. pulled $50,000 out of his pocket and carefully counted it out for the inspection of the auditor. A few days later, on March 16, 1892, a state charter was issued.

Henry Austin, Jr., and cashier Arthur Draper in front of Oak Park's first publicly-owned bank at 204 Lake Street.

The location of the new Oak Park State Bank was 204—now 1053—Lake Street. In addition to this facility, Henry Austin, Jr.

and bank vice president Henry Hansen rented offices in the Teutonic Building in Chicago at Washington and Wells Streets. "We received deposits in Chicago for many years at that office and every day a clerk would come in from the bank and get the checks which were drawn upon us," said Austin.

One of the directors of the Bank was Hiram Coombs whose office was just a few blocks away on Washington Street. One day he came to Austin greatly agitated. "He said he had a tip that the National Bank of Illinois, the bank where we had most of our money, was going to fail and we must get it out immediately," remembered Austin.

"We telephoned Oak Park to find out what our balance was in the bank. Then we started right over. There was no time to waste. We drew a check for the whole balance and I will never forget the way the paying teller looked at us as we took large quantities of bills and stuffed them into our inside overcoat pockets. He did not know what we knew, but he knew it the next day, because the bank did not open. I never carried so much money in my life. We took the money to the Northern Trust Company and opened an account immediately."

Oak Park State Bank remained at 204 Lake Street until 1899 when Simpson Dunlop died and his brother Joseph sold their bank to Henry Austin. The space occupied by the Dunlop Bank was much larger than the space on Lake Street, so Austin moved the new and larger savings facility into the Dunlop building and changed its name to Oak Park Trust & Savings Bank.

Oak Park Trust remained at that location until 1923 when Henry Austin, Jr. purchased the State Bank of Oak Park which was located in a small building on the northeast corner of Lake and Marion Streets. This well-capitalized and efficiently run bank had opened just nine years earlier. Austin was interested in the State Bank's location as much as its assets. There was no more room for expansion in his facility and he wanted to remain in the same central business location.

His solution was to absorb his competitor and move the small building designed by

HENRY W. AUSTIN, Republican candidate for State Senator from the 23rd Senatorial District lives in Oak Park, in the house where he was born 50 years ago. He is a graduate of both Oak Park and Chicago High Schools and of Williams College. President of the Oak Park Trust & Savings Bank for 22 years; Treasurer of Oak Park since 1901. He served three terms (9 years) as School Trustee and three terms (6 years) as Representative at Springfield. By education and experience he is particularly fitted to represent the 23rd District.

The Legislative Voters' League says: "Throughout Legislative service he was a champion of Civil Service and a consistent foe of pay-roll stuffing. In 45th General Assembly he was made Chairman of Committee on Contingent Expenses and resigned after a row with the Speaker, because of the latter's insistence upon appointing twenty incompetent employees, whom Austin held to be needless. The League endorsed him in its 1904 report and also in the report issued in 1906."

VOTE FOR
⊠ **Henry W. Austin**
Republican Candidate For
State Senator
23rd Senatorial District

Election, Tuesday, November 3rd, 1914
Polls Open From 6 A. M. to 4 P. M.

Legislative Voters' League Report, Oct., 1914 says: "Three terms in the House proved Mr. Austin a capable and discriminating legislator." (over)

העני וו. אוסטין וואוינט אין אוק פארק, אין האוז וואו ער
איז געבוירען פאר 50 יאהר. גראדואירט פון אוק-פארק און שיקא-
גא האי סקוהלס און פון וויליאמס קאללעדש. פרעזידענט פון אוק
פארק בענק 22 יאהר; טרעזשורער פון אוק פארק זיט 1901. גע-
ווען 3 טערמס סקוהל טריסטיע, און 3 טערמס רעפרעזענטאטיוו.

לעדזשיסלייטיוו וואוטערס ליעג זאגט: דורך דער גאנצער דיענסט
אין לעדזשיסלייטשור וואהר ער א פיינד פון דעם געשטאפטען פעי
ראל, און האט רעזיגנירט אלס טשערירמאן פון דער קאמיטע צו
מעסיגען די אויסגאבען, ווייל דער ספיקער פאדערט צו אפאינטען
20 אונפעהיגע לייט, וועלכע מר. אוסטין גלויבט מען דארף ניט.
די ליעג האט איהם אינדארסירט אין 1904 און 1906.

וואוט פאר
⊠ העני וו. אוסטין
רעפובליקאנער קאנדידאט פיר
סטייט סענאטאר
אין 23טען סענאטאריעל דיסטריקט
עלעקשאן דיענסטאג, נאוו. 3. 1914
פאלס אפען פון 6 פריה ביז 4 נאכמיטאג
לעדזשיסלייטיוו וואוטערס ליעג ראפאארט פון
אקטאבער 1914 זאגט: "דרוי טערמס אין
דער האוז האט איבערצייגט מר. אוסטין
אלס פעהיגען און קאראקטעריסטישען
לעדזשיסלייטאר. (קעהרט איבער)

Flyers promoting the re-election of Henry Austin, Jr., as state legislator in 1914 designed to appeal to all his constituents were printed in English, Hebrew and German.

Henry Fiddelke around the corner to Marion Street where it would be in the rear of his new and much larger bank. The building was jacked up and moved without a single mishap. It remained an integral part of Oak Park Trust until the 1960s when it was demolished.

Henry Austin, Jr. was an astute banker who also followed his father's lead and served in the Illinois legislature from 1902 until 1922.

The Austin home originally faced Lake Street but in 1936 Henry Austin was forced to sell this choice frontage in order to keep the bank open. The house was moved off Lake Street and turned to face Forest Avenue across the street from the Nineteenth Century Woman's Club.

Henry Austin, Jr. died in 1947. Following the death of his wife Edna in 1964 the estate was given to the Park District of Oak Park and the house demolished to create a park, Austin Gardens, which was endowed by the Austin family.

The Gale Family

For almost half a century Edwin O. Gale was one of Oak Park's most influential citizens. The large Gothic Revival house he built in 1865 at 347 Lake Street (a six-story condominium building now occupies this site) was easily as impressive as the nearby homes built by the village's other leading businessmen such as James Scoville, Henry Austin and Milton Niles.

Edwin O. Gale.

Three-year-old Edwin Gale arrived in Chicago via the Erie Canal in 1835 with his parents Abram and Sarah Gale who purchased 320 acres north of the village in what is now the Chicago neighborhood of Galewood.

After attending the College of Pharmacy in Chicago young Edwin went to work in a drug store in the Palmer House where William Blocki also worked as a clerk. Edwin Gale eventually purchased the business and, when Blocki returned after serving in the Union Army during the Civil War, the two became partners in the Gale and Blocki Drug Store.

In 1871 their business, along with most of the city, was destroyed in the Chicago Fire. When Gale went to inspect the ruins he found a single case of hairbrushes that had escaped the flames. He sold those and, with a $10,000 interest-free loan from his friend Joseph Kettlestrings, Gale went to New York to order new stock.

Kettlestrings' confidence in Edwin Gale was well founded. Within a few years Gale and Blocki expanded their business to eight drug stores including one in Oak Park on the north side of Lake Street just east of Oak Park Avenue and just two blocks from the Gale home.

Edwin Gale and William Blocki were partners in several real estate ventures, in addition to their drug stores. Gale Avenue in River Forest is part of a tract that the men owned and subdivided. They also had a real estate office on the southeast corner of South Blvd. and Oak Park Avenue that was run by Edwin's brother Whittier under the name G. Whittier Gale Real Estate.

Edwin Gale was a daily commuter to the city traveling on one of the two trains that ran to and from Chicago at that time. In the late 1860s there were only thirteen businessmen who regularly took these trains downtown. Each train consisted of only two cars and the one the commuters used was a combined smoker and baggage car. During the winter months these breadwinners were met at the station by either a servant or one of their children carrying a kerosene lantern to guide them home through the dark streets.

The number of trains gradually increased until by the 1880s there were fifteen round trips available daily. At that time the station was at Marion Street and North Blvd., an inconvenient distance for regular commuters like James Scoville and Edwin Gale who lived within a block or two of Oak Park Avenue. Their solution was to build a station at Oak Park Avenue by private subscription of property owners in the vicinity.

Edwin Gale and his wife Julia had six high-spirited sons. One night all of the Gale boys got out a stencil of two different footprints, one left and one right. They bought a can of red paint and painted footprints on every wooden sidewalk in Oak Park that led directly to their father's drug store.

And once when a teacher at Central School wrote Julia Gale a note suggesting she ought to do something about disciplining her son Oliver she got the note back with this reply written across it: "Oliver is the youngest of six boys and I'm very tired. (Signed) Julia Gale."

As the father of six sons Edwin Gale was closely involved with the management of Central School. He served as both a school director and trustee for more than fifteen years. Walter Gale, who later followed his father in the family business, had the distinction of being one of three students in the first graduation class of Oak Park High School in 1877. The other two graduates were Herbert Whipple and James Herrick, son of O. W. Herrick, the village's first teacher and later postmaster. The younger Herrick later became a distinguished surgeon.

Six sons of Edward and Julia Gale in 1906. A seventh son, Edwin, died in childhood.

Edwin Gale's house fronted Lake Street and, while his sons were growing up, the tract extended north to Chicago Avenue and was used as a pasture for grazing cows. But when each of his sons married, Gale subdivided the land, giving each son his own lot on which to build a house.

Abram Gale married Maude Bolles who lived directly across the street from the Gales in a large Victorian house at 358 Lake Street (now the site of the U. S. Post Office). The two had graduated together from Central School in 1879. They met when he was in third grade and she was in second and he used to trail after her down Lake Street on their way home from school. The newly-weds lived briefly in the little "honeymoon cottage" at 161 Kenilworth, which was the original carriage house for the Gale mansion. They later built a substantial Queen Anne house directly north at 165 Kenilworth.

Abram's brothers had more adventurous taste in architecture. Walter Gale and his brother Thomas were friends of Frank Lloyd Wright and hired the architect to design their homes. The house Wright designed for Thomas Gale in 1892 at 324 Chicago Avenue was one of two so-called "bootleg" houses because they were built while Wright was still working for Louis Sullivan.

Walter Gale's house at what is today 1031 Chicago Avenue was built in 1893 and was Wright's first completed commission after his break with Sullivan that same year. In 1907, Thomas Gale hired Wright again to design a house on a lot he had purchased at 6 Elizabeth Court. When Gale died before the house was built, his wife, Laura Gale, decided to proceed with the house which today is the famed "Mrs. Thomas Gale" house renowned for the rectilinear geometry of its exterior which is similar to another distinctive Wright house, Fallingwater in Pennsylvania.

The Gales were Unitarians and charter members of the first Unitarian-Universalist Church; a simple Gothic building built in 1872 on Wisconsin Avenue near Pleasant

Gothic Revival house built by Edwin Gale at Lake Street and Kenilworth in 1865.

Street. When that church burned in 1905 they supported Frank Lloyd Wright's innovative design of the new Unity Temple on Lake Street at Kenilworth. This building, constructed of interlocking concrete rectilinear solids, was designated a National Historic Landmark in 1969. It is presently undergoing extensive renovation and restoration.

Edwin Gale's son, Whittier, built the house directly south of Unity Temple. After Edwin Gale died in 1913, Julia Gale purchased the house from her son and presented it to the church for use as a parsonage in 1915.

John Farson

John Farson, the son of a Methodist minister, was a lawyer, self-made multimillionaire, investment banker and one of Chicago's leading financiers. But to his Oak Park neighbors Farson was better known for his kindness, generosity, extraordinary zest for life and the panache that made even his most eccentric ideas acceptable to his more conventional friends. For more than twenty years Farson alternately intrigued, charmed and shocked the public. But he was never boring.

John Farson, born in Union City, Indiana in 1855, left school at the age of twelve to help support his family following his father's death. The family moved to Champaign, Illinois where he attended the University of Illinois. The young man studied law in the Chicago office of J. R. Doolittle, a former senator from Wisconsin, and in 1880 he was admitted to the bar. The following year he married Mamie Ashworth in Chicago.

Farson organized the investment house of Farson, Leach & Co. Years later, when his son had completed his education, he dissolved his partnership with Leach and created the firm of John Farson, Son & Co. with offices in Chicago and New York.

In the late 1880s the Farsons and their two sons lived in a comfortable Queen Anne house at 237 S. Oak Park Avenue. But in 1897, John Farson commissioned Prairie Style architect George W. Maher, a one-time colleague of Frank Lloyd Wright, to design "Pleasant Home," an imposing early modern rectilinear mansion at the intersection of Home Avenue and Pleasant Street in Oak Park.

Several homes on the lots Farson purchased were razed to make room for the formal Italian garden that would later provide a backdrop for the many social events hosted by the Farsons. John Farson continued to purchase adjoining lots as they became available and eventually his estate encompassed approximately five acres. A massive steel fence surrounded the property. However, Farson never installed gates and his neighbors were always free to enjoy his grounds.

Today Pleasant Home and the surrounding estate, renamed Mills Park for its second owner Herbert Mills, is owned by the Park

John Farson.

District of Oak Park. In 1997 Pleasant Home was designated a National Historic Landmark. The ground floor of the building is occupied by the Pleasant Home Foundation and the second floor is the museum and research center of The Historical Society of Oak Park & River Forest.

Farson was an avid horseman and had Maher design a unique coach house in

70

John Farson's "Pleasant Home" designed by George Maher in 1897.

which the stalls were built in the shape of a wheel (the spokes being the stalls). The idea was to allow his family and friends to step into the center of the "wheel" to feed the horses sugar lumps without having to enter the stalls.

Even more unique was the great clock Farson installed in the cupola of the coach house. *The Chicago Tribune* detailed the reaction of residents to the chimes that sounded every quarter hour. "The clock struck only the hour at first and the full scope of Mr. Farson's innovation did not become apparent until Wednesday when the complete apparatus was in place. Then Oak Park began to realize that a disturbance of the peace was in their midst. In Oak Park where at night a pin dropped on Maple Avenue can be heard half way to Austin, the ringing of the chimes resounds like the cable car bells on Wabash Avenue."

But Farson was unperturbed by his critics and predicted his neighbors would come to like it. And he was right. As the months passed people began to set their clocks and watches by the chimes. It became such a part of their daily lives that the principal of Oak

Park High School complained to Farson that, because his clock was running late, many of his students were tardy.

However, just a few years after his coach house was complete, Farson succumbed to the lure of the "horseless carriage" and before long fine cars had replaced the horses in his stables. Farson lavished the same care on his automobiles as he had on his horses. He owned five of the first fifteen autos in the village and his chauffeur, Nels Anderson, was frequently hauled into court for making Washington Blvd. "look like a crimson streak" by exceeding the speed limit of eight miles an hour."

As president of the Chicago Auto Club and, later, first president of the Illinois State Federation of Auto Clubs, Farson favored increasing the driving speed and proposed that the organization issue members cards that would be accepted by police in lieu of bond for those arrested for speeding.

Farson had a well-known penchant for red neckties and persisted in wearing them with business attire, much to the dismay of fashion arbitrators who pronounced the combination gauche. But Farson was a law unto himself.

A friend observed: "Personal taste led him to effect red neckties. Of course they became the subject of jest. But he would not become irritated or take them off. On the contrary, he searched the earth for the reddest neckties and outdid the jokers, laughing at them. And so, his red neckties and his good humor became a landmark to everyone who had business to do with him and became, in fact, valuable commercial assets."

John Farson was charitable and far more broad-minded than many of his neighbors. He allowed parishioners of St. Edmund's to use his home for a benefit to raise funds to build the first Catholic Church in the predominately Protestant community. And he defended Rev. Sidney Strong, pastor of the Second Congregational Church, who married a divorced woman. "I have not agreed with the reverend gentleman in all things—but I must support him in this in that he has the perfect right to choose his own wife," said Farson.

In an era when the buxom Edwardian figure prevailed, John Farson was vitally interested in maintaining good health through fresh air, physical activity and correct diet. Every Saturday he loaded village youngsters into his various autos and took them for outings in the country where, as he said, "flowers grow and the air is pure." Anxiety over his wife's fragile health prompted Farson's interest in nature.

When a physician warned Farson that Mamie must live outdoors as much as possible he took the man at his word. The headlines of a Chicago newspaper told the story: "Millionaire banker fixes up a room on the roof and sleeps out of doors in all kinds of weather. He wears red pajamas."

The open-air bedroom was on the west side of Pleasant Home on the roof above the kitchen. It was provided with awnings and simple furnishings. When a reporter asked, "Do the neighbors peek?" Farson replied, "Oak Parkers are too well bred to peek."

Prior to his untimely death in 1910 Farson planned to enhance this outdoor bedroom with a hanging garden. But this did not interest villagers half as much as the Roman marble swimming pool he planned to build in his formal Italian garden. What set

The elaborately landscaped south garden in Pleasant Home.

72

tongues wagging were the nude statues of Venus and Diana that were to preside over the pool. However, they need not have worried. To protect the sensibilities of his neighbors Farson was planning to drape the goddesses in pink and white kimonos every Sunday when his grounds were usually crowded with promenading villagers.

When roller-skating became the rage Farson championed the skater's cause against those who denounced the sport as a worse evil than the speeding auto. He opened his grounds with its paths of smooth cement that were ideal for skating, and even took up the sport himself.

An article in a March, 1906 issue of the *Oak Leaves* entitled: "All Oak Park Glides Joyfully on Rollers" detailed how Farson brought round the opposition by locking them in his garage until they agreed to learn to skate themselves. The last two to yield were a Baptist minister and Mrs. Thomas Heald, (a formidable grande dame and future mother-in-law of Farson's son William) whom Farson taught to skate, well cushioned in the privacy of his garage.

John Farson's opinions were much sought after by reporters who could always count on him for a lively quote. His oft-repeated recipe for happiness was: "Live in the air, think kindly of everyone—and do what you damn please."

Farson attributed his business success to hard work, cheerfulness and the fact that he never lived beyond his income. "It is a great satisfaction to build up a business, but money is not everything in the world. My home and my friends are my main source of happiness. There are so many rich men in this country who won't even smile. They don't get anything out of life. Be cheerful!"

Scarcely a week went by that did not include an account of some social soiree hosted by the Farsons. Typical is a 1902 issue of the *Oak Leaves* that contains two social notes side by side. The first reported that a

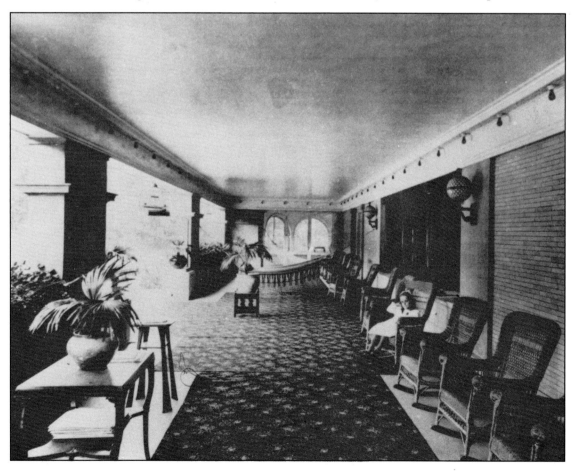

The porch at Pleasant Home was large enough to comfortably entertain a hundred guests al fresco.

reception Mrs. Farson gave for 400 women was "one of the most brilliant social events of the season" and the second was an account of a dinner John Farson hosted for the newly elected officers of the Union League Club and the Chicago Athletic Club. "Guests were conveyed from the city by a special train provided by J. R. McCullough of the North Western Railroad."

But not all of Farson's undertakings were as successful as his parties. One of Farson's most dubious distinctions was his role in introducing squirrels into the village. He was president of the Oak Park Improvement Association and, for reasons known only to themselves, members decided to raise funds to buy and "colonize" squirrels throughout the village which was totally free of the rodents at that time. For a $5 contribution, a villager was given a pair of squirrels and a "suitable squirrel house for their accommodation." But the caged animals "fought so viciously that it was necessary to liberate them to prevent further casualties." So the squirrels were freed to make their homes in trees and the result is the proliferation of the animals today.

John Farson died suddenly of a heart attack on January 18, 1910 after a two-day illness that was first diagnosed as indigestion. His death, like his life, became public property after Dr. James Herrick (an Oak Park native who achieved world prominence as the first physician to recognize coronary thrombosis) was called to treat the stricken man.

After Farson's death Dr. Herrick performed an autopsy which confirmed his diagnosis that Farson had suffered coronary thrombosis, the first case officially diagnosed as what we now call a heart attack. Farson's case history and Dr. Herrick's diagnosis were published in medical journals around the world.

John Farson's obituary lauded him as a man who, in his days of prosperity, did not forget the friends of an earlier time. "He was always democratic and was much beloved by many men who make no pretension to wealth or place. He did not get through life without making enemies, but those who knew him best knew that his dominating characteristics were kindness, gentleness and generosity."

Philander Barclay

Around the turn of the century photography was not a hobby that ranked very high on most people's list of favorite pastimes. Photographic equipment was expensive and cumbersome and the quality of the pictures they produced often left much to be desired.

Fortunately for us, Philander Barclay had both the technical skill needed to produce

Philander Barclay.

quality photographs and a finely-honed sense of history. The result is a priceless collection of over 1,000 photographs that chronicle daily life in Oak Park and surrounding communities over a period of almost fifty years. Today that collection is owned by The Historical Society of Oak Park and River Forest.

Beginning around 1902 Philander Barclay was a familiar figure around Oak Park as he pedaled through the village, his bulky black camera slung across his shoulder.

"My father's drug store was the gossiping center of the whole town," he said. "I used to listen to the jovial tales and I thought, nobody ever thinks about saving the past until the past is gone. Some day they'll be history."

To ensure Oak Park's past would never be erased ""Bicycle" Barclay, as he came to be known, did whatever he thought was necessary to achieve the effect he wanted in his photographs, including climbing trees and lamp posts and standing in the middle of dusty, unpaved streets obstructing horse-drawn traffic.

Philander Barclay's collection is invaluable to us today because, through his photographs, we are able to pictorially recreate the village street by street. Just as important, he meticulously identified every person and building in each picture and also noted the location and the date the photograph was

taken. At the time of his death in 1940, Philander Barclay's collection numbered more than 1,000 photographs. Six hundred were his own photographs and the remaining were the more than 400 photographs given to him by early residents that offer us with a rare look at village life as early as the 1870s.

Philander Barclay was born in Cairo, Illinois on September 16, 1874 and came to Oak Park with his parents in 1891. His father owned the Golden Lion Drug Store at 103 N. Marion Street. The store was easily distinguished from other Marion Street businesses by a large statue of a gilded lion that was placed atop a ten-foot-high pedestal that stood in front of the store.

As a youngster Philander came to know practically everyone in town. His father had one of the first telephones in the village and young Philander was called upon to deliver messages as they were received. As a result, he probably know more about the lives of his neighbors than anyone else.

All his life Barclay's interests and actions were seemingly at odds with one another. Nothing interested him more than village affairs and people. He knew thousands of Oak Parkers by name, yet had no intimate friend. In the half century he lived in Oak Park he never joined any group, society or club and was never a member of a church. He seemed content to hover on the periphery of village life, recording, but never participating.

As a young man, Barclay suffered from insomnia, which led him to roam Oak Park streets late at night, and in the early morning hours. He made frequent visits to the police stations and firehouses on these nocturnal walks and some of his most interesting photographs were taken during these stops.

It was during this time that Barclay also began to rely on powders and other sleep remedies that were readily available over-the-counter at his father's drug store. What was not known at the time was that these medicines contained large amounts of addictive drugs such as morphine, heroin and opium. According to Philander Barclay's obituary in the July 11, 1940 issue of the *Oak*

Leaves, "Often he was overcome by these drugs and it seemed that his frail body could stand no more, but he always recovered and

Philander Barclay standing in front of his bicycle repair shop at 1112 North Boulevard in 1912.

for months and years would use no sleeping powders."

In addition to photography, Barclay was also fascinated with the possibilities of "talking machines" and recorded the reedy voices of Elijah Hoard and Edward Robbins, two elderly members of the Borrowed Time Club, on primitive wax cylinders that could only be played on a "Gem" phonograph, a device invented by Thomas Edison in 1871. Barclay had "won" the recorder in 1891 by collecting cigarette coupons. This early attempt at oral history was accomplished after weeks of trial and error in which he recorded their voices on dozens of cylinders.

Elijah Hoard died in 1908. Robbins died two years later. Their voices were not heard again until 1927 when the cylinders were taken from a vault at Oak Park Trust and Savings Bank and played at the 25th anniversary of the Borrowed Time Club. By that time flat phonograph disks had replaced cylinders and so Barclay requested, and received a special adapter from the inventor. At the same time Thomas Edison wrote

Philander Barclay a letter warmly congratulating him for using his technology to record the voices of pioneer Oak Parkers. Some of the recordings survive and are part of the collection of The Historical Society of Oak Park and River Forest.

After his parents' deaths within weeks of each other in 1902 the drug store was sold and Philander Barclay opened a bicycle sales and repair shop. During the years he operated the shop Barclay deposited his earnings equally in all of the village banks.

Barclay never borrowed money and was not a believer in credit. Children whose fathers were among the wealthiest couldn't get their bicycle out of Barclay's shop until they had paid for their repairs. On the other hand, he would repair a bicycle without charge if he considered the owner to be unable to afford the cost.

Barclay had no business sense, however, and the repair shop was his only successful business venture. When the cycling craze finally ran its course, he found himself without income. For the rest of his life Barclay never held a long-term job and spent what little money he had on photographic equipment. In his later years he lived with his sister who shared her teacher's pension with him. After her death he relied on the charity of friends. Barclay died of a drug overdose, alone and penniless on July 7, 1940.

Although Philander Barclay never enjoyed any degree of financial success, his priceless collection of photographs rank as important a legacy to future generations of Oak Parkers as the generous gifts given to the community by wealthier benefactors.

Catherine Tobin Wright and Frank Lloyd Wright

Today there is little in the life of Frank Lloyd Wright that has not been examined in microscopic detail by numerous biographers. But few people know much about his first wife, Catherine Tobin Wright.

Catherine Tobin Wright.

Although some biographers considered her little more than a pale appendage to her flamboyant husband, Catherine was remembered by her children as being both strong-willed and caring.

"My mother was a very important force in the continuity of our growing up years," recalled her daughter, Catherine Baxter. "It was she who held us all together and was always present when the going was rough. So I have always felt for more reasons than I can list she was and is the real heroine of the saga."

"Her room was a gathering place for us all and a haven when troubled waters rose to submerge us. She participated in many civic affairs through the years she lived on Forest Avenue and was always a staunch supporter of the protection of children."

Following Wright's departure from that house on Forest Avenue he had built for his 18-year-old bride in 1889, Catherine was left to cope with tongue-wagging neighbors scandalized by her husband's very public liaison with Mamah Borthwick Cheney, a hostile mother-in-law and the financial and emotional support of six children. (Wright's fiscal philosophy was that if you "take care of the luxuries, the necessities will take care of themselves," and he also left Catherine to deal with an unpaid $900 grocery bill.)

Catherine Tobin was born in Omaha, Nebraska and grew up in the Chicago neighborhood of Hyde Park in an affectionate and close-knit family. She had three younger brothers including a set of twins. Her mother Flora was the first woman to be named principal of a Chicago public school and her fa-ther Sam worked for a Chicago dry goods firm.

Catherine met Frank Lloyd Wright at a costume party at All Soul's Church in Chicago's Kenwood community. The party marked the end of a year of study for the young adults. Dressed as a swashbuckling character from a Victor Hugo novel, Wright tripped over his sword and in the process knocked heads with the vivacious and willowy young woman.

The couple married on June 1, 1888 and less than a year later, their first son was born. The event was noted in the *Oak Park Reporter* with no recognition of Catherine's participation: "A young sculptor arrived to make his father, Frank Wright of Forest Avenue, happy on the 12th last." Frank Lloyd Wright, Jr.'s arrival was followed by the birth of three brothers and two sisters, Robert Llewellyn, the last of the Wright children was born in 1903.

Frank Lloyd Wright.

At the time of his marriage, Wright was a draftsman for Dankmar Adler and Louis Sullivan. With a loan from Sullivan, then one of America's leading architects, Wright built a five-room shingle house on the prairie, at Forest and Chicago Avenues, for his family, which he remodeled continually to meet his changing personal and professional needs. Today the Frank Lloyd Wright Home and Studio, restored to its 1909 appearance, is a National Historic Landmark.

The transition from her role as the carefree only daughter in a warm and affectionate family to a young mother beset with the care of a houseful of young children must have been difficult for Catherine. And her task was not made any easier by the presence of the formidable Anna Lloyd Wright who lived with her two unmarried daughters in the small cottage next to the young family.

The Wright children remembered their grandmother Anna as a frightening figure who was both dominating and demanding. Catherine had a dreadful fear of her mother-in-law who was so different from her own mother. After her marriage to Wright, Sam and Flora Tobin moved to Oak Park where they lived close—but not too close—to their daughter. In a letter to his children, Robert Llewellyn Wright recalled his maternal grandmother.

"The great thing about Flora was that she controlled me and everyone else around her without making us feel controlled. Her house was about a mile from ours; a well-ordered refuge always stocked with first-class food. I ate better there than at home and her house was better organized. I think my mother would have liked Flora to organize us, but Flora had the good sense not to try."

Catherine's parents must have been a great comfort to her, especially in the years following Wright's abandonment. Flora died in 1916 in Catherine's apartment above the Home and Studio and Sam survived her by just ten days. "I was instructed to let him win at pinochle, a difficult assignment," recalled Robert. "While I executed it perfectly, this fraudulent therapy failed to keep him alive. I was sorry to see him go because he had introduced me to vaudeville and given me some competence at cards."

Progressive Parenting

During those early years, Catherine established a kindergarten for her own and neighborhood children in the playroom Wright added above the kitchen in 1895. She equipped her little school with square folding tables, Froebel blocks and colored papers and painted a red circle on the floor, which the children used as a guide for "circle" games.

The Wrights believed in "progressive parenting" which meant letting the children do pretty much as they pleased. The neighbors complained the children were noisy and wild. They threw paper and toys from the balcony onto the draftsmen working below. They broke valuable art objects. They listened in on the telephone extension and disrupted important phone calls. One of their favorite pastimes was peering out the window on the second floor landing and watching their neighbors, the Harveys, eat dinner. The children thought this was hilarious.

Still Catherine had a talent for motivating her children. One spring, in an effort to rid the lawn of a blanket of dandelions, she promised the children she would make them wine from all the dandelions they could

The Frank Lloyd Wright family pose in front of their shingle-style home built by the architect in 1889 on the edge of the prairie on Chicago Avenue.

78

gather. Since liquor was never served, except on special occasions, the children thought this doubly exciting. The lawn was cleared in record time and the wine made and bottled. But what skills she possessed as a motivator, Catherine lacked as a vintner. By the time the wine was decanted, it had fermented and had to be thrown out.

To keep cool on hot, sultry evenings, Catherine and her children would sit in the open loggia or gallery that faced Chicago Avenue. They could hear people passing by and listen to their comments, but, because of the high wall, they could not be seen. And it's likely that many of the passersby made comments about the family they would have left unsaid had they known the occupants were listening.

Free Spirit

Mamah B. Cheney.

Much of their conversation probably centered on the scandalous relationship that was developing between Wright and Mamah Cheney, the wife of Edwin Cheney who had commissioned Wright to design a house at 520 N. East Avenue. By all accounts Mamah was unconventional and a genuine free spirit in an era that sought to restrict lively young women.

Mamah (she was christened Martha but preferred her nickname) was born in Oak Park and attended public schools. She received both a Bachelor and Master's degree from the University of Michigan where she met Edwin Cheney. Mamah was reluctant to give up her career but eventually agreed to marry Cheney and return to Oak Park where she was more interested in art, literature and the growing women's movement than in homemaking. One of Mamah's attractions to Wright was that her world did not revolve around her two children. While Catherine was a doting mother, Mamah's son and daughter were raised by a nurse and governess.

THE NINETEENTH CENTURY CLUB

HOME AND EDUCATION DEPARTMENT.

"Ample childhood makes rich youth, and rich youth glorious manhood, and these, taken together, form the perfect life."
HENDERSON.

MEETINGS: First and third Wednesdays, at 3 o'clock.

PROGRAM

OCTOBER 2

Parenthood
MARY S. LIVINGSTON
"The parents who truly love their children are they who can recognize through the needs of their dear ones the needs of all other children, and who feel in their inmost being the claims of childhood to happiness."

OCTOBER 16

Children's Rights and the Rights of Others
CATHERINE L. WRIGHT

NOVEMBER 6

Three Crises in Child Life
LILLIAN S. STURTEVANT

Catherine Wright presented a program at the 19th Century Woman's Club in October 1907 on children's rights.

THE NINETEENTH CENTURY CLUB

OCTOBER 21

Macbeth
Reading concluded
Witches and Ghosts
LIZZIE C. TODD
Lady Macbeth as Shakespeare Saw Her
(Both sides of the question)
LIZZIE SULLIVAN
JULIA HERRICK

NOVEMBER 4

The Sonnets
As Poetry and as Autobiography
ELEANOR J. PELLET

NOVEMBER 18

The Taming of the Shrew; Reading of the text
Three Famous Kates
MAMAH B. CHENEY

DECEMBER 2

King Lear
Reading of the text
A Study in Balance

Mamah Cheney gave a reading of Taming of the Shrew *to members of the 19th Century Woman's Club in 1908.*

Mamah was an ardent follower of the Swedish feminist Ellen Key who espoused free love and other radical ideas which were guaranteed to bring down the wrath of the community on anyone foolish enough to publicly support them. She translated Key's book *The Woman's Movement* into English and later jointly published with Wright her translation of Key's book, *Love and Ethics,* which contained many of the ideas Wright used to justify their liaison.

Mamah and Catherine belonged to many of the same civic organizations, including the Nineteenth Century Woman's Club and the two couples shared a social life. They were a familiar foursome in Oak Park, attending concerts at the Warrington Opera House as well as other social events. The 1908 membership roster lists both women as members of the Club's Home and Education Committee. That committee was responsible for the January 11, 1909 program. The topic was *Ethics in Ornament* and the speaker was Frank Lloyd Wright. But before the year was out both Wright and Mamah Cheney had left their respective spouses and children to begin a highly publicized five-year "free love" relationship that scandalized the nation.

For two years the lovers had titillated villagers with their less-than-clandestine affair. They frequently went out riding in Wright's bright yellow Stoddard-Dayton sports car and were even observed by playmates of the Cheney children "spooning" on the davenport of the Cheney library. Still their respective spouses, awash in self-delusion, refused to publicly acknowledge what everyone else already knew.

During the turbulent years between 1907 and 1909 Catherine Wright developed a friendship with Janet Ashbee, wife of C. R. Ashbee, a well-known English architect and friend of Wright's. Remembering her first meeting with Catherine in Oak Park on December 21, 1908, Janet Ashbee wrote in her diary: "If her children do not comfort her, she will be hard pressed. As yet, she is almost the girl still slender and lovely, but strongly built—and when she laughs you forget the tragic lines around her mouth."

The popular idea that Wright and Mrs. Cheney left Oak Park together is not true. What is a fact is that Mamah Cheney left her husband Edwin and their two children in the summer of 1909 and stayed with friends out west. And there is some evidence, but no proof, that she gave Wright an ultimatum to leave his wife. However, it is a fact that in September of 1909 Wright did leave his family and went to Europe where he was reunited with Mrs. Cheney. The September 25, 1909 issue of the *Oak Leaves* noted the leave taking in a single terse paragraph buried on page 32. "Frank Lloyd Wright left Thursday for Germany to superintend publication of a book to contain his architectural work. He expects to be absent a year, and the work may take even longer."

But Wright soon found himself back on the front pages of newspapers across the country after an American reporter passed on the information to friends in the U. S. that he had glimpsed the register of a hotel in Paris where "Mr. and Mrs. Wright" were staying—although Catherine was tending the children back in Oak Park.

Both the Cheney house on East Avenue and Catherine Wright's house were besieged by reporters and curiosity seekers. Catherine Wright refused all interviews saying only that Mamah Cheney was a "vampire" and Frank was merely her victim. "My heart is with him now. Frank will come back as soon as he can," she added.

"Each morning I wake up hoping it to be the last and each night I hope may prove to be eternal. To feel that an upstart should have come along and so easily drawn out my account of love with the many years of interest and left me penniless with the banker's consent and protection is pretty tough. And he seems to be so anxious to be sure I have no doubt about it. Womankind seems to be so moveable a 'feast.' Easily sold and easily bought and passed around and tossed away and no mercy except from outsiders."

Moveable Feast

Mrs. Cheney never returned to her family, but Wright did come back to Oak Park briefly in 1910. He told Catherine he would continue to live his "honest life" with Mamah and devoted himself to remodeling the home and studio to provide Catherine with income property. In October 1910, Catherine wrote Janet Ashbee: "Oh! How I wish I could find the end and unravel the snarl. Mr. Wright reached here October 8 and he has brought many beautiful things. Everything but his heart I guess and that he has left in Germany. As near as I can find out, he has only separated from her because he wishes to retain the beauty of their relationship and fears by staying with her that he would grow to loathe her."

"Each morning I wake up hoping it to be the last and each night I hope may prove to be eternal. To feel that an upstart should have come along and so easily drawn out my account of love with the many years of interest and left me penniless with the banker's consent and protection is pretty tough. And he seems to be so anxious to be sure I have no doubt about it. Womankind seems to be so moveable a 'feast.' Easily sold and easily bought and passed around and tossed away and no mercy except from outsiders."

But, despite these poignant words, Catherine Wright did learn to assert herself in later years and became active in the Suburban Civics and Equal Suffrage Club hosting many meetings in her home. When her children were older Catherine also attended classes at the University of Illinois that qualified her as a social worker. She worked for both Jane Addams at Hull House and Jessie Binford who headed the Juvenile Protection League. In the twenties she also worked with impoverished women in Appalachia for the U. S. Children's Bureau.

Frank Lloyd Wright and Mamah Cheney were destined never to wed. In 1911 he built a complex of buildings including a sprawling one-story house on 220 acres of land near Spring Green, Wisconsin his mother had given him. He retreated to this estate he named Taliesin (which means "shining brow" in Welsh) with Mamah and a handful of students. On August 15, 1914 a disgruntled servant set fire to the house while Mamah, her two children who were making a brief visit and several guests were at lunch. The man barred the doors and, as the occupants attempted to flee through the one door he left open, they were cut down with a hatchet by the deranged man.

Although Edwin Cheney had quietly granted his wife a divorce in 1911 Catherine would not agree to a divorce until the 1920s when Wright again sought his freedom so he could marry his second wife, Mariam Noel. In 1930 she married Benjamin Page and the couple lived in Rossville, Illinois until 1937 when they were divorced. "This was an unfortunate marriage and I know she regretted the move and having to give up the work she had prepared for which could have aided her independence," said Catherine Baxter.

Catherine Wright's final years were unsettled and marked by illness. She divided her time among her children who tried to keep her happy and comfortable. She died on March 24, 1959 just two weeks before Wright's death on April 9.

In a letter to his children their son Robert observed: "Instead of broadening out, my mother's road narrowed to produce the child-centered woman you know, who finally reverted to childhood herself. My father's road, however, did widen and let him go out near the top of his form. There is no moral."

Edgar Rice Burroughs

What famous Oak Park writer had his books translated into a dozen languages and made into highly successful movies? If you're thinking of Ernest Hemingway, guess again. Edgar Rice Burroughs, the creator of *Tarzan of the Apes*, also spent many years in Oak Park, but there the similarity between the two authors ends. From the time he penned his first short stories in high school Hemingway was a compulsive writer. Burroughs, on the other hand, never wrote a line until he was 36-years-old and under severe financial pressure.

Edgar Rice Burroughs.

Hemingway was a native son who left the village shortly after graduating from high school and, except for a few brief visits in the 1920s, never returned. Burroughs moved his young family to Oak Park at the beginning of his writing career and became actively involved in the community.

Edgar Rice Burroughs was born in 1875, the last of four sons of a stern but successful businessman and raised in a spacious brownstone in the 1800 block of Washington Blvd. in Chicago. As a boy Burroughs was both imaginative and undisciplined. After a vacation spent at his older brother's cattle ranch, 14-year-old Ed regaled his parents with his stories of thieves and cattle rustlers.

The elder Burroughs packed their son off to Phillips Academy in Andover, Ma. where, chafing under the strict regiment, he lasted just one semester. He finished his formal education at Orchard Lake Military Academy near Pontiac, Michigan.

After failing an exam for West Point, Burroughs enlisted in the army but was quickly discharged when physicians detected a weak heart. Burroughs had run out of options and so reluctantly returned to Chicago where he went to work for his father at a salary of $15 a week.

In 1900 he received a $5 per week raise as a wedding present from his parents when he married Emma Hulbert, his childhood sweetheart. But Burroughs still yearned for a freer lifestyle and, after three years of what he considered "penal servitude" he and his wife headed west to become part of an Arizona mining company owned by his three brothers.

Unfortunately, the company failed after a year of backbreaking work and the couple began an odyssey that took them to several towns in the southwest hoping their luck would change. But the only work Burroughs was able to find was a series of menial jobs including one as a railroad cop rushing bums out of the yard.

Edgar Rice Burroughs' life was at its lowest ebb at this point. He was 29, married for four years and still unable to support himself, let alone a family. He had never held a long-term job and his education had prepared him for nothing but a military career. Filled with bitterness he was forced to sell the furniture he and his wife had hauled around the country to raise money to return to Chicago where he held a series of jobs as a salesman. "I hated them all and I hated myself. Most of all I hated the slant-heads I tried to sell to," he recalled years later.

In 1910 when he was forced to pawn his watch to buy food after the birth of his second child, Burroughs knew he was in no position to argue when his father offered him the use of his "country place" at 821 S. Scoville Avenue in Oak Park.

However, the following year Burroughs moved his family to Chicago where he began to write out of desperation. "I began to write not for any particular love of writing. It was because I had a wife and two babies—a combination which does not work well without money," he said.

Burrough's home at 700 N. Linden, Oak Park.

Burroughs had never met an editor or publisher and admittedly knew nothing about the techniques of writing fiction. He submitted the first half of a story to Thomas Metcalf, the editor of *All-Story Magazine* and was encouraged to complete it. Metcalf purchased this first story, *Under the Moon of Mars* for $400 and published it in the 1912 issue of *All-Story Magazine*.

Intoxicated with his initial success, Burroughs began reading the works of Jack London, Rudyard Kipling and other adventure writers. He was especially intrigued with Sir Henry Morgan Stanley's book, *In Darkest Africa*. Burroughs had little confidence in a story he wrote "in longhand on the back of old letterheads and odd pieces of paper" and so was amazed when he received a $700 check for it. The story was entitled *Tarzan of the Apes* and appeared complete in the October, 1912 issue of *All-Story*.

Buoyed by this sale, Burroughs quit his regular job to pursue writing full time. "My income depended solely upon the sale of these magazine articles. Had I failed to sell a single story, we would have been broke again," he said.

But the lean years were finally over. In 1914 Burroughs purchased a large home at 414 Augusta Blvd. in Oak Park. Between 1914 and 1919, the years the Burroughs family lived in Oak Park, Edgar Rice Burroughs wrote six Tarzan books and numerous western and science fiction serial short stories for

the pulp magazines. Many of these stories were later published as books.

The writer established an office in his home and found the distractions of family life never seriously impeded his writing. "Were I afflicted with temperament, I should have a devil of a time writing stories, for now comes Joan with Helen (her doll) in one hand and Helen's severed arm in the other. I may be in the midst of a thrilling passage—Tarzan may be pulling a tiger out of Africa by the tail—but when Joan comes, even Tarzan pauses, and he stays paused, until I have tied Helen's arm to her torso again for the hundredth time." However, as the demands of his profession became more numerous, Burroughs eventually did retreat to an office on North Blvd. near Marion Street.

By the time the United States had entered World War I, Edgar Rice Burroughs had moved his family to a large home at 700 Linden. Because of his military background he was appointed a major in the Illinois Militia, a reserve group organized primarily for protection against any pro-German subversion on the home front. The September 18, 1918 issue of the *Oak Parker* lauded Burroughs' work in the militia under the headline, "Prominent Popular Oak Park Man Honored."

The article urged "every eligible man to support Major Burroughs by enlisting in his battalion. For a year and a half he has cut down his writing, and therefore his income. He sold his home at 700 Linden with the in-

tention of moving to California but abandoned the idea through a sense of duty and at great personal expense, rented another home at 325 N. Oak Park Avenue."

But, once the war ended, Burroughs did move his family to a 47,000-acre ranch he had purchased outside Los Angeles. In a farewell tribute the *Oak Parker* regretted that "Our foremost citizen and patriotic friend is going west. Major Edgar Rice Burroughs and his interesting wife and three charming children carry with them to the land of rare sunsets the very best wishes for their future happy welfare." Another article described a farewell party hosted by 11-year-old Joan Burroughs who was described as "the leader of the juvenile set in Oak Park."

Burroughs' phenomenal writing career continued to flourish in California. His company, Edgar Rice Burroughs, Inc., licensed Tarzan books, toys, comics, radio serials, movies and fan clubs. In 1934 he divorced his wife of 34 years and married a woman 30 years his junior. That marriage ended in divorce in 1940. Burroughs worked as a war correspondent in the Pacific during World War II. He died in 1950 at the age of 75 of Parkinson's disease.

Ernest Hemingway

Oak Park at the turn of the century was a setting straight out of a sentimental Booth Tarkington novel. Staunchly Republican and intellectually progressive, with one of the best high schools in the country and boasting a rich cultural and social life, villagers placed a high value on work, closely-knit family life, conservative politics and regular church attendance.

Ernest Hemingway's talented and public-spirited parents, Dr. Clarence (Ed) and Grace Hall Hemingway, fitted comfortably into the village's rigid social structure. Indeed, both were active in half a dozen social, religious and cultural organizations and scarcely a week went by when they were not mentioned in a news story or social column in the local newspapers.

Hemingway family portrait in 1905. Ernest is at the far right.

Both of Hemingway's parents were native Oak Parkers, and in fact, lived across the street from one another. Anson and Adelaide Hemingway lived in a house, now demolished, at 444 N. Oak Park Avenue, while Ernest and Caroline Hall lived at 439 (now 339) N. Oak Park Avenue. Ed Hemingway attended Oberlin College and Rush Medical College and, following a year of study in

Europe, he established a medical practice in the village.

Grace Hall was a gifted musician whose parents groomed her for a career in opera. She studied in New York with the well-known opera coach Madam Louisa Cappianni but was persuaded by young Dr. Hemingway to give up her career in favor of marriage. Although Grace and Ed both attended Oak Park High School they did not become romantically involved until he became a frequent visitor to the Hall home while attending Caroline Hall, who was terminally ill with cancer.

After her mother's death Grace Hall and Clarence Hemingway were married in an evening ceremony at First Congregational Church on October 1, 1896. The newlyweds made their home with her widowed father, Ernest Hall. Barely three months later the *Vindicator* noted: "On Saturday evening, January 8, 1897 at the home of Mrs. and Dr. C. E. Hemingway, 439 N. Oak Park Avenue, there was formed the Oak Park Choral Society. As director the society has secured the services of Mrs. Dr. C. E. Hemingway and for accompanist those of Mrs. Herbert Humphrey, both of whom are well known and equally well appreciated by Oak Park audiences. With a membership of 50 of Oak Park's best singers under the direction of Mrs. Dr. Hemingway we ought to expect good results at the opening concert next May."

Young Ernest (third from left) with Grandfather Anson Hemingway in front of Kenilworth Avenue home.

Ernest Hemingway, the second of the couple's six children, was born early on the morning of July 21, 1899 in the second floor bedroom of the Hall house. In 1974 while researching a story marking Hemingway's 75th birthday, I interviewed Ruth Bagley Burchard whose family lived on Grove Avenue, directly behind the Hemingways. Ruth recalled her mother telling her that Clarence Hemingway had promised if the baby was a boy, "I'll come out on the porch and blow my cornet." Sure enough, on that sultry July morning the sound of a cornet rang out from Oak Park Avenue and her mother called, "The Hemingways have a boy!" It was never clear to Ruth what form the announcement would have taken had the baby been a girl.

At the Hemingways

In her book, *At the Hemingways*, Marcelline Hemingway Sanford recalled growing up with her younger brother. "Mother often told me she had always wanted twins and though I was a little over a year older than Ernest she was determined to have us be as much like twins as possible. When we were little, Ernest and I were dressed alike in various outfits. I had an extra year of kindergarten while waiting for Ernest to be old enough so we could start first grade together when he became six," she wrote.

In 1905 Grandfather Hall died and, with the money she received from her inheritance, Grace began to work with architect H. G. Fiddelke designing a large stucco house at 600 N. Kenilworth for the growing Hemingway family that now included two more girls, Ursula and baby Madelaine.

The centerpiece of the 3-story house was a one-story music studio that was demolished in the 1950s. This room was actually a separate small building attached to the north side of the living room where Grace gave music lessons, recitals and soirees and where Ernest spent long hours practicing the cello. During his high school years he became more interested in athletics and gave up the cello by senior year.

Sets of the classics, Scott, Dickens, Thackeray, Stevenson and Shakespeare, filled the shelves of the family library. It was Marcelline's recollection that neither she nor Ernest skipped any of them. "We both devoured Stevenson, especially one of his lesser-known volumes, *The Suicide Club*, as well as *Treasure Island*. We both read Horatio Alger books in third and fourth grade and Ernest took them seriously," she wrote.

The works of Jack London were conspicuously missing. Their parents thought his writing coarse and common. Edith Striker, Ernest's seventh grade teacher at Oliver Wendell Holmes School, remembered the day Grace Hemingway visited and told her, "I don't think you should be reading *Call of the Wild*. It's not the kind of book young people should be reading."

Adelaide Hemingway had studied botany at Wheaton College and she passed her love of nature and the outdoors to her son Clarence who spent hours in the woods along the Des Plaines River in what is now Thatcher Woods. "Daddy would lead us on picnic hikes through the woods along the river, and he organized Ernest's and my eighth grade class into an Agassiz Club, named for Louis Agassiz, the famous naturalist," recalled Marcelline. "Some twenty or more boys and girls, including Ernest and me, went on these weekly hikes along the Des Plaines River both north and south of the North Avenue bridge."

"Daddy could make any walk into a pleasure because he knew how to look at nature. He could make you see things you had never known were there. Often in springtime we walked in the rustling leaves, and Daddy would stoop down and push the leaves aside and show us the budding wild hepaticas, pinkish lavender in contrast to the blue bells and brighter pink May flowers growing nearby."

In the winter Marcelline and Ernest also skated with their friends up and down the length of the frozen Des Plaines for a mile or more in either direction. "Ernest enjoyed skating. His ankles were strong, and often he helped me by crossing hands with me as we skated in rhythm."

High School Days

During their high school years Marcelline and Ernest were taught by Frank Platt, head of the English Department, in the oak-paneled English Clubroom. "Mr. Platt was a dignified, rather quiet man himself, but he liked our efforts at originality and his appreciation and high marks gave Ernest's and my egos a much needed boost," Marcelline remembered.

But it was in two classes taught by Miss Fanny Biggs, a course in the short story and one in journalism, that Ernest learned the most. Miss Biggs, a plain, thin woman who wore thick spectacles and screwed her hair into an old-maidish knot on top of her head, was possessed of great charm. Her warm smile made her beautiful and her keen sense of humor and enthusiasm inspired all her pupils.

Trapeze *staff. Front row, starting from left, Marcelline Hemingway, John Gehlman, Sue Lowrey, Ernest Hemingway.*

In Miss Biggs' short story class Ernest produced stories in the style of Poe, Ring Lardner and O. Henry. One of his first stories, *Sepi Jingan* appeared in the November 1916 issue of *Tabula*, then a literary monthly.

Miss Biggs conducted her journalism class as if it were a newspaper office and this training proved invaluable when her students went on to work for *Trapeze*, the school weekly. "Ernie used to do features for the *Trapeze* in the style of Ring Lardner," said Marcelline. "There would be a serious report of a football game and after it Ernie would write a 'Ring Lardner' feature on the same game in his own hilarious style, under the name of Hemingstein."

"I think I can truthfully say that the hours spent in our class in English VI, our after-school work on the paper with congenial friends, our headline writing and proofreading at the local printing office were some of the happiest hours of our schooling," she added.

In addition to his writing, Hemingway belonged to the Burke Debating Club, glee club, swim team, track team and, in his senior year, made the regular football team. Also in his senior year, he played Richard Brindsley Sheridan in the class play, *Beau Brummell.* The caption under his picture in *Tabula* reads: "None is to be found more clever than Ernie."

Ernest Hemingway wasn't the only literary luminary to emerge from the Oak Park and River Forest High School Class of 1917. Edward Wagenknecht, the distinguished literary critic, writer and teacher was the school's star public speaker and valedictorian. In 1974, I contacted Professor Wagenknecht, then professor emeritus at Boston University, for his impressions of his classmate. He responded with a charming letter in which he referred me to two of his books in which he discussed Hemingway.

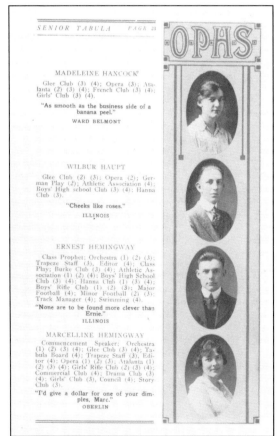

Hemingway wrote the class prophecy and, in his book of reminiscences, *As Far As Yesterday,* Wagenknecht recalled that Hemingway took his cue from my "utter indifference to all sports and games. He made me a famous baseball player and I can still remember the mischievous glance he cast at me, out of the corner of his eye, when he was reading it at our Class Day exercises."

In a chapter on Hemingway in his book, *Cavalcade of the American Novel,* Wagenknecht enlarges upon the image of Ernie as the boy-next-door. "Hemingway was a handsome, friendly and courteous boy who seemed equally enthusiastic about the sermons of the famous Dr. William Barton of the First Congregational Church and the performances of the Chester Wallace Players at the Warrington Theater," Wagenknecht wrote.

"I have since read that he was lonely in high school, that he had once run away from home and that he was sometimes regarded as a 'tough guy'. These things may or may not have been true; all I can say is that there was nothing in my contacts with Hemingway to cause me to suspect them. I had no classmate whom I recall with greater pleasure."

War Hero

After graduation Hemingway decided to postpone college. Instead he got a job as a reporter on the *Kansas City Star.* When he first arrived he stayed with his uncle, Tyler Hemingway, but later got a room of his own nearer the newspaper office and enjoyed his first taste of independent living. One of Ernie's assignments was to interview a group of Italian Red Cross officers who came to the U. S. to recruit volunteers for the American Red Cross Ambulance Corps in Italy. Ernie was delighted. At last he had found one service where his poor eyesight, which had barred him from the Draft, was no obstacle. He signed on and was sent to Italy where he served as an ambulance driver.

At that point Americans were not yet fighting on the Italian front and so when Hemingway received a number of severe shrapnel wounds he was widely heralded as a hero: the first American to be wounded in Italy. He was decorated by the Italian government and given a hero's welcome when he arrived in New York on his way home to convalesce.

Back in Oak Park Hemingway was in great demand by local organizations and churches to speak about his war experiences. In 1974 Edith Cummings Conley, who was several years behind Hemingway in high school, told me that the young soldier appeared a dashing and romantic figure when he addressed a high school assembly.

"Ernie was thin and very handsome," she said. "He came in limping with a cane and spoke so eloquently about his experiences on the battlefield that five boys immediately left school to join the ambulance corps in Italy."

In Conley's opinion, some of the animosity Hemingway was reported to have felt toward his hometown was exaggerated. "He

Photo: The Ernest Hemingway Foundation of Oak Park

Hemingway recuperating from his wounds in Paris before returning home to Oak Park.

was simply ahead of his time and couldn't live or write here under the disapproving scrutiny of his family," she said. Conley belonged to the same church as the Hemingways and she recalled that, whenever anyone mentioned that they had read Hemingway's latest book or short story, Grace Hemingway's only response was, "I never read any of Ernie's books."

In October 1921 Clarence and Grace Hemingway celebrated their 25th wedding anniversary surrounded by friends and family. Many of the guests who toasted the couple alluded to another 25 years of wedded bliss when the Hemingways would celebrate their golden anniversary in 1946. But it was not to be. None of the guests could imagine that seven years later, in December 1928, Dr. Hemingway would take his own life, while Grace would live until 1951.

The silver anniversary party was described in great detail by Belle Watson Melville, society writer for the *Oak Leaves* who noted that Dr. and Mrs. Hemingway used the occasion to introduce to their friends "their eldest son and his bride, Mr. and Mrs. Ernest Miller Hemingway, who are stopping in Chicago a short time prior to sailing for Italy."

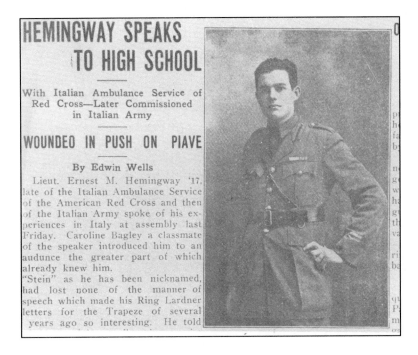

HEMINGWAY SPEAKS TO HIGH SCHOOL

With Italian Ambulance Service of Red Cross—Later Commissioned in Italian Army

WOUNDED IN PUSH ON PIAVE

By Edwin Wells

Lieut. Ernest M. Hemingway '17, late of the Italian Ambulance Service of the American Red Cross and then of the Italian Army spoke of his experiences in Italy at assembly last Friday. Caroline Bagley a classmate of the speaker introduced him to an audunce the greater part of which already knew him.

"Stein" as he has been nicknamed, had lost none of the manner of speech which made his Ring Lardner letters for the Trapeze of several years ago so interesting. He told

Hemingway did return to Oak Park for a few brief visits, including his father's funeral. But he never wrote much about Oak Park. In 1952 he was quoted as saying, "I had a wonderful novel to write about Oak Park and never would do it because I did not want to hurt living people."

Looking south from the corner of Lake and Marion Streets in 1885. Left, Lovett's Drug Store; right, Hoard's Hall.

CHAPTER IV

VIGNETTES OF VILLAGE LIFE

Residence of C. B. Ayers, 433 N. Oak Park Avenue.

An Oak Park Childhood

In November 1893 Gertrude Russell married Dr. William Lewis of Chicago in the home of her father, J. K. Russell. As a wedding gift from the bride's father the couple received a home of their own at 120 Maple. This street, just south of the North Western tracks, was lined with spacious homes built in the 1880s and 1890s for the "carriage trade" of wealthy bankers, merchants and other professionals.

In her reminiscences written more than 40 years after her wedding, Gertrude Lewis offered a glimpse of her Oak Park childhood in the 1870s. "No one was excruciatingly rich, no one put on airs. There weren't any airs to put on," she explained. "The motto of the town might have been 'plain, clean and plenty'. We lived the sweet and simple life."

"Not that we were without style," she added. "Our mothers were very well dressed. Every lady had a best black silk for Sundays and long afternoons of paying calls, for they had time for their friends then. She also had a second best black dress for missionary meetings and a summer silk for afternoon rides in the phaeton (a light four-wheeled carriage). Morning dress was frankly of calico or French percale. Little girls wore thin dresses till they were old enough for silk and then they were buttoned up as tight as were their mothers and suffered in silent elegance."

"Mrs. Brown did our hats and we wore what she gave us. Sometimes it was a trial for she would not let us grow up, and a little hat with streamers hurt our 16-year-old feelings. Then Miss Gill came. She let us wear the very latest and any color we asked for."

Flora Gill, one of the first women in business in Oak Park, opened her millinery shop on the southwest corner of Lake and Marion Streets in 1876. For the next twenty years she designed new hats and "made over" old ones for almost every woman and young girl in Oak Park. During an era when no woman ever left her house without a hat firmly affixed to her head, Flora Gill's shop was as important as a center for exchanging news and gossip as it was for the service she provided.

"Old people hadn't come into our set as yet," Mrs. Lewis continued. "Grandmothers there were, of course, who frankly dressed the part. They sat still in those days and you knew where to find them. They were dependable grandmothers with peppermints and stories, dandy ones and they were awfully good for bumps and things."

"Our mothers didn't have clubs, but they had missionary societies to enlarge their vision. The little old church and school building in the corner of the Austin yard (Temperance Hall at Lake and Forest) was the social center till Hoard's Hall was built in 1876. Mr. Austin gave all rentals from it to the Women's Christian Temperance Union and they made a good revenue from it."

MISS F. HENRIKSON

FASHIONABLE DRESSMAKING

Done in the Latest Style

Attractive Tailor Made Gowns.

A perfect Fit Guaranteed

455 Grove Avenue

Telephone 1473

1905 Oak Park Directory.

93

Four-year-old Jeanette Adland ready for the parade at Oak Park's annual horse show in 1900.

"We were not unaccomplished. We went in for classical music early. And everybody bought books and read all the time they were not riding. Naturally everybody drove everywhere. The phaeton or surrey was harnessed in the morning, the pretty mother drove and the dashboard was lined with little faces."

"When we were older we all had ponies, oodles of them. May Cook had a beauty. Laura Hulbert had a real saddle horse and took lessons but most of us just scooted. There were no pavements to impede our progress, no curbs to light on, roads were soft and easy if you unintentionally dismounted."

Barefoot boys in summer.

"Boys had the north and south prairies where they hunted and easily got birds. There was water in the river most of the time and perch, bullheads and small bass.

Wild flowers grew in the school grounds and all along the North Western tracks and everybody had cherries, apples and the small stuff children browse upon. There wasn't any Grove Avenue and along Lake Street there was a barberry hedge. But barberries looked better than they tasted. They were puckery things."

Each lady had her own "at home" day where she awaited callers who were served dainty cakes and tea from shining brass kettles. Calling was not a casual drop-in affair. Each lady arrived with great formality, gloved and with her card case in hand. After taking tea and exchanging pleasantries with her hostess and other guests, she left in the exact sequence in which she had arrived.

And, after her departure, the caller could only speculate on whether her family and foibles were being dissected by the remaining guests. One forthright lady, a newcomer to the village, took her leave at her hostess' door remarking, "Good afternoon, ladies. I leave my reputation in your hands."

Main Street Tales

"I suppose our Main Street had its tragedies and its sordid episodes. But I wish someone would write a novel to be called *The Other Side of Main Street* and if there were unhappy moments, write also of the old lady who habitually made a double batch of cookies, wondered why she did it and while they were fresh and hot just happened to think of a hungry family across and around the block.

"He could also write of the man with smallpox lifted so carefully and tended so faithfully in the days before the hospitals for contagious diseases and of the gentle lady who crept out after a great humiliation and the casual way in which everybody managed to come across the street and mention the weather to her.

"Then there is another story of the people who stripped themselves for the Chicago Fire sufferers so that Mrs. Humphrey found nothing left in her larder for the family tea; or that other time when Ida Morris, reading of the burning of the Wisconsin woods, how she and Mamie Stout gathered goods and packed barrels which Mrs. Stout rushed on through American Express."

The "burning" Gertrude Lewis referred to was the virtual tornado of flames that engulfed the small town of Peshtigo, Wisconsin on October 8, 1871, the same day flames consumed much of Chicago. This conflagration which scorched over 400 square miles and killed an estimated 1,200 people, spread so rapidly that the 800 Peshtigo residents who perished had no time to flee and most died in their beds.

In detailing the many acts of kindness shown by her friends Gertrude Lewis neglected to include her own "random acts of kindness." Although she played a prominent role in the social life of the village she never hesitated to do what she could to help her less fortunate neighbors when disaster struck.

The following social note appeared in the *Oak Park Reporter* in 1898 followed just a few weeks later by a letter from Gertrude Lewis appealing for help for a destitute family. "Mrs. G. A. Lewis, assisted by Mrs. J. T. Pither of Austin, gave a brilliant reception at 120 Maple last Friday afternoon. About one hundred ladies called during the afternoon. The floral decorations were tasteful and unique. Mrs. Lewis was dressed in white over pink with a demi-train. Mrs. Pither wore brown velvet and duchess lace with diamond ornaments. The refreshments were very elegant."

Gertrude Lewis' letter read: "Dear Friends: Two weeks ago there died in Harlem a young German who left a wife and two small children. They are not paupers nor do they wish to become so. But they are alone. No relatives in this country and no one nearer than kindly neighbors to help them. It is of the little home worth $1,200 that I wish to tell

I suppose our Main Street had its tragedies and its sordid episodes. But I wish someone would write a novel to be called
The Other Side of Main Street
and if there were unhappy moments, write also of the old lady who habitually made a double batch of cookies, wondered why she did it and while they were fresh and hot just happened to think of a hungry family across and around the block.

"He could also write of the man with smallpox lifted so carefully and tended so faithfully in the days before the hospitals for contagious diseases and of the gentle lady who crept out after a great humiliation and the casual way in which everybody managed to come across the street and mention the weather to her."

you. It is not quite paid for: four hundred dollars are still due. Of this amount the good people in Harlem have raised $228."

"A large amount for people who are paying debts and helping relatives of their own. With the home clear, the woman can live in one room, rent the rest of the house, make her little garden and care for her children. When they are old enough she can do work away from home. Will you kindly aid in this, sending any amount to 120 Maple Avenue where I will be responsible for its use. Gertrude Lewis."

Gertrude Lewis ended her reminiscences with this apt comment: "Oak Park was and is a helping place in time of trouble. Try our Main Street next time Mr. Novelist."

95

Chatelaine or Suffragette?

It takes a writer with extraordinary verbal agility to write around a subject—without once actually mentioning it! But that's just what an *Oak Leaves* reporter managed to do in 1914 while reviewing a tableau depicting the problems that could befall a young and innocent girl. Reading between the lines it was apparent that the "problem" pantomimed involved an out-of-wedlock pregnancy.

In that circumspect society ladies played an elaborate game of "I'll pretend I don't know if you pretend I don't know you know" when it came to dealing with anything outside the accepted social norm. And sex education for young girls was a haphazard affair depending on how comfortable their mothers were with the subject.

So was it any wonder that Nakama Hall was filled to capacity one Monday afternoon by women anxious to see the titillating tableau, *My Little Sister* given by members of the Home and Education Department of the Nineteenth Century Woman's Club.

"Mrs. Belle Watson Melville read the story stopping at intervals for the presentation of incidents by means of motion tableau given by women of the club," wrote the reporter. "At one of the encores, Mrs. Grace Hall Hemingway, accompanied by Mrs. Howard Simmons, added to the spell by singing that simple and well-loved old song, *Make Me a Child Again, Just for Tonight.*"

"Mrs. Melville's reading of the book was superb. She showed the girls in their simple, sheltered home life, untaught by their mothers to do anything but grow and be ladies, unguarded against financial storms, unwarned against preying powers that enabled them to fall easy victims. And then she showed with a burning vividness the trap and the tragic climax. It was a wonderfully artistic performance and it sent the women away alert to the problems so vividly presented."

Suffragettes Exercise Power

In the years prior to the 1920 ratification of the 19th Amendment to the U. S. Constitution, which gave women the universal right to vote, many ladies were beset with an identity crisis as they pondered their proper role in society. Their sheltered upbringing and education had not prepared them to form their own opinions on topics outside the realm of household management. And most had no difficulty in deferring to their husband's opinions in all things. But, at the same time, women were beginning to be more conscious of their untapped power as a voting bloc and how important it was that they understand the workings of government on the local, state and national level so they might exercise that power.

Many of these same women also became more assertive when it came to their clothing. They declared their independence from the dictates of fashion by following the lead of suffragettes such as Elizabeth Cady Stanton and Susan B. Anthony who adopted the short, and looser dresses without trains that had been introduced by Amelia Bloomer in the 1870s but rejected by the majority of women at that time. "It was so easy to go upstairs without stepping on oneself," one woman recalled. "A walk on a rainy day held

1903 Oak Park Directory.

no terrors for there were no yards of dragged skirt to clean. We had room to breath and freedom for our feet. But this healthful dress was despised and rejected by the public."

As early as 1891, Oak Park and River Forest ladies flocked to a series of political meetings held in the afternoon in Scoville Institute for the purpose of placing a woman on the high school board of education. The following year Lillie Pitkin became the first elected woman official in Oak Park when she won a six-year term on the high school board.

Yet many women found it difficult to shed their image as "shrinking violets." "Quite a number of ladies desired to exercise the coveted right of voting last Tuesday but could not muster the required nerve to crowd up to the polls with the men, and crowd back again, in order to vote," noted the *Oak Park Reporter*. "They complain that the town authorities did not provide proper accommodation. It is proposed that when a chance occurs again to vote for school officers, a parlor annex, with separate booth, shall be prepared for our feminine citizens."

These were most likely the same women who followed the advice of the editor of the *Reporter* in 1890 on how their "manipulative skills" might be used on their husbands to achieve any desired end. For example, a wife wishing to arrange a vacation was advised to "cultivate flushes and sick spells showing the need of fresh air and of transplanting to the seaside. Begin to mulch your husband with kindness and flattery. When he is ripe for picking he should have more fondling and be put into the sunlight of warm affection. This should be kept up until he begins to drop big leaves from his checkbook. When you have got all you can, turn him out of the pot and throw him into a corner to dry off."

Although women could not vote in national elections until 1920 the Illinois General Assembly empowered Illinois women to vote in local elections as early as 1913. But, once given the vote, Oak Park women demonstrated that they took the privilege much more seriously than men. Women of all ages and occupations campaigned vigorously for the right to vote. Three members of the Nineteenth Century Woman's Club, Dr. Anna Blount, Elizabeth Ball and Phoebe Butler, established the Suburban Civics and Equal Suffrage Association (later the local chapter of the League of Women Voters). The purpose of the organization was to study the workings of government in order to make an intelligent choice when they voted.

But how could the women understand the mechanics of village government when previously open meetings of the Oak Park Board of Trustees were suddenly held behind closed doors once the women showed an interest in attending. When a committee from the Equal Suffrage Association appeared at the municipal building for a board meeting they found "the lobby, the board room, the doorways and the stairways were filled with men, austere, as men are when they come to demand their rights and to protect their firesides," observed the *Oak Leaves*.

And the ladies were left standing in the hall while village business was transacted in private by the all-male board. "But why can't we go into that room?" demanded their leader. "Perhaps they do not know we are to report to our club what is being done and, of course, desire to obtain the real facts."

Dr. Anna Blount, a leader in public health whose specialty was obstetrics and gynecology, along with three other local women, Grace Wilbur Trout, Grace Hall Hemingway and Anna Lloyd Wright, were appointed to the Illinois Municipal Suffrage Commission.

Grace Wilbur Trout, who was president of both the Chicago and Illinois Equal Suffrage Association, was described as fearless, a gifted speaker and creative fundraiser for the cause. One of her most successful events was a highly publicized automobile run through Chicago and the North Shore that not only raised money, but also attracted the support of wealthy women.

Trout, who had been a prominent member of Oak Park society before turning her considerable energy to the suffrage cause, returned to the village frequently to promote women's suffrage. In 1910 the staid Oak Park Club invited her to speak. "The Oak Park Club, in compliment to Mrs. George W. Trout, invited her to come with others who advocate equal suffrage, and take possession of the club for one night," noted the *Oak Leaves.*

"Last winter Mrs. Trout was leader of the social life in the club, but since last spring has gained international reputation as a 'suffragette' and is proud of the title. Dr. Anna Blount has been equally active and has gained the same distinction. Aided by the campaigners who have been almost constantly on the stump during the summer, these Oak Park women will preach equal suffrage in their home village."

However, it was apparent to many women trying to garner information from their husbands and fathers that they had a much better grasp of the issues and were far better informed than the men in their lives. "All my husband knows about this village government is the place he pays his taxes and what it costs to break the speed laws," remarked Mrs. C. R. Erwin at a meeting held in the home of Mrs. Frank Lloyd Wright at Chicago and Forest Avenues.

But while organizations such as the Nineteenth Century Woman's Club and the Suburban Civics and Equal Suffrage Association encouraged women to grow intellectually, some ladies held more reactionary views. One woman was sure her husband wouldn't approve of a woman's club and another said she was too busy with her home duties to take on any more. Yet another didn't know what a woman's club would find to do—didn't they have their church groups already to do charity work?

In staunchly Republican Oak Park the ladies exercised their right to vote for the first time in a hotly contested primary election in April 1914. Marguerite Crook had a large sign posted on the back of her car that read: "Republicans may ride but Democrats must walk."

For one unfortunate lady, her first trip to the polling place proved fatal. "Mrs. Elizabeth Brink, wife of David Brink, 139 Taylor, died on Tuesday evening as a result of a stroke which she suffered that afternoon just after she had reached the polling place at the Ridgeland engine house," recounted the *Oak Leaves.* "She had gone to cast her first municipal ballot as a citizen of Illinois and the stroke came before she had the opportunity to vote. Her husband, one of the judges of election, sprang to her side just in time to catch her as she fell."

Thaddeus Giddings: Oak Park's Impresario

Social life in Oak Park during the 1890s was governed by an inflexible code of conduct. Everyone knew his or her place in the pecking order of society and behaved accordingly. Music teachers, for instance, were most definitely not supposed to roller skate to and from school. Nor was it considered seemly for a male teacher to knit socks for relaxation, design a labor-saving kitchen, go canoeing on the Des Plaines River with his students or entertain lady teachers at boisterous Sunday morning brunches.

Thaddeus Giddings.

But Thaddeus Giddings, the first music supervisor in Oak Park's elementary and high schools from 1896 to 1907 and one of the most colorful figures in Oak Park's past, was also one of the few people in town who could say, quite honestly, that he cared nothing for public opinion.

Giddings, an eccentric and good-natured bachelor, had the ability to make friends at all levels of village society. He was equally popular with his students and their parents who, perhaps, envied his free spirit. However, the music teacher was continually at odds with the school board that employed him, but considered music a "frill." "My students who major in music are the only high school graduates who have a skilled trade with which they can support a family from the day they leave school," Giddings told the board.

Thaddeus Giddings formed both the Oak Park High School orchestra and chorus and, under his leadership, the high school became one of the first secondary schools in the nation to grant credits for work in music, voice or instrumental with practice counting as laboratory work.

Giddings was a large man with a vigorous walk. Year round his sole means of transportation was a pair of roller skates. During the winter he wore a black topcoat that came to his heels but did not prevent him from strapping on his skates when the streets were clear. When the streets were covered with ice he used streetcars to make his rounds and became a familiar figure to the other passengers as he sat knitting gray socks either for himself or a friend as the street car slowly clanged its way through the village.

Thaddeus Giddings was a popular guest in many Oak Park homes and reciprocated by inviting teachers and other friends to lively Sunday morning brunches that he prepared himself. Seated at the head of his table the garrulous host would lead spirited discussions on a variety of topics. Villagers coveted invitations to these breakfasts, and it was considered a real coup to receive one.

Giddings lived in a seven-room flat and the extra bedrooms were always available to anyone who, in those days of only limited streetcar transportation, found themselves stranded far from home.

All of the apartments in his building at 449 North Blvd. had rear porches where, early every Monday morning, the women did their weekly washing together. According to an item in the *Oak Leaves,* when he saw all his neighbors laboring over their washboards, "he appeared on his own porch in shirt sleeves and a large apron and proceeded to do his own washing with elaborate splashing of suds and general mild burlesque of the whole process. This, of course, soon got around town and caused the greatest amount of merriment."

As a high school student Frederick Rowe recalled walking down Lake Street with Giddings one Monday morning complaining about the trouble he was having building a boat. The music teacher laughed heartily and said, "Suppose we make one and go canoeing next Saturday?" This sounded unbelievable to Rowe.

But after school Giddings went to Phelphs Grocery on Oak Park Avenue and picked up half a dozen wooden cheese boxes. These were drums about twenty inches in diameter and ten inches deep made of a sheet of split wood steamed and bent to a ring.

That night he removed their bottoms, sawed through the rings, opened out the curly peels of tough wood and these he screwed in a row to a keel strip. The next night he tacked in the canvas and gave it a preliminary coat of paint. Thursday night the boat had its final coat of paint and two paddles were whittled.

"Early Saturday morning we started off to the Des Plaines River and had a glorious day camping out," Rowe recalled. "We parked the canoe under a pile of brush and went boating again on subsequent Saturdays."

Spring Cleaning Not-So-Favorite Rite of Spring

Around the turn of the century spring could not come soon enough for Oak Park children who knew they would soon be allowed to shed their heavy lisle stockings, scratchy woolen vests and other cumbersome winter clothing.

But to their harried mothers spring meant something entirely different. The same sun that warmed the air fragrant with the scent of spring flowers also mercilessly exposed the winter's accumulation of grime and dirt in every corner of their homes and signaled that it was time for spring house cleaning to begin in earnest. This annual rite turned most households upside down for several days and prompted husbands to suddenly remember urgent business appointments that kept them away from home until order was once again restored.

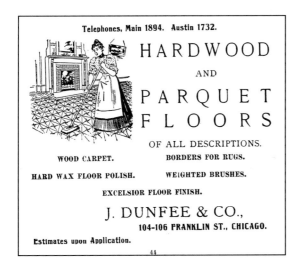

1902 Oak Park Directory.

But however wearisome she found the job, an Oak Park housewife could count on many local businesses and services that were anxious to help lighten her task. New mattresses could be made and old ones made over, custom cabinets built and old furniture varnished at the Oak Park Upholstery House, 449 North Blvd. Glidden and Sons at North Blvd. and Clinton Avenue, who came to the house to shampoo, size, wash and repair carpeting optimistically promised "satisfaction or no pay." And women weary of bending over low wash tubs could have fifty

pieces of clothing washed, starched and ironed by Brooks Laundry, North Blvd. at East Avenue, for just one dollar.

Homes could not be adequately aired until all heavy and unwieldy storm windows were removed and replaced with summer screens. Sias and Grenfell at 211 Lake Street was just one of several firms offering this service. But the Grinding Shop offered perhaps the biggest bargain of all. For only one dollar a lawn mower was picked up, oiled, cleaned, blades sharpened and returned to the customer.

But for all the attention house-proud women paid to the interior of their homes, they frequently neglected the outside. In the 1890s alleys were often used as dumping grounds for ashes and other household debris. After receiving numerous complaints about this problem village trustees decided a woman's touch was needed and appointed Mrs. F. H. Bowen, a member of the Neighborhood Civic Club, to inspect Oak Park alleys. Dressed in white and carrying a green parasol the indomitable Mrs. Bowen spent hours walking up and down every alley in the village trying to persuade residents to observe sanitary regulations.

Although business thoroughfares were generally paved with cedar blocks by 1900 most residential streets were still unpaved. To minimize swirling dust during the sum-

1902 Oak Park Directory.

mer the village's public works department regularly covered these streets with oil. But, as the *Oak Leaves* noted, "Oil on the streets has lain the dust but it appears to have also angered many domestic establishments. Commissioner Saragent has been swamped with complaints since the village began spreading oil. Children and dogs have tracked oil onto porches and into homes to such an extent that housekeepers say they have been driven to distraction."

The good news was that, after the streets were oiled, public works planned a complete cleaning of village alleys with a crew of 35 men and half a dozen wagons. "It is intended to collect at public expense all the ashes, grass and other refuse, just the same as garbage is collected now. The reduction plant will be used for disposal of all materials that can be consumed by fire and the ashes will be taken care of at some dump."

Clean-up Campaign

For several years prior to World War I the village sponsored an annual "Clean-up, Paint-up" campaign in early May. The aim of this event was the general sprucing up of both the interior and outside of homes. Horace Humphrey, the son of Dr. Simon and Elizabeth Humphrey and father of internationally acclaimed dancer Doris Humphrey, headed the campaign.

Humphrey walked the village end to end taking photographs of weed and debris-filled alleys, vacant lots and other spots he considered eyesores. These photos were then projected on the screens of all three of Oak Park's movie theaters in an effort to whip up enthusiasm for the clean-up work ahead.

A "Committee of 15" was appointed by the village president to take charge of the campaign throughout the village; each person was responsible for a half square mile. These Captains of Cleanliness pinpointed the spots in their areas most in need of cleaning and were prepared to "unleash a volunteer force in the field at the critical moment."

"Property owners and residents are urged to have their own premises in proper condition at the earliest possible date so that others may profit by their example and so that their own energies may be free for the grand wind up," exhorted Humphrey. Homeowners looking for someone to help them with their chores had only to call the Oak Park Associated Charities for the name of someone willing to work for 25 cents an hour.

Unfortunately, it appeared that a few zealots might be taking their clean-up chores far too seriously. "Has someone gone crazy about the cleaning up and beautification of Oak Park?" demanded the *Oak Leaves*. "This is the question firemen are asking. Within two weeks five barns, empty and apparently useless and which might be considered unlovely in the village beautiful, have caught fire. There is no explanation for these fires, according to firemen, except that they were deliberately started."

"As only old and empty barns are attacked by the pyromaniacs, the theory is that someone has taken this drastic and dangerous method to beautify the community and to make lanes out of the alleys and parks out of back yards."

The Sporting Life in Winter

The relatively mild winters we've enjoyed in recent years would have been a disappointment to Oak Park's early residents who were undaunted by blizzards, icy winds and plunging temperatures. These hardy souls simply strapped on their skates, dusted off their sleighs and toboggans and prepared to enjoy the outdoors.

Writing in the 1920s, Mrs. P. J. Kester recalled that 40 years earlier, winters were much colder. "The first of November was the first day of winter and was usually ushered in by a heavy fall of snow. The ground was soon covered with a thick white blanket extending east from Home Avenue and south of the North Western tracks, for miles a white plain, treeless and without a house of any kind. Nothing broke the cold silence except merry voices of skaters, jingle of sleigh bells or the dismal howl of prairie wolves as they came toward the village in search of food."

Des Plaines River in winter.

In November 1880 a number of Oak Park's young men met at Thayer's Photograph Gallery to form a skating club for the coming season. "About 30 names were enrolled and all skaters may join by consulting the president, Mr. Abe Thayer," reported the *Vindicator.* "A strip of ice half a mile long by thirty feet wide will be kept clean on the Des Plaines River above the Wisconsin Central railroad bridge."

Roller skating indoors in Steiner Hall, a large balloon frame building that could accommodate up to 500 skaters, was another popular winter spot for young people. The indoor arena, built in 1890 at what is now 157 N. Marion, was destroyed by fire just four years later. (The only picture of the rink that survives is a sketch by Albert Schneider, Jr.)

"While wails arise from every portion of the country in denunciation of the immoral 'rink,' the residents of Oak Park have naught but good words for the attraction of the sport on wheels," said the *Reporter.* "It keeps young men away from the city, and likewise enables the swain whose presence is objection to 'pater' to hold tender interviews with his best girl."

Every winter Mr. Loewy, the proprietor, held a fancy-dress carnival at the rink attended by 500 spectators and skaters. *The Reporter* covered the 1893 Carnival: "The best of Oak Park society was there in the most agreeable form. One hundred persons of both sexes appeared in becoming and varied costumes with nothing tawdry about them, making one of the most pleasant spectacles ever seen in our town."

Skaters were judged in a variety of categories including the most elegant lady's costume, the most original costume, best dramatic character, most comical costume, best clown costume and, strangely, best impersonation of an old man. Prizes included several 20-punch tickets to the rink, an elegant skate bag, a silk umbrella, a pair of nickel-plated skates and a pair of clamp roller skates.

There were other ways for a young man to court his favorite girl in winter if he was fortunate enough to have his own horse and sleigh. Horace Humphrey recalled: "When we were young fellows and wanted to take a girl for a sleigh ride we would drive sedately to the girl's home, hitch the horse to a post near the front gate, ring the bell, and when the door was opened, politely inquire if Miss Helen or Mary were at home and would she go for a ride."

Since the sleighs were open to the weather the couple depended on fur robes and a hot soapstone for the feet to keep warm. "If the snow came and buffeted our faces, if the icy winds pinched our cheeks so much the more fun. Snuggle up good and close. We'll keep warm!" Humphrey added.

Taking your best girl for a sleigh ride down Lake Street was a popular winter pastime in 1889.

After the first heavy snow, grocers who made home deliveries retired their wagons to the barn and hitched their horses to sleighs. As a boy Elwood Ratcliff recalled hitching a ride on these grocery sleighs with his friends. "You'd either ride the runners or you might even have a sled with a rope and attach it to the back end of one of the sleighs and that was really good winter sport when you were ten years old," he said.

But for the slightly older crowd, snow racing was the thing to do. According to an article in an 1888 issue of the *Argus-Vindicator,* "There will be a high old time on Washington Blvd. Saturday afternoon when all the Oak Park owners of fast steppers will meet at the corner of Oak Park Avenue to try the speed of their trotters in a series of snow races."

"Everybody knows that Duncombe and Drechsler and Einfeldt and Peterson and Dobbins and Arnold would not more miss an opportunity to prove the fleetness of their steeds than they would miss bragging about it—before the races. The boulevard east from the avenue will be used as a speedway and a few records—and a few fondly cherished hopes—will be smashed to smithereens."

During the seemingly endless winter months villagers used any occasion, however insignificant, as an excuse for a party. Using just a few props but a great deal of ingenuity they were able to create unique themes for these soirees. For instance, when Mr. and Mrs. Chester Parsons were in the midst of redecorating their house on Washington Blvd. they suddenly decided that, since their furniture was already shrouded in burlap, to hold an impromptu "hard times" party.

"Accordingly, at the appointed hour a crowd of hobos as ever wended their way through this fashionable thoroughfare arrived and took possession of the house," reported the *Vindicator.* "Card tables were hastily constructed and progressive euchre

104

enjoyed by women in faded calico waists and laundered ribbons and men who looked unutterably healthy and happy despite their patched waistcoats, ragged shirts and frayed trousers."

"Supper (which from the menu would never suggest hard times) was served on wooden plates. Tin cups were used in lieu of china and the place cards consisted of strips of wallpaper to which Mr. Parsons urged his guests to help themselves, saying that as he had to pay by the hour to have it removed it would accommodate him to have it all disappear. Dancing brought to a close one of the liveliest and most successful parties of the winter season."

Shooting pool was an acceptable pastime year round, but it was especially popular in winter. In 1893 Oak Park's lone pool hall at 104 Lake Street was transformed into a high class "billiard parlor" after it was purchased by Frank Pierce, a local entrepreneur. "Under its former management boys of all ages were allowed to play. This was not only a violation of an ordinance but rendered the place noisy and unpleasant for older and more respectable people," said the *Reporter*. "We are glad to know that Mr. Pierce, who comes to us from Englewood well recommended, has declared his intentions to conduct a quiet and respectable place in which no minors or 'toughs' will be allowed. In the past ten days he has refused admission to twelve former patrons, all under 21. No doubt the better class who want a quiet game of pool or billiards will readily appreciate the change."

Until the late 1880s when the Cicero Water, Gas & Electric Light Co. began providing electricity, homes were lighted during the dark winter months by oil and kerosene lamps. There were no meters when houses were first wired for electricity. Instead, each household was given a flat rate and could use as much electricity as family members wanted. What a boon for parents who didn't have to continually remind their kids to "turn off the lights."

B. L. Dodge, the popular principal of Central School left his chosen field of education to head the newly formed utility. In those early days when lights would flicker on and off intermittently in the course of an evening, his former pupils would laugh and say, "Mr. Dodge has taken his finger off the light button."

> *B. L. Dodge,*
>
> *the popular principal*
>
> *of Central School left his chosen field*
>
> *of education to head*
>
> *the newly formed utility.*
>
> *In those early days when lights*
>
> *would flicker on and off*
>
> *intermittently in the course*
>
> *of an evening, his former pupils*
>
> *would laugh and say,*
>
> *"Mr. Dodge has taken his finger*
>
> *off the light button."*

The Shrew and the Sparrow: A Tale of Two Oak Park Women

This is the story of two women whose husbands both worked for the North Western Railroad in the 1890s. But that was all they had in common. Mary Berry was so strong-willed that even the *Vindicator* was forced to acknowledge that "she has demonstrated the superiority of her sex in the management of men." Lena Hillman, on the other hand, was a timid woman, a homebody who was easily frightened and intimidated by strangers.

Mary Berry and her husband James purchased a large house and five acres at the corner of Ridgeland and North Avenue where, according to the *Vindicator,* "they intended to cultivate this piece of prairie and to raise strawberries, buckleberries and perhaps, other little Berrys therein."

Shortly after they bought the farm James Berry, who had recently been vaccinated against smallpox, developed a poisonous-looking scab and began to suffer other side effects from the inoculation.

"While the couple began tilling their homestead a serpent entered into this Eden in the person of John Rasmusen, a Swede who, through some legal technicality, claimed that the Berry's five acres was covered by his lease," said the *Vindicator.*

One morning Mary Berry observed John Rasmusen with a team of horses industriously plowing her five acres. She ordered him off the premises but he refused. "In her perplexity, temptation seized Mary Berry and she told a white lie, and from that moment the plot began to thicken. Her fib was very simple and very effective. "John" she said. "You had better leave this Berry patch at once for we have a case of smallpox at the house.'"

Rasmusen left quickly and began spreading the word that there was a case of Black Smallpox at the Berrys. "The news soon reached the ears of Sergeant Hacker at the Oak Park police station. Gruesome visions of epidemics, pesthouses and midnight funerals danced before the sergeant's eyes and he dispatched Officer Honrin with orders to post a smallpox card at the Berry house."

Barn in rear of farm house on north Ridgeland Avenue, similar to one on Mary and James Berry's farm.

The determined Mrs. Berry soon sent him on his way saying she would not have any nasty red or yellow cards stuck on her house without a physician's order. The policeman retired soon to return with reinforcements. Mary Berry met them at the door with a long, gleaming and very ugly-looking butcher knife The brave captain looked at the haughty woman unflinchingly, never wavering from his duty.

"If you tear the card down I will have you arrested," he said. "There are not enough policemen in all Cicero to arrest me," she replied. There was a moment of silence. Then Captain Hansberry raised his tack hammer and in an instant the smallpox card was attached to a tree in Mrs. Berry's front yard. But not for long.

"Mary Berry tore down that card in just about two seconds and threw the pieces defiantly at Captain Hansberry. Then she began carving circles and tangents in the air with the knife and begging the officers to arrest her. Every lunge which she gave with the knife seemed to fill the summer air with open-mouthed bacilli and smallpox microbes."

"After a brief consultation officers decided to wait her out. A quarantine was established at a safe distance from the house and during the evening Mrs. Berry put away her knife and became quite friendly. Taking advantage of the fact that she was quarantined, she desired the officers to do a few errands for her. This they readily agreed to and Mrs. Berry enjoyed the novel experience of sending a policeman to the market for her meat and to the grocery for her vegetables and bread. Finally, when she could make no further use of her guard she told them of her husband's vaccination and that he was not contagious. They were, not to put too fine a point upon it, not pleased to learn of her deception."

Missing Wife

The story of George and Lena Hillman, a childless couple who immigrated to Oak Park from the Netherlands about 1885, is stranger than fiction. Hillman was a railroad switchman and his wife stayed home tending their cottage and garden.

George Hillman is listed in the 1887 village directory as being a laborer living at 122 Lake Street. One day Hillman came home with two big gashes on his head inflicted by union workers incensed over his refusal to join their union. After that experience Lena Hillman became very fearful about her husband's safety. When he was gone on an errand or did not return from work at the regular time she became distraught.

One Saturday afternoon Hillman went to Christian Schlund's butcher shop on Lake Street to buy some meat for dinner. The shop was closed and he waited some time for Schlund to return and open it. In his absence Lena Hillman became alarmed and, hastily wrapping a shawl about her head, started out to find her husband. She somehow missed him and, frightened and alone, wandered for hours. The police eventually picked her up and brought her to the county hospital. Because she was distraught, difficult to understand and had no one to speak on her behalf, the medical staff judged her insane and, with no legal recourse, sent her to Dunning, the county insane asylum on Irving Park Road.

In the meantime, George Hillman returned home and found his wife gone. He searched frantically for her everywhere without success. Months passed as Hillman continued his futile search. He finally lost his job, grew disheveled in his appearance and neglected his house. Finally he, too, was picked up on the street by the police and sent to the county hospital on the suspicion that he was insane.

But, unlike his wife, George Hillman did have his day in court. "The court decided that his mind was not affected and ordered him to be sent to the poorhouse instead of the asylum. In the court there was another prisoner, John Lonson, who was found to be a lunatic and who was ordered sent to the asylum," reported the *Vindicator*.

"The bailiff in some way changed both men and the insane patient was taken to the poorhouse while the pauper was carried off to the asylum. This pauper was George Hillman, and it was the mistake of the bailiff that led to his meeting the wife whom he believed to be dead, face to face in a cottage at Dunning."

The mistake was discovered by a Dr. Loewey, the physician in charge of the men's ward. He recognized Hillman and knew that a mistake had been made. "He knew the story of Lena Hillman, having resided in Oak Park, and was acquainted with her personally. He felt sorry for the unfortunate husband, and did what he could to comfort him."

"On Wednesday he happened to go into one of the cottages occupied by female patients and was surprised to see a woman who looked like the missing Lena Hillman. Mrs. Hillman was known as 'Gretchen' in default of knowing her real name. He informed Supt. Sawyer, who notified asylum commissioners. It was decided to bring the husband and wife together and trust to fate for the rest."

"The long-separated couple were reunited and the commissioners there to witness the meeting turned away, unable to watch the poignant scene unfolding before them.

Today, of course, the couple who had suffered grievously would hire a lawyer and file suit for damages. But what actually happened to the Hillmans was they returned to their small cottage in Oak Park and began rebuilding their life together.

Villagers Made Beautiful Music

From Oak Park's earliest days it was a rare social or religious gathering that did not include some type of musical entertainment. Performances by amateur choral groups, bands, orchestras, opera societies, barbershop quartets and soloists were the mainstay of almost every event.

Mrs. Palmer Hulbert, musical director of Rubinstein Club.

The abundance of so much musical talent in one community was enough to send the society reporter of the *Oak Park Argus* into a frenzy of hyperbole in 1902. "There is no place in Illinois where there are so many musical people to the square inch as there are in Oak Park and the musicians already there are attracting others to them all the time," she gushed. "There are some people who have already attained more than a local reputation in the musical world. There are others who are fast attaining recognition. There are still others who are content to drift idly along with the great tide of musical dilettantes. All these people get together on oc-casion and have salons. This helps to thicken the musical atmosphere and more and more musicians go to Oak Park to live for the sake of the company they keep."

As early as 1880 an orchestra was formed in Oak Park under the direction of William Corbett. This group disbanded after only four years. In 1895 another group of amateur musicians organized another equally short-lived orchestra. The present Symphony of Oak Park and River Forest was formed in 1931 by violinist Gladys Welge who was later named director of the Chicago Women's Symphony.

John Farson, whose eclectic interests included a love of music, helped organize several musical groups around the turn of the century. He also encouraged George Maher to incorporate several musical motifs in the design of Pleasant Home, his Prairie Style home. These included a musician's alcove in the dining room and a music room on the landing between the first and second floor.

But even before Farson built his mansion on the corner of Home Avenue and Pleasant Street he frequently allowed the vacant tract to be used for public concerts. In 1894 the *Oak Park Reporter* noted, "The first of the series of open air concerts was given Tuesday evening at the corner of Home and Pleasant and was a decided success. The weather was perfect and people turned out in large numbers. Both streets were filled with carriages and the scene was a very gay and pretty one."

"A nice band stand had been erected and chairs were to be had for a nominal charge.

Rubinstein Club

FIFTH SEASON

1899—1900

First Private Concert

FIRST CONGREGATIONAL CHURCH

OAK PARK

Tuesday Evening, May 8, 1900.

MRS. P. S. HULBERT

MUSICAL DIRECTOR

THE CLUB WILL HAVE THE ASSISTANCE OF

MR. H. L. WATEROUS, BASSO.

...AND...

MISS GERTRUDE HILTON, PIANIST.

MISS HARRIET C. STACEY, Accompanist.

STEINWAY PIANO USED

The band, Brook's Second Regiment, Illinois National Guard, fully sustained its reputation as one of the finest in the country."

Farson was also president of the Rubinstein Club organized in 1894 to offer concerts of vocal and instrumental music. The group's first effort was front-page news in the *Reporter* in May 1894. "The Rubinstein Club scored a triumph in their first concert given in the First Congregational Church last night. Considering the short time the chorus has had to practice the results surprised everyone and speaks highly of the ability of the director, Mrs. Palmer Hulbert. Mr. John Farson, president of the club, complimented the group for their remarkable progress in so short a time."

And, of course, scarcely a week went by without mention of a performance by Grace Hall Hemingway in some local venue. On January 8, 1897 the Oak Park Choral Society was organized in the home of "Ms. and Dr. C. E. Hemingway," 439 N. Oak Park Avenue The couple had been married just three months earlier.

Prior to her marriage the local newspapers regularly carried enthusiastic account of Grace Hall's many musical triumphs. Typical was this account in the *Reporter:* "Miss Grace Ernestine Hall gave a musical tea on Tuesday afternoon at her residence for about 200 friends. The house was elegantly decorated with palms and nasturtiums. Miss Hall, who had the honor of being one of Madame Cappiani's most distinguished pupils, sang a number of classic selections from leading composers."

Municipal Band

In the winter of 1914, Joseph Farr, a plasterer by trade and cornet player by inclination, organized Oak Park's first Municipal Band for the purpose of providing villagers with a series of free concerts throughout the summer. The 24 enthusiastic amateurs held their first meeting at the Village Hall where they were welcomed by president August Einfeldt who gave them permission to rehearse in the building without paying rent. Although Einfeldt protested he had a tin ear, the players rewarded him for his support by electing him president of their group.

Summer band concert.

The Municipal Band made its first public appearance in April 1914 when they led more than 600 Oak Park suffragettes in a parade down Michigan Avenue in Chicago. The parade, which attracted 14,000 participants and an estimated 100,000 spectators, was held to thank the Illinois General Assembly for passing a suffrage bill giving women the right to vote in local elections and lobby for passage of a similar law nationwide.

Farr's Band made a lasting impression on spectators and, in appreciation for their performance, Mrs. George Plummer, president of the Suburban Civic League, promised to form an auxiliary for the Band that would raise money for uniforms, music and a permanent place to hold concerts. This was especially important because the board of the new Park District of Oak Park, formed just two years earlier, had denied Farr and his Band permission to give free concerts in any of its three parks.

The musicians had confidently expected the park board would give them the same support they received from the village. But Park District commissioners, concerned about the effect large crowds would have on the newly planted shrubs and other landscaping, refused permission. However Farr was undaunted and, at least until the end of World War I, gave many open air concerts in support of War Bond drives on the grounds of Central School at Lake and Forest and in Cummings Square at Lake Street and Harlem Avenue.

Farr was so confident about the caliber of his amateur musicians that he invited John Phillip Sousa, one of the most famous concertmasters in the country, to conduct his Municipal Band. His effort was rewarded with a courteously worded, hand-written letter from Sousa written on a U. S. Naval Training Station, Great Lakes, Illinois letterhead:

"My Dear Mr. Farr: I do hope that after our return from the Fourth Liberty Loan Drive I will have time to come over and conduct your band for an evening. I want to thank you for your most interesting article in the *Dominant*. It has evidently created an interest to a great many, for I have received from different friends copies of your article. Thank you for your many kind expressions."

Wright and Roberts: Great Architects, Opposite Temperaments

Frank Lloyd Wright was known for many things, but reticence was not one of them. Although his neighbor and fellow architect E. E. Roberts advertised his architectural services in a tasteful advertisement that appeared weekly in the local newspapers, Wright never paid to get his name in print.

Wright was a master at self-promotion and one of the ploys he used was to write incendiary letters to the editor on controversial issues. These letters were usually published on the front page—next to Eben E. Robert's paid advertisements!

In a letter that appeared on the front page of the *Oak Park Reporter* on August 23, 1900, Wright railed against a new Cicero Township ordinance requiring trees on public property be cut back in the interest of safety. Wright contended that they were being pruned because they interfered with placement of utility wires.

Frank Lloyd Wright.

Wright never saw a tree he didn't like and objected vociferously to any pruning of older trees on public parkways, referring to the cutting back as "mutilation." But the Oak Park Improvement Association had a different viewpoint: "The early settlers have left us miles of streets lined with magnificent trees. But we have neglected our heritage and today many streets are overshadowed by a sprawling growth of vegetation, shutting out completely the air and sunlight. In many places the sun never strikes the ground from spring to fall. The streets are moldy and the sidewalks are moldy. What is needed is a thorough and systematic trimming," wrote Thomas Gale, chairman of the Association and one of Wright's clients.

Wright's response was predictable: "Rows of our beautiful trees are yearly assassinated in the interest of the wires of the franchise. Oak Park in general, Chicago Avenue in particular, is groaning in helpless servitude infested with more than a fair share of offensive poles," railed Wright in his letter.

"From year to year this tree topping outrage must be repeated, for trees will grow and it seems the telephone poles will not, at least not under (John I.) Jones of Oak Park and his (Cicero Township) board. And why not? That the telephone monopoly may save the cost of raising their wires ten feet or placing them below ground where Evanston has just succeeded in placing them."

"'Bury the wires! Long life to the trees!' is a good campaign issue for the Improvement Association. A campaign of educational issues that will develop an appreciation of the priceless gift to society conferred by him who plants and fosters a tree."

Wright and Roberts were neighbors and had many things in common. Like Wright, Roberts worked out of his home at 330 Superior Street which he built for his wife Rossie in 1895. Roberts, too, employed several architects who worked in a third floor studio while he received clients in his dining room.

Between 1893 and the 1930s Eben E. Roberts designed more than 200 residences and an almost equal number of apartments, churches and public buildings in the village. Most notable were the first village hall, the north wing of the high school, the Elks Club, Masonic Block, the Colonial Club, West Suburban Hospital, Oak Park Club, Trinity Lutheran Church and parsonage and the Warrington Opera House.

Roberts advertised himself as an architect of "homey dwellings" that reflected his New England background. They were small, square buildings that Wright contemptuously referred to as "salt boxes." But despite their professional rivalry, the children of the two men were friends and played at each other's homes.

Eben E. Roberts.

E. E. Roberts' family life was vastly different than Wright's. According to his grandson, Howard Roberts Drew, the Roberts marriage lasted more than fifty years and was an extremely happy one. "Eben and Rossie had an abiding Christian faith which was of lasting influence on me," he said. "They also shared a love of music and the house on Superior Street had a music room and there were many musical evenings there."

According to Drew, his grandfather was a gregarious man active in the community whose home was often the setting for many social events. "He was fond of jokes and, on one occasion, when we had the minister to dinner Eben put a gadget under the minister's plate which made it move when he squeezed a hidden bulb. The minister's startled reaction produced the desired hilarity among the other guests."

Although both men were prolific workers, not everything they designed was built. In 1906 Charles Burton Scoville commissioned E. E. Roberts to design a massive armory on Lake Street just west of the new municipal building that would serve as headquarters for Company D, a reserve unit of the Illinois National Guard.

Plans called for the State of Illinois to pay just $1,000 annually for upkeep with the rest coming from rentals for dances, concerts, conventions and dues from the soldiers themselves. One reader rhapsodized: "Think

of President Ray presiding clothed with all his municipal dignity, think of John Farson filling the hall with his speeches of staunch loyalty to Oak Park, think of Postmaster Hutchinson in the full flight of one of his Fourth of July eagle screams for liberty, the flag and an appropriation for a new post office."

But apparently the only thing most villagers thought of was the prohibitive cost. Roberts' drawings were scrapped and Company D had to make do with renovating the third floor of Kenilworth Hall at Kenilworth and South Blvd. for use as an armory.

In 1901 Frank Lloyd Wright made a grandiose announcement that he planned to build a model community of eight houses on several unspecified blocks north of Chicago Avenue and west of Oak Park Avenue. There were to be four houses to a block, each built on a lot with a minimum width of 400 feet.

Wright's object was to build "a city man's country home on the prairie" where everything would be in harmony. "The houses will be constructed on lines to harmonize with the prairie, with low terraces and broad eaves," he said. "The design will be pleasing to the eye and suggestive of what the community will be: a settlement of people desirous of living in the country and in homes that are not an insult to the aesthetic sense."

In an interview for the July 18, 1901 issue of the *Oak Park Reporter*, Wright said that he had obtained financing for this project and work would begin in a few days. "Mr. Wright said he was not ready to let the public into his scheme and intimated that when the plans materialized, residents of Oak Park and Chicago would be treated to an architectural surprise." The "surprise," of course, was that for whatever reason, these homes were never built.

Corner of Lake and Marion Streets looking east in the 1890s. Brick Steiner Block is on the northwest corner and Schneider's grocery is across the street on the northeast corner. Spire of First Congregational Church is in background.

CHAPTER V

VILLAGE LANDMARKS: PAST AND PRESENT

Prairie Cycling Club.

Social Clubs Flourished in Village's Early Days

When Oak Park was incorporated in 1902 the social fabric of the community was a crazy quilt of clubs organized for every purpose from fellowship to philanthropy. Many of these clubs were affiliated with a church while others such as Nakama and the Nineteenth Century Woman's Club had a broader membership and so were able to build their own clubhouses.

Clubhouses for three of these social clubs, the Elks Club at 938 Lake Street, the Colonial Club at Elmwood and Lake Streets and the lesser-known Phoenix Club at 641 S. Scoville were designed by local architect E. E. Roberts.

The three-story lodge or clubhouse Roberts designed for the Benevolent Order of Elks in 1916 was a Prairie Style landmark on Lake Street until the 1970s when it was razed and a parking garage built on the site. The building was financed by Herbert Mills, owner of Pleasant Home, who agreed to take a $50,000 bond issue. At a dinner meeting to finalize plans for the club Roberts piqued the interest of the Elks in their new facility with a movie that previewed its many amenities. The movie included scenes demonstrating how to take a Turkish bath, how to dance the tango in the ballroom, how to meet one's friends in the magnificent lounge and how to sit on the broad front porch with a Havana cigar.

The Colonial Club

The Colonial Club was a family-oriented social club whose architecture was based on "Colonial" New England architecture. It was located on the site of the parking lot adjacent to Pilgrim Congregational Church at Lake Street and Elmwood where, every Saturday from June to October, the Oak Park Farmer's Market is now held. The Colonial Club was the outgrowth of another social club, the Magazine Society, organized in 1894 by several couples on south Scoville. The meetings were held in homes, but in 1902 members obtained a charter for their organization and engaged E. E. Roberts to build a clubhouse.

The three-story Colonial Club contained a billiard room, bowling alleys, parlors, clubrooms and a third floor ballroom. Boys and girls were taught the social graces in Miss May Belle Ingram's dance classes, the men played cards or billiards in a strictly masculine atmosphere and the ladies met for lunch and cards in the parlor. The Club remained active until the Depression when many members were unable to pay their dues. It was later acquired by the Village and razed in 1972 when it was determined the cost of restoring the building was prohibitive.

Phoenix Club northwest corner of Scoville and Jackson Boulevard, 1902.

The Phoenix Club

The Phoenix Club, designed by Roberts in 1902, had a steeply pitched roof, overhanging eaves, rectilinear chimney and wide porte cochre for carriages. According to an account in the November 28, 1902 issue of the *Oak Leaves* marking its opening, the 35 by 87-foot building included a lower floor

Colonial Club.

117

that housed a double bowling alley, a billiard room, lounging and smoking rooms and lockers. "The main floor contains a reception hall and library, committee and cloak rooms, a banquet hall and kitchen. The third floor is set aside for entertainment with a large ball room with a stage at one end."

The Phoenix Club was so named because it was formed from the remnants of two small neighborhood clubs in south Oak Park that had merged in 1901 under the new name. But it was a short-lived merger and the clubhouse for the Phoenix Club at Clarence Avenue and Harrison Street was abandoned about the same time Oak Park became a separate municipality.

Allen Flitcraft, "a man of stature in the community" and one of the developers of the south prairie, was among the trustees elected to the first village board in 1902. At a board meeting to consider the fate of the abandoned clubhouse, Flitcraft proposed a committee be appointed to select a site and prepare plans for a modest clubhouse to cost about what the proposed improvements on the old one were estimated to be, approximately $3,000. He offered to lend the money to build the facility to residents in south Oak Park who were interested in reviving the Phoenix Club. In 1902 Flitcraft purchased the lot at 641 S. Scoville and engaged E. E. Roberts to build a clubhouse that eventually cost $13,000.

Flitcraft leased the building to the club for three years at a rent of $50 per month. "During the life of the lease the club may make payments upon the purchase price which is to be exactly what Mr. Flitcraft has put into the venture," reported the *Oak Leaves*.

But the Phoenix Club existed as a family social club for just six years. In 1908 Flitcraft sold the property to Ascension Parish. The Church used the facility as a church and school until new buildings were completed in 1912. The building was owned for many years by the Knights of Columbus and eventually converted to a private residence. It burned in 1980 and in 1987 a new single family residence, modeled on Roberts' original design, rose Phoenix-like from the ashes of the original Phoenix Club.

The Prairie Cycling Club

In 1889 at the height of the cycling craze, a group of Oak Park men organized a cycling club that met in a cottage on Marion Street. Larger quarters were needed barely a year later when membership, in what began as primarily a men's social club, increased to

Members of the Prairie Cycling Club take a break during an afternoon of cycling in the 1890s.

118

150. In 1891 members decided to build their own facility. According to the *Oak Park Reporter*, they formed a corporation with each member becoming a stockholder. "In this way a sufficient amount of money was raised to buy the ground and put up the building, an investment of $25,000."

The site chosen was on the corner of Railroad Blvd. (South Blvd.) and Prairie Avenue (Kenilworth). The laying of the cornerstone that July was a gala event. "The boys rallied at Hoard's Hall at 7 o'clock and half an hour later nearly a hundred brightly-trimmed and lighted bicycles wheeled down Marion Street to Washington Blvd., then east and north to the corner of Prairie Avenue and the Boulevard. A temporary platform had been erected for the speakers. The orator of the occasion was Lawyer Ennis of Chicago, who traced the rise of the bicycle and cycling, closing with a glowing tribute to the club. The cornerstone was carefully lowered into place while the crowd sang 'America'. The wheelmen then formed into lines and paraded about the streets for an hour, eventually repairing again to Hoard's Hall where they ate strawberries and cream."

No expense was spared in building and furnishing the Prairie Cycling Club. "In the lower story of this three-story frame building are the bowling alleys, kitchen and steam-heated apparatus. The second floor contains the billiard, banquet, card and reception rooms while the whole of the third floor is a large hall for dancing, handball, indoor baseball and gymnasium," noted the *Reporter*. "The building is lighted by incandescent light and gas and finished throughout in hardwood."

When the Club officially opened in October the officers received their guests in the large reception room followed by an evening of dancing. "On Wednesday evening there will be duplicate whist and on Saturday there will be a stag party," added the *Reporter*.

As the popularity of cycling began to wane around the turn of the century, members of the Prairie Cycling Club were absorbed into the Oak Park Club. And when the street name "Prairie" was changed to "Kenilworth," the building became known as Kenilworth Hall. Over the years Kenilworth Hall housed a variety of tenants including C. Y. Knight, a local inventor who built the first

Willys-Knight auto in the basement around 1905 when the building housed the Oak Park Machine Co.

The ballroom of Kenilworth Hall was later used for drills by the Oak Park regiment of the Illinois Reserve Militia and as a National Guard Armory during World War II.

In 1916 Orren Donaldson, publisher of the *Oak Leaves* purchased the building and remodeled it for use as a newspaper office. For the next 34 years Otto McFeely presided as editor of the *Oak Leaves* in the first floor newspaper office in Kenilworth Hall.

During the 1920s the *Oak Leaves* office had a well-deserved reputation as a "club" where a veritable Who's Who of legendary reporters and writers including Charles MacArthur, Ben Hecht, Carl Sandburg, Vincent Starrett, Robert St. John, cartoonist Ward Savage and clergyman and Lincoln biographer Dr. William Barton were frequent visitors to McFeely's office in Kenilworth Hall.

Oak Park Golf Club grounds south of Madison Street between Home Avenue and Carpenter. In the early 1890s this was the baseball grounds for the Oak Park Club.

Westward Ho Golf Club

Although the term "networking" had yet to be coined, that was one of the primary activities engaged in by some of Oak Park's most prosperous businessmen as they negotiated the fairways of the village's first—and only—golf course laid out on the prairie south of Madison Street and east of Harlem Avenue between Home and Grove Avenues.

The membership roster of the Westward Ho Golf Club included Thomas Gale, Henry Austin, Dr. John Tope, Paul Blatchford, Arthur Heurtley, Willis Herrick, William

Furbeck and Nathan Moore. Another charter member was an ambitious young architect named Frank Lloyd Wright. It's interesting to speculate that the details for several of Wright's most important homes were worked out on the nine-hole golf course with clients like Fricke, Gale, Moore and Heurtley.

The golf club was organized in 1898 under the name of the Oak Park Golf Club. It was later changed to Westward Ho Golf Club because it was so often confused with the Oak Park Club that had been formed in 1890. The new name, and the club itself, was modeled after a well-known English golf club. Only three charter members of the club had ever played golf before. One of them was Miss Johnnie Carpenter, considered one of the best woman golfers in the country.

It isn't clear whether she owned the large Victorian house at 535 Carpenter which, at that time, stood alone on the south prairie or whether she was merely instrumental in purchasing it for use as a clubhouse. Whatever the circumstances, it soon became the focal point for the club's social calendar with facilities for dining and dancing for members and their guests.

But, barely a year after the club opened, it became apparent that larger facilities and more land to expand to an 18-hole course were needed. At the same time there was pressure from builders like Seward Gunderson who wanted to subdivide the prairie into lots for new homes for middle-class families. Within the next ten years the small golf course was subdivided and new streets cut through from Madison to Roosevelt Road. The street on which the first club house still stands (now a private home), was named "Carpenter" in recognition of the woman who created a setting for a sport which, at that time, belonged exclusively to the wealthy, on the site of what later became a middle-class neighborhood.

In 1901 members of the Westward Ho Golf Club built a substantial clubhouse at Ridgeland and North Avenue in Galewood on the site of an old apple orchard. But before the year was out the new clubhouse burned to the ground. It was replaced with a new structure the following year. The location of the Westward Ho Golf Club was considered inconvenient by many so the directors offered a "wagonette" or carriage which shuttled members several times a day from Oak Park Avenue.

In November 1911 the second clubhouse was also destroyed by fire. The building was insured for $16,000 but sustained $25,000 worth of damage. It was decided not to rebuild on the site because by then it was evident the course would be surrounded by new homes within the next few years. The club moved to a new location near Melrose Park, but lost many members when the Oak Park Country Club was formed in 1914. It finally ceased to exist as a club in 1922.

Oak Park Club

In 1890 George Landis Wilson sent a postcard to 60 Oak Park families to determine their interest in forming a "first class family club." At that time the churches were the only social outlets in the community and it was felt that, as the village grew, there was a need to bring more people together to exchange ideas and further community development.

Charter members met soon after to consider two offers for a clubhouse. J. H. Hurlbut offered to sell the fledging club his three-story mansion on the northwest corner of Railroad Blvd. (North Blvd.) and Park Place (Forest Avenue). The other bid came from James Scoville who intended to retire to California and so offered to rent his furnished home (which stood on the site of today's World War I monument in Scoville Park) to the club for two years for only $2,000.

Scoville's offer was accepted. Officers were elected with J. H. Hurlbut the first president, a charter was applied for and, on July 4, 1890, the club opened with fireworks and a gala party. By September the *Vindicator* announced: "The Oak Park Club is now fully organized, ready for its formal opening when the bowling alley and ballroom (occupying a one-story addition between the house and the barn) will be open for the first time. Some six billiard and pool tables will be in place for the gentlemen. All things necessary for creature, as well as intellectual comforts are attended. Alleys, 70 feet in length are so contrived that they are easily transformed into a dance floor. Ten strikes are now in order."

The Oak Park Club was located in this mansion at North Boulevard and Forest Avenue from 1893 to 1920.

At the end of two years membership had increased so rapidly the club officers decided to accept Hurlbut's original offer and purchased his residence for a permanent home. The house was remodeled and an addition built to provide a ballroom, billiard room and bowling alleys. (Today this site is occupied by a parking lot and several commercial/apartment buildings.) The new home of the Oak Park Club was occupied on November 14, 1893.

The Oak Park Club served as the social hub of the community for almost one hundred years. It was described as one of the few private clubs in the country designed for the entire family. Or, as one member put it, "There are about 700 husbands in Oak Park who don't go to their club when they want to get away from their families." Thursday was the maid's night off and so the club always offered a special family dinner every Thursday that was very popular with the women.

Events and programs for members of all ages were coordinated by a social director. The season's calendar included bridge tournaments, formal dances, lectures and classes. According to one young matron, if you belonged to the Oak Park Club you did not socialize anywhere else because you had all you could do just to keep up with all the programs.

But on January 10, 1920 disaster struck when the club was destroyed by fire. The club leased Kenilworth Hall while plans could be drawn for a larger three-story brick facility built on a lot members purchased at 721 Ontario Street. This building, completed in 1923, remained a force in the community until the 1960s when membership began to decline. In 1988 the building was purchased by the Habitat Company and the space converted into condominiums.

Oak Park Theaters Offered Only Wholesome Fare

Today the Lake Theater, an Art Deco movie palace that opened in 1936, is Oak Park's only movie theater. But between 1900 and 1920 half a dozen theaters, offering a repertoire that included grand opera, stock companies, vaudeville and movies, all flourished in Oak Park.

The first, and most elegant theater in Oak Park was the Warrington Opera House, a musical Taj Mahal on the southeast corner of South Blvd. and Marion Street. The theater, designed in 1902 by E. E. Roberts, promised "only the very best refined and high class acts."

No trace of E. E. Robert's original design remains on the façade of the building that now houses the Mar-Lac House, a banquet facility and several retail businesses. The Marion Street side of the building was covered with cement after a fire in the 1950s and, while the original brick front remains on South Blvd., all of the geometric ornaments have been removed.

The Warrington Opera House presented a far different picture on October 16, 1902 when a 200-voice chorus accompanied by 40 members of the Theodore Thomas Orchestra marked its opening with a performance of Rossini's *Stabat Mater*.

"According to an account of the event in the *Oak Leaves:* "The auditorium presented a scene of great brilliance with its mural decorations in red and cream, its blaze of electric lights and its crowd of handsomely dressed ladies and gentlemen." Among the box holders were E. E. Roberts, John Farson,

The Warrington opened in 1902 as an opera house but eventually made the transition to a popular movie theater.

William Fricke, C. W. Dunlop, the theater's owner and Dr. John Tope, one of the founders of Oak Park Hospital.

Unfortunately it proved difficult to maintain such ambitious musical programs and the Warrington soon became home to several popular stock companies including the Grace Hayward Stock Company and the Chester Wallace Players. Parents knew that when they sent their children to a matinee performed by either of these companies they had little to fear. Who could argue with a repertoire that included *Rebecca of Sunny Brook Farm, Polly of the Circus* and *Yankee Girl?*

In fact, to show their appreciation for such wholesome fare, the Woman's Society of First Baptist Church prepared a luncheon for the Chester Wallace Players which was served on the Warrington stage one Saturday between the matinee and evening performance.

"The two long tables were set across the stage and a congenial company gathered round them. Mr. Wallace beamed benignly upon members of his company and especially upon the guest of honor at his right—his mother. When all had done fullest justice to the meal, chatting cozily and enjoying the hour's relaxation and had lingered over the delicious homemade cake served with ice cream, the tables disappeared as magically as they had come, and everybody hustled to make ready for the evening performance."

Avis Dooley, who moved to Oak Park in 1909, recalled attending Saturday matinees at the Warrington featuring the Chester Wallace Players. "As a Saturday afternoon custom neighborhood children under the guidance of an elder walked to the matinee. After the audience had settled down, young men strolled the aisles carrying trays laden with candy, salt water taffy, popcorn and peanuts. Through the week we saved our pennies for this special treat."

"We never considered a play successful unless the villain made his appearance slyly fingering a glistening pistol and shooting blank cartridges which sent us crawling under the seats," she added.

"The actors disregarded the fourth wall on the set and left it open in their minds for personal contact with their audience. Many a snide remark sailed out to friends in the box seats. In fact, we all knew the players names

Warrington Theatre
SEASON 1915 — 1916
Chester Wallace Players

Offer for Thanksgiving Week Beginning

MONDAY EVENING, NOV. 22nd

A Timely Thanksgiving Offering.   A Play of Happiness and Contentment

"THE COUNTRY BOY"

The Play that Established the Record Run of Two Years on Broadway, New York

PRICES

Nights
Lower Floor 50c and 35c
Balcony 25c

Matinees
Adults 25c
Children . . . 10c

Special Matinee Thanksgiving Afternoon [Thursday]

Evenings
Curtain . . . 8:15
Motors . . ' . 10:40

Matinees
Tues., Thurs., and Sat.
Curtain at 2:30

MR. CHESTER WALLACE

Seats are now selling for the entire week. Reservations can be made in person at the box office or by calling Oak Park 132. Mail orders will be honored when accompanied by a remittance.

TONIGHT LAST TIME   "A BACHELOR'S ROMANCE"   Sol Smith Russell's Great Success

Following the regular policy of the Warrington, Thanksgiving Matinee at 3 o'clock.
Prices the same as evening, 25c, 35c, 50c; box seats 75c

Ad for Chester Wallace plays in the Oak Leaves.

so well that often, in a crucial moment during the drama, onlookers would shout, 'Walter, don't go in there—he has a gun!'"

The Warrington was eventually forced to make the transition from live performances to talking pictures to attract audiences who were mesmerized by this new phenomenon. An *Oak Leaves* reviewer marveled, "All kinds of sounds are reproduced in perfect unison with the pictures and so naturally as if they were really being seen and heard in the original."

Oak Park goes to the movies

One of the Warrington's greatest competitors was The Playhouse, designed by E. E. Roberts in 1913 and located just around the corner at 1111 South Blvd. The exterior of this small and exquisitely detailed movie house was carefully restored in 1989 and the interior reconfigured for use as office space.

The Playhouse boasted a fifteen by thirty-foot skylight or open roof which was patterned after the Hippodrome Theater in London, a feature not found in any other American theater until that time. According to the *Oak Leaves,* "In the ceiling is a skylight that is open to the sky. A cover, operating by electric motor, slides on and off this opening as the needs of the audience may require. The opening will admit daylight at every intermission, permit the rapid discharge of all used air and a system of fans will draw in fresh atmosphere."

The Playhouse served as a movie theater until 1918 when it was purchased by Atlas Educational Film Company. Before its 1989 restoration it passed through many hands, suffered a devastating fire and was subdivided into retail space.

The Oak Park Theater is a name that is probably unfamiliar to many villagers who, nonetheless, do remember the Lamar Theater at 120 S. Wisconsin (now the site of the Family Service and Mental Health Center of Oak Park and River Forest at 120 S. Marion). But the two are actually one and the same.

The Oak Park Theater opened in 1913 as a movie and vaudeville house. It was built by three Maywood men who spared no expense in creating a worthy rival for the Warrington and The Playhouse. By 1930 the name of

123

The Playhouse.

Wisconsin Avenue had been changed to Marion Street to correspond with the street of the same name north of the tracks. It was at this time that the name of the theater was also changed to Lamar (an abbreviation of Lake-Marion).

But perhaps the Lamar's greatest claim to fame was that it was the first theater in Oak Park to show a movie on Sunday. The film selected for this groundbreaking event was *Abraham Lincoln*, a subject even the staunchest opponent of Sunday movies couldn't object to.

The question of Sunday movies appeared on ballots in Oak Park in 1917, 1923 and 1925 and was defeated each time. This was due in large part to the impassioned rhetoric of opponents such as the Superintendent of Oak Park Elementary School District 97 who declared, "the wide open Sunday with theaters, poolrooms and dance halls will destroy the mental, moral and physical efficiency of Oak Park children."

Acceptance of Sunday movies in 1932 reflected both changing attitudes and the effect of the Depression. Villagers who could not afford more expensive entertainment were glad to forget their troubles, if only for a few hours, in their neighborhood movie house.

As Seward Gundersen, Thomas Hulbert and other developers began building large tracts of homes south of Madison Street, several other movie houses opened including the Elmwood Theater at Harrison Street and Gunderson Avenue and the Southern Theater, 828 S. Oak Park Avenue.

The Plaza Hotel

In the years preceding the 1993 fire that destroyed much of the historic Plaza Hotel at 123 S. Marion, this once elegant building had gradually deteriorated into a transient hotel. But today the hostelry, now fully restored to its former glory, is again offering hospitality to guests just as it did more than a hundred years ago when visitors who came to Chicago in 1893 to attend the Columbian Exposition in Chicago's Jackson Park stopped there. This elegant hotel, now fully restored, opened in May 2000 as an annex of the adjoining Carleton Hotel.

The Plaza Hotel was built in 1892 by George Mayo who recognized that many out-of-towners coming to the Exposition would prefer to stay "in the country," far removed from the dirt and congestion of the city. The original four-story building known as the Plaza Lodge had twenty rooms and a lobby with two large bay windows. A second section was added a year later increasing the number of rooms to fifty-three. Business was so brisk that Mayo purchased two nearby Queen Anne homes on Maple Avenue to accommodate the overflow of guests.

Throughout the Gay Nineties and well into the next century the hostelry, renamed the Plaza Hotel, was one of the village's most fashionable gathering places with both guests and villagers who came to dine in the hotel's elegant dining room. Wealthy horse owners whose horses were running at the Harlem Race Track in Forest Park also stayed with their families at the Plaza Hotel during the season.

The Plaza Hotel.

According to Philander Barclay, the Plaza Hotel was Oak Park's first skyscraper and offered a certain social cachet. "At the Plaza in horse and buggy days, guests and others would sit on the sidewalk during the afternoon when the sun was behind the building, and especially in the evening when the men were home. What a glorious time the guests and the villagers had in talking about events of the day during that leisurely period."

For many years the Plaza Hotel's homelike dining room was one of the most popular places to dine. "As many as 200 villagers as well as the hotel patrons would take their Sunday dinner there," said Barclay who recalled when Marion Street from South Blvd. to Pleasant Street was lined with fine horses and carriages during the summer and sleighs and cutters in the winter.

But one Saturday evening in the fall of 1895 the hotel received unwanted notoriety when a waiter stabbed a guest to death with a French carving knife. According to the *Oak Park Times*, there had been ill feeling between the waiter, George Spiller, and the murdered man, L. L. Letts, for several days over the good name of a certain young lady.

"Mr. and Mrs. Letts and their young son sat at a table in the dining room and were discussing Spiller when the latter entered from the kitchen and overheard his name. Seizing a large French carving knife from the kitchen he confronted his enemy. Letts leaped from his chair and in a few seconds lay dying on the floor, the blood gushing from two hideous wounds. At the police station Spiller said all he had done was in self-defense and it seemed to him that he had not struck a blow and that Letts must have run into the knife and thus committed suicide."

The 1993 Plaza fire was not the first time the Hotel suffered fire damage. On November 25, 1900 "the biggest fire Oak Park has seen for many days gained headway in the rear portion of the Plaza Hotel and, but for the superb work of the fire department, would have swept away the building," said the *Times*.

"The conflagration spread rapidly breaking out in several places. When the alarm was sounded it interrupted a card party in progress. Many of those who but a minute before had been contemplating jacks and ten spots now rushed to their apartments in a mad endeavor to save clothes and other valuables. The Hotel was stripped of everything that was not fastened to the floor."

During the long winter months The Plaza was a popular destination for sleighing parties of young people who would arrive at the hotel in large bob-sleds with two men on the seat, one the driver, the other the footman. After dropping the young people off at The Plaza these men would drive over to the livery barn at 130 N. Marion where they would unhitch the horses, water and feed them and then head over to the saloons in Harlem for a few steins of beer before it was time to make the return trip.

At that time almost every house and business in the village had a hitching post for the horses out front. And many buildings, including the Plaza Hotel, also had stepping stones at the curb for the convenience of passengers alighting from their carriages. However, by 1922 horses were long gone from village streets. So when Marion Street was about to be widened and repaved, Clarence Fowler, then manager of the Plaza, proposed that the contractor dig a hole and bury the stone because it was too difficult to break it up into small pieces.

Philander Barclay was present at the burial and recounted that the stepping stone was buried directly opposite the main entrance of the Plaza Hotel about fifteen feet east of the building. This would put it just about in the middle of Marion Street today.

Scoville Institute

On your next visit to the main Oak Park Public Library take time to notice the words, "Scoville Institute" carved in stone on the lintel above the main entrance. This inscription, along with the large oil portrait of James Wilmarth Scoville painted by Frank Pebbles that hangs on the second floor landing of the Library and a plaque inside the front door, are the only visible reminders that remain of the man who so generously funded Oak Park's first library.

In 1883 James Scoville announced he would donate $75,000 for the formation of a cultural and civic center that would be financed by dues paying members. Villagers were asked to subscribe to a library fund that would be used to purchase books. This was the first serious attempt to create a repository for books that would benefit all residents.

Ten years earlier a group of businessmen met at Pebbles Paint Store to organize a social club. They wanted to make it a smoker but since smoking was a vice discouraged by their wives they decided to substitute books in place of cigars and formed instead the Oak Park Library Association. This privately subscribed library was located in one of the storefronts of the Holley Block at 125-7 Lake Street. When the Scoville Institute was completed in 1888 the Association turned over its collection of 1,655 volumes to the new library and disbanded.

James Scoville asked 13 prominent men to serve as trustees of the new library which was built on land he donated at the corner of Lake Street and Grove Avenue adjacent to his home. (The present library now stands on the site of this first library and Scoville's home has been replaced by the World War I Memorial on the crest of the hill in Scoville Park.)

Articles of incorporation were written and architect Normand Patton's design for a distinctive Romanesque building of Bedford stone was accepted. The cornerstone was laid on September 4, 1886 and by the time the building was dedicated in October 1888, Scoville's gift for the building, lot and endowment totaled $115,000.

Scoville Institute was an immediate success. By 1890 more than 1,000 library cards had been issued and throughout the Gay Nineties it served as the center for much of Oak Park's social and cultural life. On any

Cornerstone is laid for Scoville Institute in 1888. Home of James Scoville is in the background.

127

Scoville Institute

given day a villager could choose a book on the first floor, attend a lecture, meeting or other activity on the second floor and even work out at the Institute's gymnasium on the third floor. (However, the gym was soon abandoned after complaints that it was too noisy).

Unfortunately it was soon apparent that Scoville Institute's endowment fund was insufficient to keep pace with increased costs and, under the terms of Scoville's gift, no charge could be made for the use of the books or building. By 1891, just three years after Scoville Institute was completed, it was already facing a deficit. The community was growing rapidly and the trustees felt that a building, which opened its doors to all, should not be supported by a few. They enlisted the support of local newspapers to lobby residents to increase their donations to the Institute's endowment fund.

Children's Room in the Scoville Institute.

The *Oak Park Reporter* informed its readers the good news was that about 800 new books had been purchased and the library was in good shape as far as the book fund was concerned. But the downside was that the permanent endowment did not provide enough revenue for current expenses and increasingly the trustees were unable to make ends meet.

128

"The usefulness of the Institute is crippled because of this lack of funds, and it ought to be remedied," said the *Reporter*. "In a community of prosperous and public-spirited people like Oak Park there should be no trouble in securing all the money needed for such a noble educational center as the Scoville Institute. With a permanent endowment of $50,000 or $100,000, the trustees could greatly extend the usefulness of the institution. Let our people be thinking about it, and see what can be done."

Scoville Institute continued to operate under a deficit until 1902 when Oak Park separated from Cicero Township and became an independent municipality. The following year voters agreed in a referendum to submit to a tax for support of a public library. The referendum provided for a Library Board to be elected and two mills out of every dollar of state taxes were to be used for support of the library.

Most villagers are unaware that from 1903 until 1961 when it was decided to demolish Scoville Institute and build a new library, there were actually two library boards. The Scoville Board held actual title to the building and land but its members had no voice in policy-making decisions, while members of the elected library board were responsible for all library policy.

In 1961 the Scoville Board dissolved itself and turned its assets over to the elected board with the stipulation that the words "Scoville Institute" be carved in stone on the lintel above the main entrance of the new one-story library which was completed in 1964. The second story addition was added in 1977.

Hephzibah Children's Association

For more than 100 years Hephzibah Children's Association has been a beacon of hope for the abused, neglected and otherwise disadvantaged children who pass through its doors. Through the years this not-for-profit agency at 946 North Blvd. has earned the respect of state and private social service agencies who regularly refer difficult cases to Hephzibah because of its reputation as a home that truly makes a difference in the lives of troubled children.

Although Mary Wessels is acknowledged to have founded Hephzibah, the home would most likely not have succeeded without the enthusiastic support of Dr. Emily Luff, an Oak Park physician who tended the children when they were ill and encouraged Mary Wessels with both financial and moral support long before the community recognized the valuable service she provided.

Mary Wessels, the well-educated daughter of a wealthy Canadian businessman, was the head nurse in an orphanage for boys in Franklin Park. In 1895 the facility burned to the ground and the boys were transferred to other homes.

Wessels, described by those who knew her as "a caring, unselfish, motherly person who was never happy except when brooding over a sick child," lived in a small house on Maple near Chicago Avenue. Finding herself at loose ends, she contacted a Chicago social service agency that sent her two boys to care for. A postcard addressed to a friend is the only record of the actual formation of Hephzibah. It read: "I have begun my work. I have two boys, ages 6 and 7."

Mary Wessels chose her mother's name, Hephzibah, which has a Biblical meaning of "comforting mother" for her home. The first sign bearing the name was hung out in front of the small house on Maple which, in those days, was called Menominee Street. The sign, which had belonged to Dr. Luff, was

Children at Hephzibah Children's Association enjoy a visit from Santa.

covered with paint and the words "Hephzi-bah Home" printed over it.

Dr. Luff lived on Chicago Avenue, just around the corner from Mary Wessels' home and was a frequent visitor late at night on her way home from her calls. She often found Miss Wessels with a croupy child in her arms. "We worked over a child without saying a word and she always did exactly as I told her to. Brown sugar and hot water saved the life of a strangled baby one night and we worked until midnight to keep him alive."

The first Christmas in 1895 found Mary Wessels with nine children plus a tenth infant who arrived on Christmas Eve. The baby, whose mother had been put out of a house in Chicago for lack of rent, was so ill they could not refuse to take the child in. Dr. Luff made a bed out of a large box and Christmas morning the newest addition to the home was carried downstairs with great ceremony.

"We had a turkey and cranberry sauce and all the fixings and I made a great bowl of apple foam so that the children could have a dessert that would be good for them," recalled Dr. Luff. "We brought the baby in the shoe box right down the table and we all had a lovely time. We had a tree and gifts for each child."

Raising money to feed and clothe her brood was a continual challenge for Mary Wessels. Although neighbors and churches came to her rescue on occasion, there was no regular source of income. Dr. Luff tried to interest her patients and friends in supporting Hephzibah but never asked for more than a dollar and often received this amount in quarters. One patient gave her a dollar every week for soup while another well-to-do family sent their coachman to the home to deliver fifty cents tightly sealed in an envelope.

When the house on Maple Avenue became too crowded Mary Wessels used her own funds, left to her by relatives, to rent a house on Lake Street two doors west of today's Calvary Memorial Church. With a larger house and more work to do she frequently took in both the mother as well as the child, giving both a safe haven.

In its new, more visible location Hephzibah Home began attracting more attention.

Contributions trickled in on an ongoing basis but, as the number of her charges increased, it became obvious that this sporadic support was not enough. In 1902 Hephzibah was put on a more stable financial footing with the formation of a board of directors consisting of some of the village's most prominent citizens including Henry Austin and Dr. Emily Luff. Proceeds from the Oak Park Horse Show held annually for several years in the 1900s also benefited the children's home.

The creation of a board of directors was the result of a walk Dr. Robert Johonnot took one day down Lake Street. The clergyman stopped to read a placard attached to a turkey hanging in the window of a grocery. The sign said the bird was being raffled for the benefit of Hephzibah, something he felt was illegal. Dr. Johonnot confronted Mary Wessels with this fact. "She replied that someone offered to raise funds in that way and she had not thought it illegal. She very sweetly offered to give it up, but added that they were in dire need. The result was a guilty feeling on the part of the minister and a new interest in the home. He went to one of his parishioners, Mary Gerts, who helped him organize the board," recalled Dr. Luff.

Mary Gerts and her sister Kate gave a reception in their home. "With eight of their friends they received virtually all of Oak Park's social set and many friends from Chicago. Every visitor left a card for each hostess. The week following the reception Miss Gerts drove out in her brougham and, calling at each house, she sold back to her guests their own calling cards at one dollar each. This fund was probably the largest nest egg the home had ever seen," reported the *Oak Leaves*.

A sad footnote to the history of Hephzibah is that Mary Wessels seemed to drop from sight after she was called back to Canada because of the illness of her father. She wrote several letters to Dr. Luff. Then the letters stopped. Because of the great friendship between them Dr. Luff felt that nothing but death would have ended the correspondence.

131

A Tale of Two Streets

At first glance it doesn't appear that Humphrey Avenue, a north-south street that runs the length of the village, and Elizabeth Court, a curving one block east-west thoroughfare, share many similarities. But the common thread that binds them are their names. Each was named after one half of a prominent couple who exerted a powerful influence on the religious, social and intellectual fabric of the village from the 1870s until the turn of the century.

formed Vassar College for women. She turned it down, choosing instead to move to Wisconsin where her husband had been offered a post at Beloit College and she accepted a teaching position at nearby Rockford College.

Several years later Dr. Humphrey, a Congregational clergyman, was offered the job of district secretary of the American Board of Missions, an international organization with offices at 151 S. Wells Street in Chicago. It was a job he held for the next thirty years.

Woodcut of Elizabeth Court and grounds of the home of Dr. Simon Humphrey. The street was named for his wife Elizabeth.

Both Dr. Simon James Humphrey and his wife, Elizabeth Emerson Humphrey were descended from a rich New England vein of Puritan stock that included scholars, poets and theologians. On his mother's side, Humphrey's lineage could be traced back to the Mayflower and William Brewster while Elizabeth was a cousin of the Transcendentalist poet and essayist Ralph Waldo Emerson.

The young couple met while Humphrey was a student of Elizabeth's father, Professor Ralph Emerson, at Andover Theological Seminary. Elizabeth, a graduate of Oberlin College, was exceptionally well educated for a woman of that era. In 1867 she was offered a position on the first faculty of the newly

The Humphreys moved to Oak Park in 1870 at a time when the small community with a population of just under 500, was beginning to grow because its location close to the city. They immediately became influential leaders in shaping the social, intellectual and religious life of the community.

Elizabeth Humphrey in particular set the standard for behavior that was copied by many other women in the community. She was an experienced educator and, according to the *Vindicator*, "Her visits to the school were frequent and her advice eagerly sought by the teachers. Her home was one of the centers of the boy and girl life of the village." She founded the Woman's Board of Missions, was an arduous worker for the Women's Christian Temperance Union and First Congregational Church and raised her daughter and four sons with a firm hand. For his part, Dr. Humphrey was deeply disturbed that Oak Park was given over to "card parties and frivolity" and ministers who, for the most part, preached on topics of which he did not approve.

The Humphreys purchased a large parcel of land from Joseph Kettlestrings on what is now Elizabeth Court and in 1873 built a Gothic style home with vertical board-and-batten siding surrounded by an unpainted picket fence. The lot for this house at what is now 2 Elizabeth Court originally stretched to Forest Avenue until Humphrey sold the southeast corner of the lot to Paul Blatchford who built a house at what is now 250 Forest about 1887. The Humphrey's house, which originally faced Forest Avenue, was remodeled by later owners into a Dutch Colonial façade and its original Gothic design obliterated.

As the village grew residents recognized the need for a more formal delineation of streets. Forest Avenue homeowners agreed but asked that "one curved thoroughfare, even if only a block long," be incorporated in the plan. So the street that was named Elizabeth Court in 1892 came into being as a narrow, curved street which originally was open to traffic at both Kenilworth and Forest Avenues.

The street was officially dedicated on July 8, 1892 by the trustees of Cicero Township in a move intended to help retain the bucolic ambiance of the street. The proclamation stipulated that the street "shall be used only for carriages, buggies and light vehicles and that loaded teams shall be excluded from passing through it; and it is further stipulated and agreed that the driveways and sidewalks of said court shall be retained unchanged in the present form."

Dr. Humphrey, whose great passion was landscape gardening, is credited with laying out and landscaping the street with the help of neighbors who purchased tracts of his parcel and built their own homes. And, by unanimous consent, the street was named after his wife Elizabeth.

But deliverymen were less than enthusiastic about Elizabeth Court because the numbers were totally out of synchronization with adjoining streets. As a result of their complaints Cicero Township trustees approved a name change from Elizabeth Court to Erie Street several years later. This made Erie a contiguous street—albeit with several jogs—from Austin Blvd. to Harlem Avenue in Oak Park.

However, the residents of Elizabeth Court, with the support of many of their neighbors, raised such a storm of protest that the trustees reversed themselves and restored the original name. Today Elizabeth Court is the only street in the community that still retains the original numbering system from west to east. All other east-west streets were changed by 1915.

In the 1892 Oak Park directory Humphrey Avenue is called "Cicero" but by 1894 the name of the street had been changed to Humphrey. The name change was primarily because of Dr. Humphrey's association with James Scoville in developing the community of Ridgeland and was not due to his position as a minister.

The Humphrey's son Horace was the only one of their children who spent most of his adult life in Oak Park. Horace Humphrey was a likeable gadfly who flitted from job to job and never achieved his potential. In 1892 he married Julia Wells, a concert pianist whose father was also a Congregational minister. But the carefree young couple was not really very religious. Julia must have scandalized her in-laws when she learned to ride a bicycle, gave up corsets and wore tights.

For the first five years of their marriage they lived in several different homes in Oak Park. In 1895 their daughter was born at 315 N. Grove. Doris Humphrey would later achieve international acclaim as a pioneer in modern dance.

In 1898 Horace Humphrey, whose career included jobs as a reporter and photoengraver, was hired as manager of the Grand Palace Hotel at Clark and Grand Streets in Chicago. The family occupied a cramped apartment in the basement. In later years Doris Humphrey recalled, "The Palace Hotel catered to a middle-class, theatrical clientele. It was always full of homey people, who happened to be on the stage. It was anything but impressive or smart. It occupied one corner of two cross streets; the other three cor-

Doris Humphrey.

ners were blooming with saloons. Our corner clanged with trolley cars and drunks at all times of the day and night."

The Humphreys wanted only the best for their daughter. They sent Doris to the very progressive, for that time, Francis Parker School for kindergarten through high school. She showed an inclination for dance at an early age so Julia arranged for lessons with eminent ballet masters. However, her real inspiration came from Mary Wood Hinman who taught dance at Francis Parker.

Horace Humphrey was not a very good manager and carried residents on the books for weeks when they were out of work. The hotel was eventually sold and the family moved back to Oak Park to live in two third-floor rooms in the home of the Standishes, family friends who lived at 409 N. Grove.

After graduation Doris and her mother supported the family by opening a dance studio in Oak Park. Julia was the business manager and accompanist. The school was an immediate success offering classic, gymnastic and ballroom dancing for children and a Saturday evening ballroom class for young adults.

Many of Doris' classes were held at Unity House, the social hall attached to Unity Temple. She also lent her talent to choreographing programs given to benefit local charities. One of the most memorable performances was the story of Demeter and Persephone told in music and dance. The program, performed June 20 and 22, 1914 as a benefit for the Wellesley College endowment fund, was attended by hundreds of villagers entranced by the vision of dozens of young women dancing in skimpy Greek costumes on the lawn of Henry Austin's estate. Among the participants was Mrs. Catherine Wright who, according to the reporter, "made a lovely Demeter."

The *Oak Leaves* rhapsodized, "Miss Humphrey's dancing, well known in Oak Park, always gives keen enjoyment, but was probably never more alluring than in its graceful out-of-doors setting on Mr. Austin's lawn."

Fortunately her very staid and proper grandparents were not there to disapprove of this "frivolity" even though it was performed on the grounds of one of Oak Park's most respected citizens.

Oak Park Incinerator Stirred Lively Debate

Anyone who suffers from respiratory problems can, literally, breath a sigh of relief that the "garbage crematory" or incinerator at North Blvd. and Euclid Avenue that belched dense black smoke into the atmosphere for more than fifty years is a thing of the past.

In 1907 a majority of village trustees rejected several more distant sites for the incinerator and voted to build the 200-foot high smokestack in the center of the village to save hauling costs. Officials reached their decision despite the bitter opposition of residents who pointed out the obvious health risk the incinerator posed to all villagers, especially the young people who attended Oak Park High School located near the incinerator plus the certain loss of value of property in the immediate vicinity.

From 1835, when Joseph Kettlestrings most likely dumped the ashes from his fireplace into the woods behind his log cabin, until 1899 when Cicero Township passed the first garbage ordinance, the disposal of trash was completely unregulated in the village.

Housewives deposited raw garbage in uncovered wooden boxes and crates and placed them in the alley, according to John Lewis, township supervisor. "The alley is regarded as a common dumping ground. There weeds, ashes, leaves, grass, paper, manure, stumps, brush, wood, tin cans, scrap, glass bottles, broken crockery, old furniture, mattresses and bed-springs, plaster, stone and rubbish of every imaginable description clog these thoroughfares," lamented Lewis. "In some places manure has been spread about the alley until it forms a mire 12 to 18 inches deep. Ashes are also deposited in piles until they form a serious obstruction."

Lewis was instrumental in passing the ordinance that required all homeowners to provide their own sturdy receptacle with a tightly fitted lid that had to be stored on their premises. Homeowners had their choice of receptacles although it was suggested they use a galvanized 20-gallon can

Village incinerator at North Boulevard and Euclid Avenue spews pollutants onto Oak Park Avenue. Photo was taken in 1903 from Oak Park High School located just a few hundred feet away.

selling for $1.50. Under the old system the householder forced the village to remove any and all garbage by simply dumping it in the alley. However, under the new ordinance, if the homeowner wanted his garbage picked up, he was compelled to place it in an approved receptacle or the "gleamers" or scavengers would not remove it on their weekly rounds.

In 1899 Cicero Township passed another ordinance banning the emission of dense smoke from any locomotive, chimney or smokestack. But by 1902 Oak Park had separated from the township and so was not subject to any of its laws, including the ban on "dense smoke."

At that time village officials had no compunction about dumping the town's trash in adjoining communities that were still part of Cicero Township. The *Oak Leaves* applauded the move: "The village board each year makes an appropriation for a village dump where all sorts of refuse, by law, is required to be deposited. This dump is located in the southeasterly part of the village and, if we are not in error, is located just inside the town of Cicero. It is good sanitary foresight of the board to arrange for this dump and we commend it for so doing."

In 1906 Oak Park had a contract with Berwyn to deposit trash in that community. When it expired Berwyn officials sensibly refused to renew it. Oak Park trustees then attempted to open a new dump at Oak Park Avenue and Division Street but the ground was so soft it could not be used. So, without consulting officials in River Forest, the garbage contractor, Mr. Palmer, was directed to deposit Oak Park's garbage across Harlem Avenue in River Forest.

"When River Forest authorities discovered this they promptly arrested Mr. Palmer and put themselves in vigorous communication with the Oak Park Board," reported the *Oak Leaves*. "Palmer was let off as not to blame in the matter. The village has since been dumping its garbage and burying it in one of the streets in the northwest corner of the village (now Greenfield Park) which, in turn, has raised a howl of protest from the people living in that vicinity."

So in 1907 as they saw their few remaining options disappear, village trustees concluded that the most effective way to dispose of garbage would be to burn it. Hence, their decision to build an incinerator. Their plan might not have been opposed quite so vigorously if it were not for its proposed location on a lot at North Blvd. just east of Euclid Avenue. This site, just a few hundred feet from the first Oak Park High School and in the center of the village's residential and business area, drew a quick and negative response from citizens when it was proposed in April 1907.

However, Board President William Einfeldt said that after spending a day at a Joliet incinerator and corresponding with officials in other cities that had incinerators, he was satisfied that a properly constructed facility would not pose a health risk in Oak Park.

But Trustee Henry Magill, who had also visited the Joliet incinerator, came away with a completely different picture. "We found an institution that could not be tolerated in our beautiful village," he said. "It was foul smelling and unsightly. From the smokestack smoke was constantly rising which could be seen from hundreds of feet distant. It was a windy day and some of this smoke swirled down toward the base of the stack and drifted by at just about the right height to give our high school students the benefit."

Magill interviewed the Joliet health commissioner and manager of the incinerator and while they spoke highly of their operation, they were surprised at the idea that anyone would seriously consider locating one in a residential area.

According to Magill, in cities surveyed by the trustees, none of the incinerators were in residential areas and "we have been unable to find a single town where the crematory is located in proximity to homes, schools and churches and we feel sure that the citizens who live in the threatened locality are doing a service to the entire village in their attempt to head off what would be a very serious mistake," he added.

But, mistake or not, the incinerator was eventually built on the site selected by the trustees and was in operation for the next fifty years. It was finally closed on January 1, 1959.

Villagers Tarred by Local Tabloid

One of the earliest newspapers that served the small communities of Cicero Township was *The Vindicator,* a weekly published by William Halley, the feisty and opinionated editor who had no qualms about editorially clubbing anyone of whom he disapproved.

Halley began publishing his broadsheet on Halsted Street in Chicago in 1863. Initially it covered news of both the city and suburbs. But by 1894 the name was changed to the *Oak Park Vindicator* when Halley moved to Steiner's Hall on Marion Street and devoted himself exclusively to publishing the news of Austin, Oak Park and River Forest.

Halley regularly engaged in the kind of scurrilous character bashing that today would have his victims taking him to court for libel. One of his targets was Dr. Orin Peake, a physician, respected Civil War veteran and the village's first druggist who built his store at 206 Lake (now 1051) in 1873. In 1886 Peake helped compile the village's first directory by opening a registry in his store and asking everyone who stopped in to record their name and address.

In an 1886 issue of the *Vindicator,* Halley noted that "Dr. Peake's directory is almost completed. The work has proven so fatiguing that the good doctor has taken to excessive drink. While this reporter cannot say that Dr. Peake is consistently under the influence of spirits, yet he can prove that he often leaves (dry) Oak Park with an empty demijohn (a large bottle with a short narrow neck), always heading toward Chicago. His friends say that this is left at Central Park to be filled with artesian water and that its use has greatly benefited the genial doctor."

Then there was the hapless young man whose offense, in Halley's eyes, was attempting to grow a mustache. "Our verdict is that it was an utter failure. We would advise the young man to stop thinking that it makes him better looking to wear a few weak hairs on his upper lip, which droop over and dry up for want of nourishment," sneered Halley.

And you might have thought twice before opening a business on Lake Street in 1898 after reading Halley's litany of the death of prominent merchants. "Oak Park businessmen seem to have a fatality attached to them. During the past few months the death of Arthur Scales has occurred, Charles Garling was killed by the dummy engine, F. S. Goodman suffered a paralytic stroke and the recent death of Richard Mette has added another to the list of diseased and disabled tradesmen."

But some readers were astute enough to realize that the way to Halley's crotchety heart was to tempt him with culinary delights. Halley wrote glowingly of the "superb dinner" he had enjoyed with the family of Mr. and Mrs. O. W. Turner of River Forest. "When a newspaperman gets an opportunity to vary the monotony of a fifteen-cent restaurant meal by an invitation to dine on strawberries and cream, with an abundance of other good things to tempt the appetite, he needs no second bidding."

As a result of this not-so-subtle schmoozing with the Turners, Halley enthused that "the expensive cottages, the width and depth of the grounds, the exclusiveness of its inhabitants from everything which can offer the least impediment to standing in society or morality, the harmony that prevails, the accommodations of trains to and from the city and the fine drainage makes this, to the overworked businessman, an 'Arcadia' if one can be found on earth."

Halley contrasted this 'Arcadia" to its neighbor Harlem (Forest Park). "A quaint village entirely devoted to the propagation of children, fowls, garden products and gravestones."

"The air is pregnant with the odoriferous perfume of beer, switzerkase and onions. The women have entire charge of the truck patches and not one of the 'lords of creation' was observable while numerous women with their heads enveloped in a turban and arms bared to the elbows were busily engaged in hoeing the succulent potato and fragrant onion." The "gravestones" Halley referred to so disparagingly were the soft limestone markers cut for gravestones in Forest Home Cemetery.

Oak Leaves formed

In 1902, Orren M. Donaldson purchased both the *Oak Park Vindicator* and the *Oak Park Times*. About the only thing he retained from both tabloids was their subscription list. The newly formed *Oak Leaves* had loftier goals.

"*Oak Leaves* is just what it purports to be. There is no ulterior motive in its publication" proclaimed Donaldson in the newspaper's premier issue. "There is no man or body of men behind it with an ax to grind. It represents no clique or faction. It represents no one's interest but the publisher's and he means that his interest shall be identical with that of the community."

Donaldson made several innovative changes in the format of the new paper including abandoning the bulky oversized newsprint used by most papers at that time in favor of a trim "magazine" size. He also introduced a distinctive new look in which oak leaves were intertwined in the *Oak Leaves* logo.

The *Oak Leaves* like its predecessors, was printed in the city. But within a short time Donaldson formed the Oak Leaves Company and installed his own printing press in the newspaper's office at 204 Lake Street.

Five years later the business was reorganized as the Donaldson Publishing Co. Orren Donaldson was president, Alfred MacArthur was named vice president and Telfer MacArthur served as business manager. The company was moved to a three-story building at 1114 North Blvd.

In 1916 Donaldson retired and sold the *Oak Leaves* to Telfer MacArthur who became the guiding spirit of the newspaper for more than 40 years until his death in 1960.

Telfer was the brother of playwright Charlie MacArthur and John MacArthur, founder of Bankers Life & Casualty Co., and one of the wealthiest men in the country who later formed the MacArthur Foundation which annually endows non-profits and charities with millions of dollars.

But Telfer MacArthur was content to spend his life in Oak Park. He was a charter member of the Oak Park Rotary, president of the Chamber of Commerce and a supporter of many civic and charitable causes.

MacArthur's first move was to name Otto McFeely editor of the newspaper. In 1942 the offices of the *Oak Leaves* were moved to Kenilworth Hall (formerly the Prairie Cycling Club) at the southeast corner of Kenilworth and South Blvd. The building was remodeled and the offices of the *Oak Leaves* remained there until 1971 when the building was deemed obsolete and demolished.

First office of Oak Leaves *in room at the back of Dunlop and Co., Realtors, 204 Lake Street.*

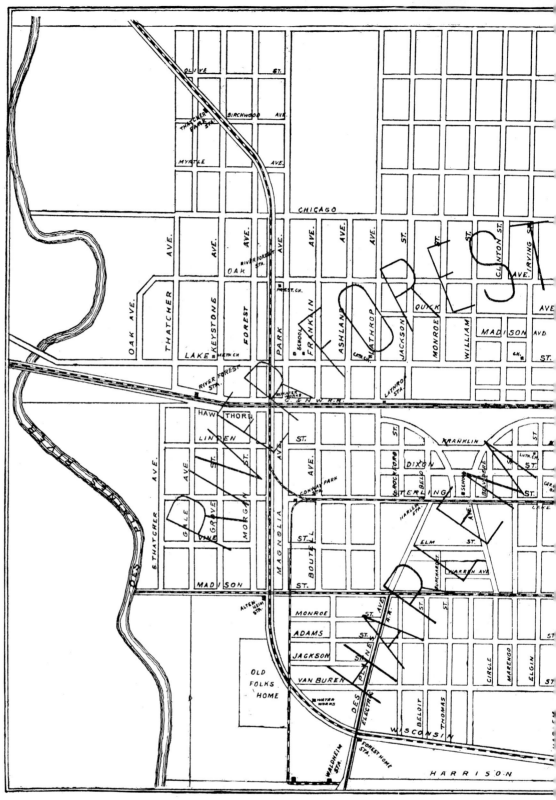

Map of Oak Park, Ri

... PRESE

FRANK

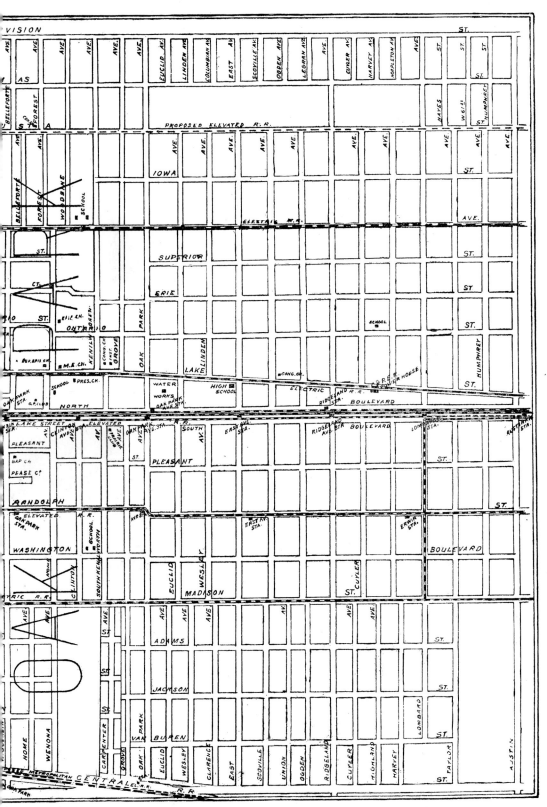

Forest and Harlem.

Map of Oak Park, River Forest and Forest Park published in the 1903 Oak Park Directory.

CHAPTER VI

OAK PARK DEALS WITH DEATH AND DISASTER

SS Eastland *capsized at the Clark Street dock of the Chicago River, July 24, 1915.*

Villagers Mourn Iroquois Fire Victims

On December 30, 1903 most Oak Park homes were still festively decorated for the holiday season as families prepared to welcome in the New Year. But within the space of just half an hour on that Wednesday afternoon the village, along with the entire nation, was plunged into mourning.

An overflow crowd of 1,830 persons jammed the newly opened Iroquois Theater on the corner of Randolph and Dearborn Streets in Chicago, Many in the audience may have been reassured by the words "Absolutely Fireproof" printed in bold letters on the day's program announcing the musical farce, *Mr. Bluebeard* starring the popular comic Eddie Foy. They should not have been.

Iroquois Theatre - ABSOLUTELY FIREPROOF

IROQUOIS THEATRE CO., Props.
WILL J. DAVIS and HARRY J. POWERS, Resident Owners and Mgrs.
THOMAS J. NOONAN, Business Manager and Treasurer.

Special Notice To South Side Patrons

The Illinois Central Suburban service now includes E x p r e s s Theatre Trains leaving Homewood at 6:56 p. m. and Hyde Park at 7:44 p. m., arriving at Randolph street station at 7:55 p. m., and leaving South Chicago at 7:13 p. m., arriving at Randolph street at 7:45 p. m.

After the Theatre Trains, S o u t h Bound, leave Randolph street as follows: 10:30, 11:05 express, 11:40 p. m. and 12:30 a. m. for South Chicago; 10:50 p. m. and 12:00 night for Homewood; 10:50, 11:10, 11:20 express and 11:25 p. m., 12:00 night and 1:00 a. m. for Grand Crossing; 11:20 p. m. express for Blue Island; 11:25 p. m., 12:00 night and (except Monday) 1:00 a. m. for Burnside.

Telegraph and messenger calls in the ticket office.

Special calls for Owen Fay's carriages apply at the ticket office, or to doorkeeper.

Ladies' reception-room and toilets to the left of the foyer. Gentlemen's smoking-room in basement to right of foyer.

Ladies' wraps will be cared for by an attentive maid in the reception-room.

Gentlemen's check-room adjoins the smoking-room.

Telephones in ladies' reception-room and gentlemen's check-room.

All articles found in theatre should be returned to doorkeeper or to ticket office.

Ticket office open continuously from 9:00 a. m. to 9:45 p. m.

N. B.—Our patrons are entitled to, and should receive, the courteous and respectful attention of every employe. The management invites information of any incivility or inattention.

SEAT AND BOX SALE—PRICES. Orchestra, entire lower floor, $1.50. Dress Circle, first four rows, $1.50; remaining rows, $1.00. Balcony, first five rows, 75c; remaining rows, 50c. Boxes, seating six, $15.00.

MAIL ORDERS will at all times receive prompt attention, if they contain certified check, postal or express order, payable to IROQUOIS THEATRE. If party desires tickets mailed, self-addressed return envelope must accompany order, thus avoiding possibility of error. Special attention will at all times be given to out-of-town orders.

Everything in the imposing granite, Bedford stone and glass façade of Chicago's newest entertainment palace was flammable, including the scenery, drapes, carpeting and plush covered seats. In addition, all but three of the 30 fire exits were locked, electric arc lamps were not enclosed, there were no fire extinguishers, the ventilation and sprinkling systems did not work and the staff had no idea what to do in case of a fire or widespread panic.

About 3:15 p.m. as a double octet sang the lyrical number *In The Pale Moonlight* a floodlight began to give off sparks, which quickly ignited a small portion of the heavy scenery. As the tongues of fire began to spread through the theater that had opened just thirty-eight days earlier Eddie Foy, incongruous in tights, floppy shoes and a smoldering red wig, tried to calm the audience. "Please folks, there's no danger! Just be calm!" he pleaded. He could not have been more wrong.

When a stagehand tried to lower the asbestos fire curtain it snagged when only partially closed. Then a draft from the open door backstage suddenly created a wind tunnel that acted like a tremendous suction and sent a huge ball of flame shooting under the curtain and over the orchestra pit. The audience, now in a panic beyond Foy's control, rushed for the locked exits. Within the space of half an hour 602 people, mostly women and children, had died in the worst theater fire in American history. During the next few weeks hundreds of theaters, including the Warrington Theater in Oak Park, closed for installation of fire-prevention devices. The Iroquois fire also led to the adoption of the first national fire codes for public buildings.

Oak Park Weeps for the Sad Death of its Children was the headline in the black-bordered January 2, 1904 issue of the *Oak Leaves*. "When the first news of the awful Iroquois Theater disaster reached Oak Park it was hoped that while this community might mourn with those who mourn, it would have no occasion to sorrow for its own dead. But as further reports came in it became evident that this could not be the case."

Then followed accounts of the fire by villagers who had managed to escape the conflagration and a sad listing of those who had perished in the fire.

Lloyd and John, the two sons of Mr. and Mrs. Frank Lloyd Wright of Chicago Avenue, with their grandmother, Flora Tobin, had seats within three rows of the front and came out without injury by staying calm and obeying the counsel of Eddie Foy.

However, Dr. and Mrs. T. E. Roberts were in a state of suspense for several hours. "Their daughter Elizabeth, accompanied by Mrs. Richard Sears and her daughter, had intended to attend the matinee at the Iroquois. Mr. Sears (founder of Sears, Roebuck and Co. and an Oak Park resident), in his busy rush of business, neglected to secure sittings at the Iroquois and so decided to obtain tickets for Mrs. Sears and the children at another theater."

Other young people were not so fortunate. Fifteen-year-old Ruth Payson of 1 Elizabeth Court, a sophomore at Oak Park High School, along with her cousins, Glenn and Helen Bickford of Rogers Park, all perished in the fire.

A double funeral was held from the home of Mr. and Mrs. T. W. Winder, 201 S. Harvey for their sons Paul 17 and Barry 12 who were both burned to death. The family had recently moved to Oak Park where they had come largely for the sake of their children, reported the *Oak Leaves.*

Another double funeral was held at 34 Forest Avenue for 7-year-old Earl Pridmore Martin and his aunt, Edith Pridmore. "The boy and his aunt sat in the fourth row of the first balcony and, because of the terrific jam at the doorways, were unable to get out. The bodies when found were almost untouched by fire and the identification was positive as soon as Mr. Martin went to the scene."

Mrs. Minnie Christopherson, 231 S. Harvey, and her sister Lydia Hanson had seats near the front of the first balcony. "With the outburst of the flames they fled to the rear of the balcony where they were caught in the crush and where Mrs. Christopherson undoubtedly met her death. Miss Hanson, who was badly burned, survived."

Nellie Dawson, a teacher at Lowell School, suffered a fate far worse than death. Badly burned over much of her body, she survived for more than a month before succumbing to her injuries. Miss Dawson had gone to the theater with her mother and 7-year-old niece who both perished. Her home was in Barrington but, during the school year, she lived with the Furlong family at 239 Harvey. She

had urged Miss Furlong to accompany her and her invitation would doubtless have been accepted, surmised the *Oak Leaves*, but for the preparations that were being made for New Year's in the Furlong home.

Except for a few victims killed by people leaping from the balconies, those on the main floor had time to reach the exits. But in the balconies there was only fire and panic. As the wires shorted the electricity went out and inky blackness enveloped the theater. The stampeding crowd found the exits that were not locked opened inward. Also, the gates at stair landings were padlocked to keep those in the balcony from getting down into the dress circle. The result was victims piled five and six deep at these barricaded exits.

The balcony, packed with hundreds of children, had gone mad. Women attempted to drag out as many as they could, frequently losing their small charges in the clawing crowd where they were knocked down and trampled to death. As doors and windows burst open and shot out flames, some victims became human torches. Still hundreds of children were found dead in their seats where they had remained, choking to death on smoke. Many had fallen forward, with their heads resting on the seat ahead of them, as though in prayer. A crowd of 60 persons raced from the balcony down an unmarked hall with a locked exit at the end. All were trapped and found later in terrible heaps, burned and suffocated to death.

Two months after the fire George Leach, a freshman at Oak Park High School who had gone to the theater alone that fateful day, wrote an account of his experiences in the *Tabula* which, at that time, was a monthly newspaper and not, as it is today, the high school year book.

"The performance was in keeping with the building: they were both beautiful. These thoughts were going through my mind in the second act when suddenly a yellow light appeared at the left of the stage. There had been so many different colored lights used during the afternoon that I thought this one a part of the play, until small pieces of flimsy drapery fell to the stage floor burning," wrote Leach.

"At this point a quiet murmur ran through the audience but there was no shrieking or yelling. Suddenly a man appeared and tried to put it out. But, finding this impossible, he turned to the audience motioning for everyone to remain seated. This I did until it seemed foolish to stay there any longer and then turned up the aisle, leaving many people who by this time had become petrified with fear."

"On the first floor the shrieking of women and children had become the chief noise, with the exception of the explosions which I heard. Perhaps the building would blow up, and with that thought I went out the front entrance into the most panic-stricken crowd I was ever in. I stepped across the street and climbed up on a hose wagon to get a better view. The street was crowded with hatless women, chorus girls in stage garb and little chil-

---

THE IROQUOIS THEATER HOLOCAUST.

Fire broke out in the flies of Iroquois Theater, Chicago, at the matinee performance of "Mr. Bluebeard" on Wednesday, at which a large proportion of the 2,000 in attendance were ladies and children. The great destruction of life that occurred in a few minutes following the discovery by the audience is simply appalling. Thursday morning papers gave the number of dead at 550, the injured 350, reported missing 250. These figures may be changed some, either reduced or increased, but in any event the number will be close to 1,000 dead, fatally or partially injured.

Our local records up to this time show nothing more dreadful—not even the sinking of the "Lady Elgin" in Lake Michigan, July 4, 1861, when about 300 persons were drowned, nor the great Chicago fire, Oct. 9, 1871, though the property loss amounted to many millions, yet the recorded loss of life was only about 300. So that the fatalities at the Iroquois Theater fire were horribly in excess of either.

Several Oak Parkers are among the victims, but up to this hour all the dreadful details are impossible to collate.

Ruth Payson, aged 15, daughter of Mr. and Mrs. Edward Payson, 1 Elizabeth court, and her two cousins, Glen Bickford, aged 17, and Helen Bickford, aged 15, of Rogers Park, were found among the dead, evidently from suffocation, as no injury was found on their bodies. The funeral of Miss Payson will be held at Third Congregational Church next Sunday afternoon at 2 o'clock, and the funeral of her cousins will be held at Graceland Chapel, Chicago, Saturday, at 11 a. m.

Miss Edith Pridmore, of Chicago, sister of Mrs. Z. E. Martin, of Oak Park was at the theater with Mr. Martin's son, Earl P., aged 7 years. Miss Pridmore died at the Sherman House Thursday morning, but up to the latest account Earl had not been found.

Paul Windor, aged 16, and his brother, Berry, aged 12, who reside at Pleasant street and Harvey avenue, were both burned to death. Drechsler's ambulance brought their bodies out Thursday afternoon.

Miss Francis M. Lehman, 525 N. Austin avenue, sister of H. J. Lehman, the letter-carrier, perished in the fire. Miss Lehman was teacher in the Chicago public schools.

Dr. and Mrs. T. E. Roberts were in great suspense for several hours on account of the fact that their daughter, Elizabeth, accompanied by Mrs. K. V. Sears and her daughter, started for the Iroquois Theater. Mr. Sears, in his busy rush of business, neglected to secure sittings at the Iriquois, and because he could only obtain seats in the very front row, decided to take Mrs. Sears and the children to another theater. There was rejoicing by Dr. Roberts when he found his daughter safe and well at the Northwestern depot at Avenue just as he was about to start for the city in search of her.

Ralph, Chester and Percy Skillin, Orson and George McClary and George Shipley were in the theater when the fire broke out, but they all escaped without injury.

The entire world sympathizing with Chicago at this time shows how much akin we all are, and as it comes close to our own doors our hearts go out to those who have so suddenly and so sadly been afflicted.

Headline of Reporter-Argus, January 2, 1904.

dren lost from parents; confusion reigned here supreme."

"I saw the wounded carried out and sent away in ambulances. Next came the dead, one after another was carried out of that terrible hole of death and laid on the sidewalk like so many sacks of flour, faster than they were able to be carried away. When I had counted 40 I left, fully conscious of my narrow escape."

There was a firehouse in the next block and within fifteen minutes firemen were pouring tons of water into the theater. When they were finally able to reach the interior they found a scene from Dante's *Inferno*. Some of the most hardened reporters from Chicago's tabloids fainted as the dead and dying were dragged out and laid in rows along the curb. The counting of victims dragged on for another day and a night as relatives searched frantically for their loved ones.

Aftermath of Fire

Instead of welcoming in the New Year with a round of parties, Oak Park, along with Chicago and surrounding communities, was plunged into mourning. There was scarcely a family in the village that was not in some way affected by the fire. Most of the villagers who died were buried in Forest Home Cemetery in Forest Park and for more than a week there were sad processions to that cemetery as the victims were laid to rest.

The aftermath of the Iroquois Theater tragedy resulted in the passage of a new set of safety codes for public buildings including the requirement that all doors open out. Immediately after the fire many churches and theaters, including the Warrington Opera House in Oak Park, were closed for inspection. Three weeks later the Warrington was reopened. "During the past weeks a large force of men has been at work rearranging the seats, fire-proofing the stage, putting in additional exits, fire-proof curtains and fire-fighting appliances. The Warrington has always been considered safe, but with these improvements, it will rank as one of the safest in Illinois," reported the *Oak Leaves.*

The manager of the Iroquois Theater and several public officials including the Mayor were indicted. But there were no convictions. It was a case of graft-as-usual Chicago style. Building and fire inspectors had failed to inspect or worse, had been paid to ignore obvious deficiencies.

A footnote to the history of the Iroquois: The archway which formed the stone front of the theater was a copy of a monument built in Paris to commemorate the death of 150 victims of a flash fire at a charity bazaar there in 1857. It had been a prophetic design.

Titanic Tragedy Touches Oak Park

On April 10, 1912 the newly commissioned luxury liner *Titanic* left Southampton, England on her maiden voyage to New York. The magnificent 66,000-ton vessel could carry about 3,000 passengers but had lifeboats for only a fraction of that number. But this didn't seem to matter because the ship's owner, the White Star Line, had confidently labeled it "unsinkable." Her cargo included a priceless copy of the *Rubaiyat of Omar Khayyam* and a list of passengers collectively worth $250 million. Five days later, on the evening of April 15, the *Titanic* struck an iceberg and within three hours went down in the icy waters of the North Atlantic with the loss of 1,502 lives.

The magnitude of this maritime disaster was beyond the comprehension of most people. There was scarcely a village or town in the country that was not touched in some way by this tragedy. Although no local residents were passengers on the *Titanic* there were several people in Oak Park who lost family members.

Mr. and Mrs. Fred Kenyon, the sister and brother-in-law of Mrs. George Baldwin of 309 Linden, were among the passengers. The couple who made their home in New York had visited the Baldwins just four months earlier at Christmas. In the days following the disaster confusion reigned and families like the Baldwins had no way of knowing who had survived and who had perished.

The fastest way to end the suspense was to go to New York and meet the *Carpathia*, which was steaming slowly toward New York with her tragic cargo of survivors that her crewmen had plucked from the water. And that is what George Baldwin did. "Knowing that the crowds would be very great and that the authorities were strict about tickets to the Cunard dock, Mr. Baldwin wired ahead for tickets of admittance," noted the *Oak Leaves*.

"Mr. Baldwin and a friend made their way through a drenching rain to one block east of West 14th Street where they had to pass through three cordons of police with fully a thousand or more automobiles lined up for the survivors."

Baldwin later described the scene to the newspaper: "On arrival at the second floor of the dock where the vessels unload their passengers there was a concourse of fully 1,500 people massed around the entrance which was railed off. A pin could have been heard had it been dropped and millionaires like J. Pierpont Morgan Jr., the Astors, the Seligmanns and the Guggenheims were rubbing shoulders with men in the most modest walks of life. It was a sight never to be forgotten and agony was etched in almost every face."

"A short time later the United States Senate Committee sent from Washington elbowed its way through the gates to be ready to go aboard to interview Mr. Ismay." (Bruce Ismay, owner of the White Star Line, managed to find a place in one of the lifeboats and spent the remainder of his life reviled by the public).

"At last the great moment had come when the covered gangplank was passed on to the vessel and the people were to know who was there and who was not. The survivors came out in single file; there were first two men and then a woman with a hood; I saw her face, it was Mrs. Kenyon, but I did not know her; behind came a man and woman and then little Mrs. Astor in a white turban and sweater. All faces seemed the same, devoid of understanding."

TITANIC DISASTER

Oak Park Touched by Greatest Shipwreck—Carelessness on Lake—The Atlantic Wreck of 1873

Oak Park, like hundreds of other communities, was closely connected with the Titanic disaster.

Mr. and Mrs. F. R. Kenyon, who visited in Oak Park at Christmas, and Frederick J. Banfield of England, who visited Edward M. Rowe, assistant superintendent of Oak Leaves composing room, a few weeks ago, were aboard the great vessel. Mrs. Kenyon is a sister of Mrs. George P. Baldwin of 309 Linden. Mr. Baldwin went to New York to meet the survivors and Mrs. Kenyon came ashore safely. Mr. Kenyon has not been heard from since he placed Mrs. Kenyon in the lifeboat. Their home is in New York.

Oak Leaves.

147

"Fearing I might not be near enough to see her, I went around to meet the first of the survivors again as they were coming through the lines and again looked into the face of Mrs. Kenyon but did not recognize her, so swollen were her features from weeping. But I recognized the four-leaf clover on her hood and called her by name and caught her as she staggered out of line. I asked her if she came alone and she could only bow assent; and I knew she was a widow."

"The heart-rending scenes on that dock would be impossible to convey on paper and I don't think there was a man or woman on the dock that night who was not shaking and who will not be a little kinder through life to humanity in general."

Mrs. Kenyon later told Baldwin that the shock of the impact was very loud and heavy, but that none of the passengers felt they were in any danger. Still she and her husband who had retired for the night dressed and put on heavy coats before going on deck.

"There was apparently no system, as the first few boats had been lowered without their full capacity. She was in the eighth boat, which had 60 people because, by that time, passengers were awakening to the peril. She asked Mr. Kenyon to accompany her, but he said he would not go while there was a single woman or child left on the ship. He insisted that she go and said he would probably join her the next day; and kissed her good night. There was a sailor and three men on the boat and the rest were women and children. The men had gotten aboard with the understanding that they could row, but when they reached the water it was found that none of them had ever handled an oar. So Mrs. Kenyon and another lady helped row the boat miles through the ice drift."

"At half past two in the morning she saw a blinding flash, heard a loud explosion on the *Titanic* and then all became dark and soon after the ship sank. At half past six in the morning Mrs. Kenyon was picked up by the *Carpathia* and given a stateroom, the privacy of which did much to hold her mentality from the terrible scenes of sorrow at all times in evidence in the salon."

Frederick Banfield, an Englishman and friend of Edward Rowe, assistant superin-

TITANIC VICTIM HERE

August Wennerstrom, Swedish News paper Man, Who Floated Historic Life Raft, an Oak Parker

August Wennerstrom, who escaped from the Titanic after the decks were awash with icy waters, is employed at the home of H. S. Mills, Pleasant street and Home avenue.

In Sweden he was a newspaper man, but now he is working in the garden and learning English. Mr. Wennerstrom was a passenger on the Titanic and had no opportunity to get into a life boat. He said the women of the steerage in many cases refused to leave their men, and so went down with the ship. His manner of escape is a fine commentary on the chaos and lack of discipline prevailing on the largest ship afloat, which had put to sea with a full complement of bartenders, cooks, dishwashers and other hotel help, but short handed as to seamen. What seamen were aboard had never been drilled, according to evidence submitted in Europe and America. Mr. Wennerstrom was wandering about the decks and had given up hope, when, with four other men, he discovered, lashed snugly in its place, a collapsible canvas life raft. The crew and officers, in spite of the fact that hundreds were unable to get into the life boats, had forgotten the raft or had never known of its existence.

As the deck sank under their feet Mr. Wennerstrom and his companions discovered the forgotten raft and this frail

June 1, 1912 Oak Leaves.

tendent of the *Oak Leaves* composing room, who had visited the Rowe family in Oak Park a few weeks earlier, was aboard the *Titanic* when it went down.

Banfield, who had accompanied Mrs. Rowe and her two small children to England, was making the return trip to America. "I do not expect to hear from him again," said Edward Rowe. "I know he would have waited until the women and children had their chance and then there was none for him."

Charlotte Collyer and her 8-year-old daughter Marjorie who were among the survivors took refuge after the disaster with her husband's American relatives, Mr. and Mrs. E. Y. Horder, 6411 Washington Blvd. in Oak

148

Park. According to a front page story in the May 4, 1912 issue of the *Oak Leaves,* "Mr. and Mrs. Collyer had sold their little business in Bishopstoke, England and intended with the proceeds to begin life in the new country with some members of Mr. Horder's family in Idaho. But when the catastrophe took place Mr. Collyer was one of those for whom there was no room in the boats and all their savings and railroad tickets went down with him."

When the alarm was first sounded Charlotte Collyer didn't bother to put up her hair, just tied it back with a ribbon. Her daughter Marjorie had a steamer rug around her shoulders. Mr. Collyer took little trouble dressing because he expected to be back soon --he even left his watch lying on his pillow.

But Collyer never returned to his stateroom. A seaman yanked Mrs. Charlotte Collyer by the arm, another by her waist and they dragged her from her husband Harvey. As she kicked to get free, she heard him call, "Go, Lottie! For God's sake, be brave and go! I'll get a seat in the next boat!" But, of course, he never did. Mother and daughter recuperated from their ordeal with the Horder's in Oak Park before continuing their journey to Idaho.

August Wennerstrom, a Swedish citizen, was a third-class passenger on the *Titanic.* His reason for coming to the U. S. is not clear. But by the end of May, just six weeks after the disaster, he was employed as a gardener by Herbert Mills at Pleasant Home. Mills had purchased the estate from John Farson's widow after Farson's untimely death in 1910 and used the spacious ground to entertain just as lavishly as the previous owner.

In the June 1, 1912 issue of the *Oak Leaves* Wennerstrom detailed his escape from the *Titanic.* "Mr. Wennerstrom was wandering about the decks and had about given up hope, when, with four other men, he discovered lashed snugly in its place, a collapsible canvas life raft. The crew, in spite of the fact that hundreds were unable to get into the life boats, had forgotten the raft or had never known of its existence."

"As the deck sank under their feet Mr. Wennerstrom and his companions discovered the forgotten raft and this frail vessel saved more than 20 men. They ripped the raft loose and opened it and it floated on the deck. (This was at 1:45 a.m. barely half an hour before the ship went down.) The men climbed in and in a moment were in the sea. Mr. Wennerstrom said they picked up other men from the sea, but that when the raft was so over-crowded it was ready to sink, someone fired a pistol at all who tried to climb aboard."

After the collapsible raft had been washed clear of the wreck, a trickle of exhausted swimmers began to strike out for it. Hauling themselves over the low canvas side, they sprawled in the bottom of the boat. Two of the swimmers were his friend Edvard Lindell and Lindell's wife. Wennerstrom held his hand out to her, only to find he didn't have the strength to haul her aboard. Desperately he hung on, hoping someone would help him, but finally his strength gave out and Mrs. Lindell slipped into the water. Heartsick, Wennerstrom turned to Mr. Lindell, afraid to tell him what had happened. It wasn't necessary. By this time Lindell had frozen to death.

At the end of his interview with the *Oak Leaves* Wennerstrom agreed to give a further account of his experiences on the *Titanic* at a later date. He never did.

Sinking of the *SS Eastland*

July 24, 1915 was a day eagerly awaited by the 2,500 employees of Western Electric's Hawthorne plant in Cicero. That was the date set for the company's annual summer excursion. Michigan City was chosen to host the event and for several days an advance party of employees had been in that town preparing for the festivities. Streets were decorated and floats readied for a parade that was never held.

S.S. Eastland after disaster – Chicago River.

Shortly after 9 a.m. the excursion steamer *Eastland*, filled to capacity with the workers and their families and friends, was preparing to cast off from the Clark Street dock where the ship was anchored. Without warning the boat capsized and, within minutes, sank at dockside just a few feet from dry land. More than 844 people drowned. Most of the victims were trapped below deck and had no time to escape.

The sinking of the *Eastland*, was the greatest maritime disaster involving a single ship on any of the Great Lakes. In terms of lives lost it was also the worst disaster in the history of Chicago, surpassing the Chicago Fire in 1871 where an estimated 300 to 400 peo-

ple died and the 1903 Iroquois Theater fire where 602 people perished.

The majority of Western Electric workers were young and of Czech origin. They lived in Chicago and suburbs surrounding the Cicero plant including many from Oak Park, River Forest and Forest Park.

Little Gertrude Stork, 1037 Circle, Forest Park, had reluctantly boarded the *Eastland* with her father and brother. After the tragedy her father recalled that, a few minutes before the accident, she expressed a feeling of fear that something was going to happen. "Almost as soon as she had given expression to her thought, the boat capsized and Gertrude sank into the water, never to come up alive," intoned the *Oak Leaves*.

Two young men who were working for the summer at the Cicero plant were more fortunate. Ralph Doran, 461 Park Ave., River Forest and Arthur Hoover, 733 Woodbine, Oak Park, both recent graduates of Oak Park and River Forest High School, were both on the top deck when the boat listed.

According to the *Oak Leaves*, they made a rush toward the land side but the deck rose too steeply for them and they were flung headlong across the deck. "Doran was able to clasp a wire support for the mast and swung to the top of the boat where he was taken off by a tug. Hoover's slide across the deck was arrested by a bench and he was unhurt."

The boys went to the office of Arthur's father, G. W. Hoover a few blocks away. As soon as the elder Hoover heard of the disaster he rushed to the scene to hunt for his boy. After several futile hours he gave up hope and returned to his office, only to find the boys drying their clothes.

Martha Bross, 415 Beloit, Forest Park, went on the excursion with her friend Emma Bohles, 192 Franklin in River Forest, a Western Electric employee. After their rescue she gave this account of their ordeal. "We went aboard the Eastland about 7 a.m. and went up to the third deck, but it was already so crowded that we went below. It was so close there and so many men were smoking, that we went up to the third deck again and stood a few feet from the rail."

EASTLAND DEATHS

Oak Park and Forest Park People Die in Catastrophe—Many Have Narrow Escapes

When the Eastland capsized in the Chicago river on Saturday ten Oak Park and Forest Park people were carried to a tragic death. All of the bodies were recovered on Saturday and Sunday. Many Oak Park people barely escaped with their lives from the disaster which brought death to 1,300 Chicagoans on an outing of Western Electric company employes and brought sorrow into more homes than the Iroquois theater fire, Chicago's greatest holocaust.

Residents of the community who lost their lives were:

LESLIE SIMMONS, 722 North Kenilworth.
WILLIAM SYKES, 1134 South Harvey, and two children, Harry and Margaret.
EARL DAWSON, 1113 South Taylor
RALPH ROSSOW, 1141 South East.
MATHEW BONGA, 829 Wisconsin.
HERMAN A. RISTOW JR., 1041 Home, and brother, WILLIAM F. RISTOW, 939 Lathrop, Forest Park.
GERTRUDE STORK, 1021 Circle, Forest Park.

The following were reported as Oak Parkers in the list of dead and missing given out by the information bureau, but their homes were across Twelfth street in Berwyn:

James Skrivanec, 1538 South Grove.
Mrs. A. C. Anderson, 1409 Wenonah.
John Humpal, 1524 South Oak Park avenue.
H. C. Waller, 1214 Highland.
Mrs. Ludwig, 1619 South Taylor avenue.

Oak Leaves, *July 31, 1915.*

That decision saved their lives. "By the time the boat was ready to start I noticed that it leaned over to the north a little as soon as it started and then, in a few seconds it was reeling in that direction with such force that I could not hold onto the railing. I got a small finger hold of the wall but it was enough to keep my head above water. Then a man trampled on my fingers but I held on as tight as I could and soon my friend, Miss Bohles, got a man to help me to a better place on the side of the boat out of the water. We then helped others near us, and finally we got onto the wharf."

Others were not so fortunate. A double funeral was held for William Rostow, 939 Lathrop, Forest Park, the father of three small daughters, and his brother Herman, 1041 S. Home Ave., Oak Park. Both were Western Electric employees. "Herman had as companion for the day Miss Ida Jutci. The announcement of their engagement was expected soon. The party of young people were on the first deck on the river side of the boat and were all thrown into the water together."

One of the most notable acts of heroism was performed by Frederick Willard, 506 N. Elmwood in Oak Park, who pulled his father to safety through a porthole. "The young man then tied a rope about his waist and plunged into the water from which he had just escaped. He grasped many of those sinking and pulled them back to shore. After he had saved 60 in this manner, according to a man who assisted him, Willard fainted and was forced to give up the work."

Other villagers rushed to help. Oak Park police Captain George Lee volunteered the services of several Oak Park policemen for rescue work and Oak Park businessman Frank Strickland was one of those who threw empty chicken crates into the water to save those who could not swim. Morris Rogers, son of Sampson Rogers, one of Oak Park's most prominent citizens, was downtown when he learned of the disaster. "He went to the scene and got through the police lines with his hospital card and offered his services. For the next 24 hours he worked with doctors in caring for the injured."

One of the first physicians to arrive was Dr. Thomas Carter of the Chicago Health Department. He examined unconscious victims as they were brought to the wharf, attempting to find a pulse in the neck. If one was detected he called for a pulmotor. If he could find no sign of life, he merely said, "Gone," and proceeded to the next person.

Injured survivors received medical attention in a building directly across the street from the Clark Street Bridge while bodies recovered from the *Eastland* were sent to a makeshift morgue at the Second Regiment Armory. People who had reason to believe their relatives were among the dead were admitted to the armory shortly before midnight, 20 at a time. A weary Red Cross worker assisting them later commented, "The heartrending scenes of the Armory had better be left undescribed."

Equally emotional were the reunions with their families of those feared lost. "At the same time that many families were gathered about the lifeless forms of the deceased, communions just as sacred were held in dozens of Oak Park homes where husbands, wives, brothers and sisters were united again after hours of despair in which it was feared that loves ones were lost."

Most of the accounts of the *Eastland* disaster which were telegraphed around the country were the work of young Charles MacArthur of Oak Park, brother of Telfer MacArthur, editor of the *Oak Leaves.* Charlie MacArthur, the prototype of the hard drinking, wise-cracking newspaperman who later collaborated with Ben Hecht in writing *The Front Page,* worked for the City News Bureau and happened to be at the Clark Street bridge when the *Eastland* capsized. In addition to reporting the tragedy the young reporter also spent the next two weeks with other rescue workers helping to recover bodies.

In the weeks following the disaster there was a steady stream of funeral processions down Madison Street as families buried the victims in Forest Home, Waldheim, Concordia and Mount Carmel cemeteries. There were so many burials that these processions did not stop at dusk, but continued until late in the evening.

The aftermath of the catastrophe was a massive relief effort by Western Electric, the Red Cross, United Charities, the City of Chicago and many individuals to provide funds to bury the dead and offer assistance to orphans and other survivors who had lost a breadwinner.

But there were exceptions. Relief workers sent to disburse money to destitute families often discovered that loan sharks had been to many homes before them with offers of "help" to the bewildered survivors in the form of large loans at exorbitant rates of interest.

Another unsettling development was the hordes of unemployed workers who stormed the Western Electric plant hoping to replace workers who had perished on the *Eastland.* This occurred despite published notice by the company that survivors of victims were to be given first choice of vacancies. The work force of many sections within the plant was completely decimated. On one bench where 22 young women previously worked, only two reported for duty when the plant reopened; the rest had died. And one of the "twine rooms" where women worked on the wrapping material for telephone wires was entirely wiped out.

A film of efforts to rescue victims on the Eastland was barred from Chicago movie theaters by city censors. However, this film was shown several weeks later at the Oak Park Theater. "Manager Hodgson cut out much of the gruesomeness of the scenes, but even the hurrying lines of police carrying covered bodies in a continual procession on stretchers was enough to raise protests from any who witnessed the film," scolded the *Oak Leaves.* "The objection was that such a disaster ought not to be shown for money, especially while so many hearts were stricken with sorrow. But Mr. Hodgson thinks this is met by the fact that the profits on the picture were pledged to the *Eastland* Relief Fund."

Who or what was to blame for the capsizing of the *Eastland?* Over the years there have been many theories. One held that the disaster occurred because most of her passengers suddenly rushed from starboard—the wharf side—to port as the ship began to move. Another suggested that the *Eastland* was stable when she was built in 1903 but was reduced to only marginal stability by later modifications that were required by maritime authorities after the sinking of the *Titanic* three years earlier.

Victorian Decorum Hid Domestic Violence

Around the turn of the century village boosters like William Halley, editor of the *Oak Park Vindicator,* accentuated only the positive aspects of village life. Oak Park, he proclaimed, is a bower of beauty. "It is the home of luxury and refinement. Here education flourishes and religion and temperance triumph. There is no place for anything that savors of discord or disorder."

Yet the reality was that women and children were often the victims of domestic violence at the hands of loutish husbands and fathers whose abuse was often concealed by their victims for fear of reprisals. It was only when the mistreatment was so blatant and could no longer be ignored that neighbors intervened.

In 1894 Halley reported two such cases in his newspaper: "For several weeks it has been known that the 10-year-old son of William Flack has been horribly maltreated under the pretense of paternal discipline. The lad has been frequently driven from home by the severity of these attacks and at last has been taken by Charles Flynn to his home on Maple Avenue. Several gentlemen, including Mr. Flynn and Rev. C. P. Anderson have interested themselves in the case and it is expected that justice will be done." The following week the newspaper reported that Flack had been arrested and fined $25 and costs by Judge White. However, the fine was suspended to await the decision of Judge Scales on the application of Flynn for custody of the boy.

In the same issue, the *Vindicator* also reported the death of Mrs. Matilda Kramer. "The case has attracted much attention because it was alleged that her illness was due to maltreatment at the hands of her husband. The woman was left destitute, but was cared for by several Austin ladies who interested themselves in her case."

"Dr. Mary Kearsley attended her and secured her removal to the hospital. In addition to the bruised condition of her body, she had a serious attack of fever that finally caused her death. A coroner's inquest was held Tuesday and Mr. Kramer was not charged. Mrs. Kramer was 36-year-old and leaves several children."

Mrs. Kate Burridge was much luckier. She filed suit to compel her husband who had left her to continue to support her and their four young children "as he is well supplied with this world's goods." According to Mrs. Burridge, her husband had treated her harshly for more than ten years. "Several times she was obliged to flee to the home of her mother and, in her absence, Burridge misbehaved himself with two ladies by the name of Alice Savory and Carrie Huene. With the latter, it is claimed, he went so far as to give her a power of attorney, authorizing her to draw checks upon his bank account while refusing to support his family."

In a community where a woman's social status was inexorably linked to her married state, a single woman was especially vulnerable. If the lady had no particular skills that would enable her to earn her own living she was usually dependent on the sufferance of her relatives. In the best of circumstances she was a respected and productive member of the household. But her position was far more tenuous if other family members looked upon her as nothing more than a drudge, a "poor relation" that was a source of unpaid labor.

Reading between the lines that attitude may have sealed the fate of 56-year-old Susan Slocum who made her home with her niece in a house on south Harvey. In its July 15, 1894 issue the *Vindicator* reported that she was found dead in her room on Sunday morning. The cause of death was asphyxiation from gas she had turned on by her own hand.

"For the past five years Miss Slocum had made her home with her niece Mabel Morey and her family. It is said that arrangements had been made to send the aunt to the old ladies' home and that owing to the impending change Miss Slocum became despondent. It is thought that she resolved on her rash act in a fit of melancholy."

Another tragic death that same year was the suicide of an unnamed young maid who also asphyxiated herself when the father of her child refused to marry her. A penciled note was read at the inquest into her death held at Postlewait Funeral Home. It read: "Dear Walter, The gas is turned on. I can

Life was often difficult for women who worked long hours as domestics and clerks, often for low wages.

hear it hissing as it escapes. I grow weaker. You will live to regret your actions."

The "Walter" in question, a 19-year-old youth, testified at the inquest that he gave the woman a diamond ring as a present and not as a pledge of their betrothal. When her pregnancy became obvious he began avoiding her and did not take her threat to commit suicide seriously.

The girl's employers stood by her and tried to arrange a wedding. "But the shame was so great it blotted out two lives. The finger pointing at the unmarried mother and the common belief that certain births are disgraceful, tortured a young woman and her babe into an untimely grave."

Oak Park "Baby Mill"

In 1914 an unmarried mother, shunned by her family and stigmatized by society as a "fallen woman," had few options if she wanted to keep her child. In Oak Park many women who found themselves in this position were forced to place their infants with Lois Kennedy, a harridan who charged them for child "care" that included malnourishment, abuse and even death.

It was not until eight of the babies died while living with Kennedy that state and local officials finally raided her "baby farm" at 425 Maple, removed the remaining children they found and arrested Kennedy who was indicted by a Cook County grand jury and held for trial.

This doting couple is typical of the majority of parents around the turn of the century. But unfortunately some children were mistreated at the hands of their parents.

Although the village had granted Kennedy a license for her "boardinghouse for babies" there was never any stipulation about the number of children she could take in at one time. Nor did any officials make any home visits to monitor the quality of the care they received.

Kennedy's house was, in reality, a baby mill. She was free to accept as many children as she wished and, later, when their parents made no attempt to reclaim them, there were no laws to prevent her from handing them over to any stranger who expressed a willingness to provide a home for the abandoned child.

However, after several mothers did return for their babies and found them gone, they complained to Oak Park police who investigated and found 14 children hungry and living in filthy conditions. Led by Dr. A. F. Storke, a local pediatrician and Police Chief Lee, several nurses and local women removed the children who were taken to Cook County Hospital for examination.

"On Wednesday Judge Pinckney of the juvenile court heard the cases of the 14 babies," reported the *Oak Leaves*. "He said it was the worst case he had ever heard and declared he would do all he could to prevent Mrs. Kennedy from ever going into business again. When she was ordered to jail by the judge after the hearing, Mrs. Kennedy fought four deputies and finally rolled into the gutter in Clark Street, much to the amazement of spectators. According to jail authorities,

she was the most rebellious prisoner ever in the institution."

Jealous husband shoots wife in Oak Park boardinghouse

The *Vindicator* also printed a detailed account of the attempt by Frank Raynor, a clerk at Martin's grocery store to kill his wife. Raynor, who was regarded as a model employee, lived with his wife Anna in Mrs. Kerr's boardinghouse and was "insanely jealous of his wife and without good reason."

"It seems that Mrs. Raynor, who is only 22-years-old, was until a year ago Miss Anna Poston of Westville, Indiana. Her parents wanted her to marry Raynor, but on the eve of the ceremony she refused to do so, having learned that he had a divorced wife still living and two children. At the point of a revolver he compelled her to again consent to the marriage, and their life has been anything but happy ever since."

"Goaded by inordinate jealousy, it is said that Raynor locked his young wife in her room and more than once threatened to kill her. About three weeks ago he refused to pay her board and she became the guest of Mrs. Kerr."

Anna Raynor had made up her mind to return to her parents. But the night before she was to leave Raynor pushed his way into her room for a final talk. "His wife held to her resolve and, incensed beyond reason, Raynor drew his revolver and shot her in the right breast. She fell in the hallway and he fired two more shots, neither of which took effect. A number of boarders were on the porch when the shots rang out. They started for the stairs where they encountered Raynor with a pistol in his hand. He waved them back and made his escape. The police have an excellent description of him and his capture is only a question of time."

Villagers Afflicted by Addictive Drugs and Disease

In a town powerfully influenced by the Women's Christian Temperance Union the notice in an 1894 issue of the *Oak Park Vindicator* that J. W. Schoening had put a new soda fountain with twelve syrups in his drug store must have been greeted with great enthusiasm. "All the tubes and cylinders are of the best black tin, silver lined. He will have it ready for business within a week." noted the *Vindicator*.

But one of Schoening's clerks, evidently looking for something stronger than a root beer fizz, decided to sample some of the many addictive drugs that were readily available over the counter and without prescription in his employer's drug store.

"Some excitement was created on Tuesday evening by a young drug clerk who indulged freely in the druggist's strong waters after which he endeavored to sober himself with powerful drugs. The combination evidently had an entirely opposite effect, as he proceeded to raise a most unseemly disturbance even to the length of perforating the drug store ceiling with a number of shots from a revolver. Officer Blundin arrested him and Judge Amerson imposed a heavy fine which was suspended on promise of good behavior."

At the turn of the century truth in advertising was an idea whose time had not yet come and many of the bottled medicines available in Oak Park drug stores contained large amounts of addictive and potentially-lethal drugs such as morphine, heroin, powdered opium, codeine and chloroform.

Worse, most of these "remedies" which claimed to cure common childhood illnesses were packaged under deceptively reassuring names such as Koepp's Baby Friend (morphine), Dr. Moffett's Teething Powder (powdered opium) and Dr. James' Soothing Syrup (heroin) that masked their active ingredients.

Lovett's Drug Store on the southeast corner of Lake Street and Marion Avenue.

156

Newspapers were equally cavalier in carrying advertisements for these products. Dr. Eline's Great Nerve Restorer for all brain and nerve diseases promised: "Fits stopped free. No fits after first day's use. Insane persons restored. Infallible if taken as directed." Lydia E. Pinkham's vegetable compound assured relief for all "those painful complaints and complicated troubles common to our wives, mothers and daughters" while Pitcher's Castoria guaranteed a quick cure for diarrhea, fever and stomach pain.

By 1910 the federal government was beginning to take an active role in attempting to control both the exaggerated claims and the products themselves. Although the industry was still unregulated there was movement to have druggists enter into a voluntary agreement not to sell these harmful drugs without a prescription. "An attempt is to be made to have a resolution to this effect adopted at the next meeting of the National Retail Druggists' Association," reported the *Oak Leaves*.

"All publicity possible should be given to this list," added Dr. Robert Savage, director of the Oak Park Board of Health. "In my own experience among the poorer people in the hospitals, I have found children imprisoned by these patent cures. In Oak Park people have more opportunity to learn, and I have not seen any mother who would knowingly give such a deadly concoction to her children."

Poisons easily available on demand at the corner drug store were also used frequently by despondent individuals to end their lives. "The people of Harlem (now Forest Park) were greatly shocked at the death of Miss Emma Troost, which was caused by poison administered by her own hand," reported the *Vindicator*. "The coroner's jury decided that she had committed the act while temporarily insane. Miss Troost was 18-years-old and had been betrothed to Mr. William Murray who had recently broken their engagement. He is greatly afflicted by the sad tragedy."

Deadly Diseases

Infectious diseases, such as smallpox, were another scourge that was greatly feared because most had no cure. Whenever there was an outbreak, victims and their families were quickly quarantined in their homes, schools were closed and public gatherings suspended to prevent the spread of the deadly disease.

Chicagoans unfortunate enough to contract a contagious disease were taken from their families by force to "pest houses" where they received minimal care and usually died of their illness. During a particularly virulent outbreak of smallpox in the city in the 1880s one Oak Park resident suggested in a letter to the *Vindicator* that Cicero Township prepare for the expected outbreak by opening its own, more humane hospice to care for these infected patients.

"Referring to the alarming spread of smallpox and the fact that the city authorities have lost all control of it, and that anyone is liable to take the disease from infected rail or street cars, it would be a good thing if Oak Park and Austin joined hands to do what some suburban villages south of Chicago have already done."

"These people do not propose to allow any of their people to be taken to sure death at the city pest house. They have secured an isolated residence, fitted it for patients, provided medicines, bedrooms, food, etc. and have arranged for nurses and doctors to be called when the need arises. We should be ready to do the same and not be compelled to the brutal system of taking the helpless patient by force from his family and almost certain death at the city pest house."

Workers and Employers Clash in Wage Disputes

By 1900 many of the workers employed by businesses in Oak Park and surrounding communities had successfully organized their own unions. And relations between labor and management were generally marked by civility. The Cicero Council, No. 11 of the Butchers' and Grocery Clerks' Association of Illinois made a point of thanking employers in the *Oak Park Reporter* for favors granted: "The members wish to thank the employers who have made the 7 o'clock and Thursday afternoon closings possible."

However, in the summer of 1899, there was considerable unrest among skilled carpenters who considered themselves woefully underpaid. These were the artisans who created the meticulously hand sawn and carved millwork that was such an important part of the large Queen Anne, Greek Revival and Italianate homes being built at that time.

The June 22, 1899 issue of the *Oak Park Times* chronicled a meeting between the carpenters and contractors who met to discuss a new contract. The carpenters were demanding a 10-cent an hour increase to 42 1/2 cents an hour.

"Mr. J. P. Willing explained the view of the contractors. He said he did not consider 42 1/2 cents per hour to be too much for a good carpenter, but too great an advance at one step; that a large abrupt increase would check building progress and it would be better to move to a more satisfactory scale by degrees. He proposed 35 cents an hour as a compromise. The carpenters considered this offer and on a vote of 31 approving it and five opposing, there the matter stands."

But the action taken by disgruntled carpenters over the next few weeks rendered this vote meaningless. "The union men have been keeping a sharp watch on buildings this week in an endeavor to induce workmen to go out or not help the contractors," reported the *Times*. "While their efforts have not been wholly successful they have materially checked construction and are holding back contracts about to be let."

Bedard and Morency, a large millwork on South Blvd. near East Avenue, and one of the largest employers in the village, found itself caught in a no-win situation between the warring factions. "Twenty-seven contractors met on Tuesday and decided to notify Bedard and Morency that they must either deliver the millwork ordered by said contractors for buildings or such material will be purchased elsewhere," said the *Times*.

"Bedard and Morency is a union mill and the union has ordered the firm to deliver no work to contractors who refuse to agree to

1905 Oak Park Directory.

the union scale of 42 1/2 cents per hour and other requirements. If the mill yields to the contractors the millhands will strike. If they do not the contractors will withdraw patronage. This makes the mill a victim in spite of its desire to agree with all parties and have no trouble. It seems like a case of punishing the unoffending to get at someone else."

The union carpenters resorted to other action guaranteed to attract the attention of both the contractors and the general public. "The carpenters strike took a new turn on Sunday night. Harry Hogan, 303 Iowa Street, was made the victim of one of the worse pieces of malicious meanness Oak Park has ever known," said the *Times*. "He has three buildings under construction and some miscreants sneaked in and out, gouged and defaced the woodwork to the value of more than $500. There is no sympathy for that sort of deviltry in this town and the hope is that the fellows who are guilty will get the full extent of the law."

But instead of abating, the violence escalated. In July the newspaper noted that the new building under construction by Andrew Blackstone at Scoville Avenue and Pleasant Street was vandalized by persons in sympathy with the striking carpenters. The new floors, casings and doors were cut and gouged in more than fifty places."

At that point homeowners and contractors began hiring watchmen to protect their property at night. This didn't deter three men who returned to the Blackstone property ready to inflict more damage. However, they were discouraged when the watchman fired several shots over their heads.

Norton Bros. Can Works

Labor unrest was also rampant in Maywood where many Oak Parkers were employed at the Norton Bros. Can Works (This plant was the predecessor of the now-demolished American Can Co. factory at 9th Avenue and St. Charles Road.)

In July 1900 all 1,300 factory workers walked off the job. "The cause of this strike arose from the refusal of Ray Norton to take back some of the men who were laid off Monday afternoon and also from his refusal to recognize any committee sent from the union that was organized several weeks ago," reported the *Vindicator.*

The immediate cause of the strike was trivial. "Twenty-three boys working in the tinshop quit work Monday noon on account of the heat and did not report again till the next morning. The superintendent filled their places with men who were given from $1 to $2.50 a week more than the boys received. When the boys returned half of them were given work in other departments and the remainder were promised the first vacancies that occurred."

"The union took up the case of the boys. A meeting was called at Maywood Hall at which a committee was appointed to wait on the firm and demand the reinstatement of the boys at the wages paid their successors. It was voted that if it was refused all members of the union were to strike Tuesday morning. Wednesday night the committee reported back that not only was their demand denied, but Manager Ray Norton declined to receive the men as representatives of the union. Accordingly, every employee of the works was ordered out. The true object of the walkout is to force the firm to recognize the can makers' organization."

But that would never happen because the Chicago Federation of Labor would not help the men organize a union while they were on strike. Subsequent issues of the *Reporter* chronicled the sorry plight of the workers. "The trouble still continues at Norton's factory. The strikers get on the cars, stopping them, and prevent the workingmen from getting seats. Numerous fights have occurred. The saloons in Melrose have been forbidden to sell beer in pails or to be drunk outside their places. A free soup house for the benefit of the strikers has been established and a number of them are patronizing it."

The Norton brothers were apparently able to break the union by replacing strikers with other workers who quickly lined up to take their jobs. The news account noted that "new men are being taken in as rapidly as possible." And a careful reading of the *Reporter* for the next year turned up no follow-up articles on either the strike or the plight of the workers whose wages had been cut and had no way to vent their grievances.

Corruption and Graft Taint Rarefied Air of Oak Park

Once Oak Park had distanced itself from a Cicero Township Board that many felt was corrupt, most villagers confidently expected that the officials they elected to run their newly formed municipal government would have the integrity and honesty that was lacking in the Cicero Board.

Unfortunately, this was not always the case. But, despite convincing proof that some officials engaged in much the same political chicanery as their Cicero counterparts, most people refused to believe it. "Rumors of graft in Oak Park are in the air. Shame on such rumors. Outrage to even think of such rumors in our village," huffed the *Reporter-Argus* in 1906. "Let the circulator of such rumors be cremated in front of the new post office on any weekday at high noon and put an end to such foul and libelous rumors floating around on the pure air of the beautiful village of Oak Park."

Tell that to the judge who dismissed charges against 19 prominent Oak Park men accused of gambling in the Condon racetrack in Forest Park. "The manner in which the case fizzled was a disappointment to those who scented an opportunity to connect respectable residents with the gambling and drinking which takes place in the race track owned by a notorious gambler," reported the *Oak Leaves*.

"Judge Schumacher refused to divulge the names of his prisoners who cheerfully paid him his fee of $3.50 and went their way. One man returned later and asked that a set of poker chips confiscated by the police be returned to him, as they were the gift of a dear friend. The judge refused to give him the gambling paraphernalia, but referred him to the desk sergeant who told him to drop in during the evening and see the chief."

In 1913, Henry Lembke, an Oak Park policeman, presented the village board with evidence that many officers were drinking and gambling while on duty. President Einfeldt's response was to inform the officers that, off duty, they had all the rights of other citizens but, for the sake of peace and discipline, they had to agree to quit card playing and drinking on the job. The president added that to punish policemen for doing what leading citizens and board members did for entertainment would be a miscarriage of justice.

But Einfeldt's mild rebuke did not go far enough to satisfy O. C. Doering, a trustee who hired two detectives at his own expense to come to Oak Park and entrap the offenders in an undercover sting operation. "With regular gumshoe methods, these sleuths approached Police Chief George Lee and proposed to put him on their payroll for $50 a month. His duties were to keep still and to help the gamblers remain under cover and, at the same time, do a profitable business with the many villagers who engaged in gambling."

Captain Lee appeared to take the bait but instead informed President Einfeldt, and the two officials planned their own counteroffensive. When the detectives arrived at

Race Track
GAMBLING

An Important Issue in Cicero Spring Election

Lines are Distinctly Drawn.   No Question How the Respective Candidates Stand on this Issue

VOTERS OF CICERO NOW HAVE AN OPPORTUNITY TO ACT AT A TIME WHEN UNITED ACTION WILL BRING SUCCESS IN AN EFFORT FOR MUCH NEEDED REFORM

Law Abiding Citizens Have Demanded for Years that Race Track Gambling at Hawthorne be Stopped by the Town Authorities of Cicero. The Resolutions Passed in 1898, Found on the Following Two Pages, Still Express the Sentiments of Berwyn Citizens

The Citizens' Ticket is Pledged to Bring About This Reform

Vote the Citizens' Ticket
on April 3, 1900, as follows:

For President,	**John I. Jones**, Rep.,	of Oak Park
For Supervisor,	**Edward H. Duff**, Rep.,	of Oak Park
For Four-Year Trustee,	**Edward M. Cole**, Rep.,	of Berwyn
For Three-Year Trustee,	**James W. Carter**, Dem.,	of Oak Park
For Assessor,	**Frank E. Ballard**, Dem.,	of Oak Park
For Town Collector,	**George A. Walters**, Rep.,	of Clyde
For Town Clerk,	**Jacob R. Drent**, Rep.,	of Berwyn

Race track gambling.

Captain Lee's house that evening arrangements were made to arrest them as soon as money changed hands. But the men were tipped off by an informant and made no further attempt to contact Chief Lee.

"Neither Captain Lee nor President Einfeldt are taking any credit for defeating the detectives whose work was coarse and led the police chief to know them for amateur

Oak Park police Sgt. George Lee and Officer Ernest Speedsman pose for a simulated arrest in this Philander Barclay photo.

detectives just as if they had tin stars on their coats," said the *Oak Leaves.*

But the Captain had other problems with Chicago gamblers that used Oak Park as a clearinghouse to transmit race results. "Captain Lee and the police force have not yet found any way to block the transmission of racing results through the Western Union telegraph office in the North Western Station at Wisconsin Avenue," reported the *Oak Leaves.*

Results of races in Juarez, Mexico, Tampa Bay and Jacksonville, Florida and Oakland, California arrived at the telegraph office in ci-

pher. As soon as they arrived, a messenger took them to a Forest Park saloon where bookies then phoned these results to scores of other saloons in Chicago and other suburbs. Since the Oak Park police had no authority in Forest Park and the Forest Park police turned a blind eye to the gambling, Captain Lee's options were limited.

"Captain Lee cannot see how he is to get hold of the situation for the messages are all in cipher. He laid the information he has secured before assistant Chief Schuettler of Chicago and that official could not suggest any steps to be taken by the Oak Park police."

The Sheriff of Cook County was just as uncooperative. "It has been the open boast of the gamblers that Forest Park officials will do nothing to molest them. For this reason Captain Lee looked to the Sheriff. 'Why do you Oak Park people want to go around with a red light looking for trouble,' was the reply he received. And so the highest officer in Cook County, the Sheriff does nothing to enforce the law in Forest Park which is within his jurisdiction," the *Oak Leaves* noted indignantly.

But if Oak Park officials were unable to insulate citizens from gambling and other vices the very least they could do was to protect them from the corruption that was sure to follow any viewing of "immoral" movies. In 1913 village trustees suspended parliamentary rules and unanimously passed an ordinance establishing a Censorship Board that consisted of twenty citizens. This ordinance decreed that no picture could be shown in village theaters without first obtaining a permit issued by the village clerk only after the picture had been reviewed and approved by the board.

The cost to the exhibitor for each film reviewed was fifty cents per picture and, once approved, the permit had to be displayed in the theater's lobby. The Censorship Board turned thumbs down on movies it deemed "immoral, vicious, obscene or tending to disturb the peace or displaying any unlawful or riotous scenes."

Six bridesmaids and a flower girl attended Laura Leonard at her 1900 marriage to Bert Ball.

CHAPTER VII

OAK PARK CELEBRATES THE HOLIDAYS

Young people at Second Presbyterian Church in Oak Park celebrate Halloween.

Leap Year

In the 1890s a little mild flirting at well-chaperoned parties was about as far as any young woman of marriageable age could go to signal her interest in a particular swain. But every four years during Leap Year, particularly around February 29, all bets were off and unmarried women were encouraged to go on the offensive in search of a husband.

This time-honored tradition had its origins in a 1288 Scottish law that allowed women to propose marriage throughout Leap Year. The spirit of this law was followed for centuries in Europe and the U. S. as women signaled their intention of finding a husband by wearing a scarlet petticoat, the edge of which was visible under their dresses. Tradition further held that if a man chose not to accept the woman's proposal he had to pay her a forfeiture of a silk dress.

It's not known if the young ladies of the Oak Park Cycling Club were wearing scarlet petticoats at the gala Leap Year party they held on Christmas night in 1892. "The ladies are expected to supply the gentlemen with flowers and all the attention that their admiration for the timid young men can call for," reported the *Vindicator*. "As to whether the ladies will have the courage to take their partners home remains to be seen. We hope the young men will demand all they are entitled to in the way of gallant attention."

Could these young ladies be planning Leap Year socials designed to attract eligible bachelors?

That same year the young ladies of the First Methodist Church in Oak Park organized a Leap Year sleigh ride for their gentlemen friends. Again, the *Vindicator* covered the event: "The party started from Oak Park under the most amiable circumstances, but after Chicago was reached the sleighing gave out and walking was undeniably more pleasant than riding. The home of Will Crafts on Van Buren Street was the objective where an oyster supper awaited them, after which the young people started back in the moonlight. And for those who like that sort of thing it was a triumphant success," grumped editor William Halley, an inveterate bachelor.

In the same issue of his newspaper Halley, tongue firmly planted in cheek, offered his own estimate of the town's most eligible bachelors. "Now that it is Leap Year the ladies may not have a full list of the acceptable young men. So the editor takes the opportunity to present a few of the most desirable parties to their notice."

"Gus Keefer is a very good type of manhood with a dark mustache and who is an amateur photographer. Ladies, this is a chance not to be thrown away. Louis Lunsford is a very congenial fellow all around. He is sure to be taken this year. J. R. McGregor, known among the boys as 'Skeets' has short fair whiskers and among the young ladies is known as 'Smiling Rod'; he is sure to go off among the first and is a bargain."

"Dr. Roberts, whose professional ability is known to all, is also a rare catch and as he is too busy to attend to such matters, some of the fair ones should attend in his case for him. Dr. W. G. DeVere extracts teeth without pain; he is tolerably good looking and should not be neglected. P. G. Kennedy we are somewhat doubtful about, but we think he may safely be put on the list."

In the 1896 Leap Year sweepstakes two young ladies discovered too late that it's never a good idea to make assumptions in affairs of the heart. During that Leap Year the two unnamed women, "one residing on South Humphrey, Ridgeland and the other residing on Lake Street in River Forest, gave a Leap Year party to two young gentlemen of their acquaintance, one residing at Oak Park and the other at Hinsdale."

"They invited them to the city where they took them to a place of amusement, which was, under the circumstances, proper enough. But the young ladies had forgotten the consequences of such a proceeding during Leap Year. They expected, of course, the young men would display their usual gallantry and pay all the expenses. But they were seized with consternation when they found their male companions were not putting their hands in their pockets but simply whispering, 'Leap Year.' The ladies, to their great chagrin, had to stand all the expenses incurred and have not yet done worrying over it."

In that same issue of the *Vindicator* was an account of the tribulations of Daisy Wixom, daughter of a wealthy coal merchant in Cooperstown, New York who married Fred Budlong during Leap Year after a short courtship. The couple moved to Oak Park where the bride had plenty of time to regret her rash decision.

Both Fred and his brother George worked for Daisy's father in the family business. They were advancing rapidly and the father was thinking of taking his son-in-law into partnership, reported the *Vindicator*. "But in an evil moment the boys succumbed to temptation and Fred forged his father-in-law's name to a check for $10,000. Then, taking his young wife who was ignorant of her husband's action, Fred and his brother fled to Chicago."

The trio changed their surnames to Williams and moved to Oak Park. Soon Fred was driving a coal wagon for Johnston & Co. on Lake Street while George worked in Wright & Congleton's livery stable on Marion Street.

"They might have remained in hiding forever had it not been for the young wife. Her suspicions were aroused by her husband assuming the name of Williams and forbidding her to write to her father. At last she was determined to find out for herself and so wrote to her father telling where she was living and under what name. In reply she received information of her husband's perfidy and money for transportation home. Sheriff Ward was notified by Wixom and the arrests followed. All three left for Cooperstown on the same train Friday night, the husband and his brother in irons and ignorant of the fact that his wife was in the car next to him."

Lincoln Centennial Celebrated in 1909

In 1909 the usual observances of Abraham Lincoln's birthday on February 12 took on special importance because that year marked the 100th birthday of the Great Emancipator. Throughout the nation elaborate patriotic programs were planned to mark the birth of a President who was still very much alive in the minds and hearts of Civil War Veterans and other now-elderly citizens whose lives had touched Lincoln's, however briefly.

A February, 1909 issue of the *Oak Leaves* covered the various local celebrations. "Oak Park paid its tribute to Abraham Lincoln Friday night in the largest gathering of citizens in the annals of the village. The Warrington was crowded and an overflow meeting was held in the First Baptist Church. Everyone who attended appeared to feel refreshed for a new and better civic life. On the stage was the high school chorus and orchestra of more than 150 boys and girls. In the front seats sat Veterans of the Civil War. Between these two extremes of youth and age were men and women in all periods of

Tabula *cover February 1909.*

life. The old soldiers have done their work and proved their patriotism and the others are yet to do their work."

The Phil Sheridan Post of the Grand Army of the Republic presented pictures of Lincoln to both the high school and all grammar schools. At Lowell School H. S. Kimball raised a flag used in a Massachusetts town during the War to signal news of battle to families awaiting word of their soldiers. And during a Lincoln Assembly at the high school a bronze bust of the President purchased by students in all the history classes was presented to Principal Mark Hanna.

Z. P. Hotchkiss who lived in a large Queen Anne home at 237 S. Kenilworth, had learned how to operate the telegraph as a young boy. In his job as a telegraph operator he had several historic encounters with Abraham Lincoln. His first meeting was in a dingy office in the Cherney House in Springfield in 1860 when he informed Lincoln that he had been elected President.

"My recollection of this meeting may be a little clouded by the memory of the thick tobacco smoke at the Republican headquarters of the new political party," Hotchkiss recalled. "The telegraph line direct from Washington was on a big Caton sounder that was liable to drop a dot in the yells that announced the climax of one of Lincoln's stories."

"As the final bulletin started I held up my left hand pleading for silence. Mr. Lincoln saw the signal of distress and said, 'That reminds me of a story...' and the impulsive boy telegrapher impudently said, 'Story nothing, hush up!'."

"The Great Man reached across the counter and grasping the little hand of the little boy said politely, 'I beg your pardon.' Yes, Abraham Lincoln once begged my pardon for being saucy. I held that great big strong hand as I wrote down the final figures and, getting upon my tiptoes, whispered, 'Sir, you are elected President of the United States.'"

Hotchkiss' next met Lincoln several years later at General Grant's headquarters at City Point at the close of General Sheridan's campaign in the Shenandoah Valley. Lincoln had come out to meet Grant and to learn firsthand of Sheridan's progress against the

Tabula, *February 1909, page 52.*

Confederates. Hotchkiss was working in the telegraph hut when a messenger arrived with a dispatch from Sheridan for General Grant. He had come through Confederate lines at Richmond and was gaunt, hungry and splattered with mud.

Hotchkiss requested both Grant and Lincoln come to the tent to receive the message, which turned out to be written in code. Puffing an unlit cigar, General Grant said, 'Mr. President that is government cipher. Let's go back to our lunch and let the operator get busy.'"

At the tent entrance Mr. Lincoln turned to the messenger, "Are you hungry?" he asked. "I am a private soldier, Mr. President and would not dare," the man replied. Lincoln saw his chance of cutting red tape in the army. "General Grant, have this courier commissioned a captain, so he can eat with his brother officers," he said.

"The last time I ever saw Abraham Lincoln was when he went arm-in-arm with the tall courier, with General Grant holding up the tent fly as he said to me, 'Mr. Operator, hustle.'" And Hotchkiss hustled in translating General Sheridan's official report of his great victory in the Shenandoah Valley."

Another compelling speaker who addressed the pupils of Unity Church Sunday School was Mrs. Francis Low of 415 S. Wesley. Although she was then in her nineties, Mrs. Low told her audience how, as a bride she and her husband were entertained by Lincoln and his wife Mary. Francis Low was both a friend of Lincoln's as well as one of his first clients.

"My acquaintance with Mr. and Mrs. Lincoln began at the beginning of 1860 while we were stopping for several days in Springfield on our wedding journey. Mr. and Mrs. Lincoln spent each evening with us during our stay," she recalled.

"I was completely captivated with his conversation. His great fund of knowledge upon all subjects and his humor and droll stories fascinated and charmed me. His homely features and awkwardness, which we hear so much about, made no impression upon me. I saw only the light of his intelligence and great tender heart shining through his rugged features."

Following Lincoln's nomination as the Republican candidate for President at the Wigwam Convention in Chicago an enormous political rally was held in Springfield. The Lows were invited by Lincoln to spend the day at his house. "It was a day long to be remembered. I sat at an open window on the second floor of his home where I could look right down upon Mr. and Mrs. Lincoln standing on their little front porch and so was able to hear all that was said while that immense procession filed by."

"The gaudily decorated floats and gaily gotten-up men and women on horseback and on foot, with banners of every device imaginable, axes and rails and log cabins and 'ruralites' splitting away at those rails for dear life. In fact, there was everything conceivable to typify the hardships of that masterful man through all his poverty-stricken years."

"Flags were flying and bands pealing forth their patriotic airs all along the line. As each delegation came opposite Mr. and Mrs. Lincoln they would stop and given vent to their enthusiasm by vociferous hurrahs and cheers and calls for speech! speech! speech! And all heard something which seemed to enthuse them to the bursting point."

The Glorious Fourth Observed in Both Villages

Around the turn of the century the Glorious Fourth of July was observed with day-long celebrations marked by oratory, picnics, parades, pageants and sporting events. The highlight of every Fourth of July came in the evening in both villages when families living within a certain area would combine resources for a fine display of pyrotechnics in their neighborhood. In 1894 the River Forest Women's Club organized the kind of Fourth of July celebration that typically occurred in towns and villages throughout the country. "The beautiful hickory grove of six acres fronting the Thatcher homestead on Lake Street afforded abundant room for the crowd of 500 who were in attendance," reported the *Argus*.

"A large stage covered with bunting had been erected and flags floated everywhere. The featured speaker was Miss Ada Sweet, president of the Women's Club of Chicago who gave a stirring review of patriotism in 1864 and 1894. Mrs. Buell, president of the Club, read the Declaration of Independence faultlessly. Members of the Phil Sheridan Post who were Veterans of the War came in full military dress with drum and bugle corps and were seated on the grandstand in a place of honor. The guests brought their own lunches and at noon intermission these were disposed of."

Fourth of July Collision

Two years later thousands of residents of both Oak Park and River Forest celebrated the Fourth by gathering on the South Prairie at Ridgeland Avenue and 16th Street in Berwyn to witness the deliberately planned collision of two steam locomotives and several trains belonging to the Chicago and Northern Pacific Railroad. That railroad began in Cicero to serve local manufacturers and according to an early map of Berwyn, it zigzagged through streets in both communities including 16th Street.

In its edition the week after the Fourth of July in 1896 the *Oak Park Reporter* gave a full account of the collision of the two trains meeting under a full head of steam. No mention is made of the engineers on either train and at what point they jumped clear before impact.

"The trains stood on the tracks facing each other about 30 feet apart. The engines were designated as 99 and 100. They each weighed 35 tons, both were about 16 years old and, despite their shiny coats of new paint, they would both be commonly called scrap engines."

The Baird brothers, 738 S. Lombard, celebrate the glorious Fourth.

Billboard at Harlem Avenue and Lake Street advertising 4th of July railroad collision.

"After the long but inevitable delay peculiar to such occasions the engines backed away each a mile distant. Then the crowd waited, their excitement at white heat, for the reappearance of the doomed trains. Presently the two engines came puffing toward each other as lightly and gaily as if no danger impended. Nearer and nearer they came and in a moment, Crash!

And the wreck was complete. There was a lofty pile of broken iron and splintered timbers, amid a cloud of steam and smoke. It was a fine spectacle and everyone regarded it as an entire success. The crowds ran forward and the relic hunters soon covered the pile of wreckage seeking suitable souvenirs to carry away with them."

Fireworks provide excitement

The Fourth was always made a little livelier in Oak Park because of the unlimited supply of explosives that were readily available at Sam Lee's Laundry at 122 Lake Street (now 1127). Philander Barclay recalled standing on the sidewalk in front of the Hoard Block at Marion and Lake Streets surrounded with homemade cannons purchased from Sam Lee.

"Of course, this was always on the night of the third for the village kids wanted to get the ball rolling bright and early. In those days you could hear the bang of those dangerous objects at the Des Plaines River and as far east as Central Avenue in Chicago."

A favorite trick of some kids was to throw a long string of firecrackers over the trolley wires of the Cicero and Proviso streetcars, a deed that effectively tied up traffic in both directions. Streetcars would stop on either side of the firecracker rope and both passengers and spectators would be treated to an unscheduled display of exploding fireworks.

One July in 1913 a bunch of Sam Lee's firecrackers became separated from the main string and landed on the steps of the Women's Christian Temperance Union reading room across the street from the laundryman's store on Lake Street. "As this was a day when most every kid in town would risk his life for the sake of obtaining a free bunch of these noise makers, within two seconds a bunch of lads were doing a little football stunt in the doorway to see who could grab them first," recalled Barclay. "It

Fourth of July flag-raising ceremony in River Forest.

170

was little Billy Wilder who was the lucky chap that secured these dangerous playthings and, hiding them in his hat, had enough crackers to set off the following day."

That same year Dick Scales, proprietor of a general store on Lake Street, introduced a new form of excitement on the Fourth using his ample stock of paper balloons. According to Barclay, "Balloons were sent up with cards attached giving the name and address of the sender and asking the finder to note the time when the paper bag was discovered as well as the location. The following day I received a call from a River Forest lad saying he had found my bag in the top of a tree in his yard near Park and Oak. It was a great disappointment that my bag had landed so near home, for I had hoped it would land in some farm yard as far away as Iowa or Nebraska."

By 1913 a number of local Improvement Clubs had been organized to serve the various neighborhoods that had recently sprung up on Oak Park's South Prairie. That year the South Side Improvement Club which served the southwest end of the village held their Fourth of July celebration on Harrison Street. The day began early with the ringing of the fire bell and included races, games and a tug-of-war. When darkness fell Japanese lanterns illuminated every lawn as residents sat in front of their homes with their neighbors enjoying the display of fireworks.

A few blocks further east the Jackson Improvement Club held a daylong celebration at Ridgeland and Madison Streets for everyone who lived in the southeast section of the village. Their day included a baseball game that pitted the single men against those who were married, activities for children, speeches and patriotic music performed by the Oak Park Concert Band.

A Great Thanksgiving Marked end of the Great War

Thanksgiving 1918 was an especially meaningful holiday for villagers who just a few weeks earlier had taken to the streets in jubilation upon hearing the news of Germany's surrender which marked the end of World War I. By the time the con-

The Public Press, no less than Public Office, is a Public Trust

OAK LEAVES

Once a week by the
PIONEER
PUBLISHING
COMPANY
1114 North Blvd.
Phone Oak Park 6000

Subscription price
TWO DOLLARS
AND ONE-HALF
PER ANNUM
IN ADVANCE
For a Single Copy, 5c
Back Numbers, 10c

Entered at the postoffice at Oak Park, Illinois, as mail matter of the second class

Oak Park, Illinois   Saturday, November 23, 1918.   Vol. XXXII, No. 47

MILLIONS TO SING AT 4

Oak Park and River Forest in National Chorus at High School on Thanksgiving Afternoon

"A Great National Festival of Song," the people of all the cities and towns singing at the same hour, is the plan for Thanksgiving afternoon. The hour is 4 o'clock.

Oak Park and River Forest will sing in their largest auditorium, the High School Theater, and admission is free.

There are 1,500 seats. "Come and sing your thanks for this great victory which we have won. Raise your voice in praise and thanksgiving for the many blessings our country has been made the recipient of during this last year," says the announcement.

Glenn Dillard Gunn, newly elected director of the High School Musical Department, will present the High School Glee Club of 150 members in a group of American folk songs. The Glee Club will also assist in singing community songs.

George Lee Tenney will direct the community singing, and two of the Liberty quartets will sing. Mrs. Fredericka Gerhardt Downing of Oak Park, the contralto, recently approved and engaged by Sig. Campanini and his staff of critics to be a member of his great Chicago Opera Company, will sing Allitson's "A Song of Thanksgiving" and a new song, "Joy," by Mrs. George M. Scott of Oak Park. The song received immediate approbation when sung recently in Orchestra Hall, Chicago, by Mabel Garrison. There will be a short expression of thanksgiving and praise by Col. P. E. Holp of Chicago, Chautauqua orator and lecturer.

Especial reservations will be made for Gold Star mothers and fathers and friends, and the roll will be called of those who have made the supreme sacrifice.

"Come early and have a seat, and bring the children and visitors," is the invitation. Promptly at 4 o'clock on this day of thanks great choruses and masses of people will be singing our national anthem in every village, town, and city as well as in the camps.

Naval Officer Weds in East

The marriage is announced of Miss Constance Billington of Jersey City, N. J., and Ensign George A. Gibson, formerly of Oak Park but now attached to the U. S. S. Winding Gulf, which took place in the east on October 25.

THANKSGIVING DAY

The Pastors' Union, believing that in this notable year our whole community should express its gratitude to God in one great union service, announces the following program:

Community Thanksgiving Service will be held in the First Congregational Church on Thursday evening at 9:30, Rev. William E. Barton, D. D., pastor, presiding. Music will be rendered by the choir of the First Congregational Church. The topic of the day will be "A New Thanksgiving." There will be three brief addresses, as follows:

"A New Thanksgiving for the Community and State," Rev. Charles K. Carpenter, pastor First Methodist Church.
"A New Thanksgiving for the Church," Rev. John M. Vander Meulen, D. D., pastor First Presbyterian Church.
"A New Thanksgiving for the Individual," Rev. Carl D. Case, D. D., pastor First Baptist Church.

There will be recognition of the heroic service of the men of Oak Park who have participated in the splendid fight that has brought victory to our armies and peace to the world; recognition also of the faithful service of many organizations and many hundreds of people who have contributed time and effort to the various forms of war work at home.

The offering of the day will be for the Oak Park Associated Charities.

NOTICE—A HOLIDAY

Oak Leaves office and plant will be closed all day Thursday— Thanksgiving day. Therefore news and advertising copy must be in this office on or before Wednesday night. The office will be open till 9 o'clock on Wednesday evening.

Buy War Savings Stamps. Promote thrift. If funds are not loaned the cost will be paid in taxes.

CAPTAIN SACKETT KILLED

Oak Park Graduate of West Point Falls in Battle—Four Others Reported Wounded, None Seriously

Casualty reports this week included men of this community as follows:

KILLED IN ACTION

Capt. George Wilbur Sackett, commanding Company F, Eleventh Infantry, Oct. 15; nephew of Mr. and Mrs. G. W. Trout, graduate of Oak Park High and West Point in 1917.

WOUNDED

Arlo A. Mingus, 132d Inf., Oct. 8, recovering.
David E. Weswick, Co. D, 131st Inf., recovering.
Lieut. Julian Jacobs, Inf., slightly.
Fred E. Madsen, 123d Heavy Field Artillery.

Capt. George Wilbur Sackett, commanding Company F, 11th Infantry, 5th Division, 10th Brigade, was reported killed in action on October 15. However, his wife and his relatives were not informed of the fact that he had died in action, presumably in the last great drive in the Argonne woods, until the day after the armistice was signed. His company took part in the St. Mihiel victory.

Captain Sackett graduated from Oak Park High School and afterward from West Point in the 1917 class. While at the army school he distinguished himself as an expert gymnast and swimmer, being a member of both the gymnasium and swimming teams. He was also a good boxer, a very proficient cavalryman, and received a badge as an expert rifleman. Upon graduation he was sent to Fort Oglethorpe, Chickamauga Park, Ga., where he demonstrated marked ability in making good soldiers out of raw recruits. His company was one of the two best in the regiment. While at the fort he was awarded badges for expert marksmanship and pistol shot. On July 18, 1917, he married Miss Antoinette Cooper, daughter of Mr. and Mrs. W. H. Cooper of New Rochelle, N. Y. He was commissioned a captain on August 5, 1917. He embarked for France on April 21, 1918.

In reference to the war he said: "Oh, this war is great to read about. The predominating features of this business, as I see it, are dirt, hunger, thirst; more dirt, cold rain; still more dirt and, above all, enervating fatigue. Still we exist in spite of bullets, shells, gas, long, heartbreaking hikes, and concentrated filth. Man is a tough proposition to kill. Was Sherman right? I think he didn't go far

flict ended more than 2,000 young men from both villages were in uniform, 600 men and women had served overseas in various volunteer capacities and there were few civilians who were not engaged in some type of war work on the home front.

Although the Armistice was not signed until November 11 the War officially ended on November 7 when the Hindenburg line was broken in the Battle of the Argonne in France. "Oak Park celebrated victory in the Great War on Thursday afternoon. The rumor, afterward denied, reached the community about noon and was taken as fact," reported the *Oak Leaves*.

"Within an hour the celebration was on. Stores were closed. Flags appeared as if by magic and many walked down the street carrying the colors. About 2 p.m. pupils in the grade schools 'struck' and marched in the streets waving flags. People stopped to shake hands and everyone appeared to feel a great happiness that the terror began by Germany in 1914 was ended."

Thanksgiving Celebration

A great National Festival of Song was held in cities and towns across the country on Thanksgiving Day to celebrate the Armistice signed just a few weeks earlier. The 1,500-seat Oak Park and River Forest High school auditorium was filled for a celebration in which Glenn Dillard Gunn, director of the music department, led the audience and Glee Club in song.

A special place of honor was given to Gold Star mothers and fathers and the roll was solemnly called with the names of the young men who made the supreme sacrifice. Among them were two men who perished in the closing days of the War. They were Lt. Frank Sturtevant who died in action in Verdun and Rev. Hedley Cooper, rector of St. Christopher's Episcopal Church at East Avenue and Adams Street who served in the front line as a chaplain. The previous June, Rev. Cooper had come back to Oak Park to marry his childhood sweetheart Ruth Ketcham of 412 Wesley.

Shortly before his death Cooper wrote his father: "I am in the trenches, living in a dugout and going up into the front line every day. War is certainly all that Sherman said it was, and then some, but it has its compen-

sations and in the last analysis one always has God and what a cheerful and consoling truth this is. God always with you in dugout and trench, on bright days and stormy nights."

Henry Austin, Jr., chairman of the Patriotic and Defense League, urged villagers to attend Thanksgiving church services. "Do we fully realize that in the 300 years since Thanksgiving Day was established there has never been a time when we have greater cause for Thanksgiving than at present. This country has had two great wars before, but no war which daily took such a toll in human life as this terrible struggle. And ending as it does at the time of year when we are accustomed to set aside a day to consider the good things God has given us, why cannot we hold the day especially sacred and give the church services such an attendance that it will be a historical event in the annals of Oak Park and River Forest?"

Although the guns were silenced the War Savings Drive was still collecting money. In fact, a new campaign to raise $800,000 began Thanksgiving Day. According to Mrs. L. E. Yager, chairwoman of the campaign, "If the nation does not invest in War Savings, it will have to make up the deficit by raising taxes, as the financial authorities based their estimates upon a certain amount from War Savings."

In the euphoria following the Armistice, the local newspapers were filled with accounts of the heroic deeds of young men from both communities who served in the War. Lt. Alan Winslow, son of Mr. and Mrs. William Winslow of River Forest received the Croix de Guerre from the French government for being the first U. S. airman to down an enemy plane in France. Winslow, a graduate of Oak Park and River Forest High School, was a student at Yale when the War began. Along with many of his friends he enlisted in the Navy and later became an Army flyer trained by the French Corps. (Winslow's parents are best known for their massive Prairie Style home on Auvergne Place designed by Frank Lloyd Wright in 1894.)

James Kearins of 317 S. Elmwood in Oak Park was one of the many unrecognized heroes of the War. Serving as a volunteer ambulance driver he ferried badly wounded soldiers from the front to a base hospital behind the line. On one occasion he was forced to place his patients in a dugout to save them from the rain of shells falling around them. Darkness fell but he could not sleep hearing the moans of the suffering men. "Is there anything I can do for you?" he asked. "Try and sing something funny," came the reply.

So Kearins sang. He sang every funny song he had ever heard and when he got through he told them every joke he knew. When daylight came one wounded man tore a red ribbon from his tunic and gave it to Kearins. "This decoration belongs to you, not me," he said. "You're the bravest man I've ever seen."

Today many villagers are familiar with the Charles Roth American Legion Post but have no idea who it was named for. Shortly before the Armistice was signed the *Oak Leaves* reported: "Major Charles Roth of the 108th Engineers is on his way home from France. Mrs. Roth this week received a telegram from her husband with the brief message: 'Coming home to be promoted'."

"Major Roth, who has been in France since May, has seen some hot action recently

Private Edward Robbins (second from right) with his comrades at Camp Grant in 1917 prior to going overseas.

northwest of Verdun. A dispatch to a Chicago paper told of the feat of the 108th Engineers in building a bridge over a marsh, which allowed the infantry, artillery and ammunition to pass over. The Yanks met the Prussians when they crossed over and one of the decisive actions of the offensive took place. Major Roth was in the thick of it, and he has sent home two helmets worn by the Kaiser's crack troops as souvenirs of the occasion."

Even after the War had ended sentiment against the "Huns" and all things German persisted. The result was that many loyal Americans with German surnames were forced to change them. In River Forest John von Pien, whose father came from Germany and fought for the Union in the Civil War and whose son was a U. S. naval officer, went to court to have his name legally changed to "Pine." "I desire my friends and neighbors to know that we are thoroughly American by birth and by all the loyalty we have to give," said the former Mr. von Pien.

Ghosts of Christmas Past

When Joseph Kettlestrings built a small cabin on Lake Street in 1835, Christmas was a legal holiday in only one state. Americans celebrated the day quietly and Joseph and Betty Kettlestrings, devout Methodists, were no exception. There were no other settlers in the immediate vicinity and so, as the prairie wolves broke the cold silence with their howls and the snow piled up around their cabin, Joseph and Betty and their children most likely observed the first Christmas in their new home with Bible readings and perhaps the exchange of small handmade gifts.

After the Civil War Oak Park's population increased dramatically as Union Veterans such as Anson Hemingway settled in the community which, in the 1870s was still little more than a country village. Years later Hemingway recalled these Christmas' past:

"On Christmas Eve everyone used to pile in the sleigh and drive to the Christmas celebration, which was held in the old schoolhouse on the Austin property at Lake and Forest," he said. "The village had a population of about 1,000 and my wife and another lady, usually Mrs. James Scoville, always called on every newcomer. So everyone knew everyone else when we got to the party. Children spoke pieces and we had a tree and presents for everyone."

Hemingway also recalled a holiday sport that more closely resembled shooting fish in a barrel. "The men assembled on Christmas Day at north Oak Park Avenue near Augusta and shot turkeys. The fowls were boxed so the marksman had only to take aim. If he landed a bullet in the neck, he could take the bird home. Shooting prairie chickens on Madison Street was also a popular sport."

January 1, 1911, 12:45 a.m. Guests at "Hard Times" party given by the Ollier family in River Forest welcome the New Year.

Christmas cards were not widely used and gifts and small remembrances were exchanged instead. Children and their parents went from house to house on Christmas to personally deliver their greetings and leave small gifts. Families and their friends usually gathered around fireplaces after a sumptuous Christmas dinner and visited while the little ones popped corn and played games.

Hemingway concluded his look back with a poignant observation: "Families were bigger in those days. We had more snow and cold weather, we worked harder, we knew each other better and we were happier."

Christmas remained a low-key affair for the next several decades. A week before Christmas in 1897 the *Oak Park Times* noted, "Oak Park will have a quiet home Christmas. Children will be remembered at home and in the churches, Santa will visit every house where there are boys and girls. And the Christmas dinners with the festive turkey and stockings full of candy, the green trees, the graceful festoons and picturesque holly, all will be seen in Oak Park homes. There will also be a morning delivery from the Oak Park post office on Christmas day. Arrangements have been made for a wagon delivery during the holidays of such packages that are too large for the carriers."

By the turn of the century Christmas was more widely celebrated with family and friends in homes, community halls and churches in a spirit of camaraderie and friendship. Modest gifts were exchanged and "shop till you drop" was an expression yet to be coined.

Quite the contrary. Merchants did not advertise their holiday goods or foods until just a week or two before Christmas. In 1890 the first advertisements for the holidays did not appear in the *Vindicator* until December 13. Typical was the tasteful advertisement placed by Miss C. Druhl of 129 Holley Court who had rented a portion of Senne's Furniture Store at 108 Lake for just two weeks so she could offer villagers "a handsome stock of holiday goods, including tidies, baskets, pockets, handkerchiefs, cases, glass boxes, toilet sets, sofa cushions, rib-

bons, yarns and fancy embroideries. Ladies will please call and examine."

Albert Burgess who owned the Avenue Bakery at 140 Lake Street was the purveyor of holiday decorations including popcorn strings, penny candy canes, tinsel, glass balls, wreaths, holly, mistletoe, candles and, most important, fresh Christmas trees delivered to the customer's home. His bakery was also the place for housewives, overwhelmed with holiday chores, to go for fresh-baked fruit cakes, plum puddings, macaroons and layer cakes.

However, after the holidays some local merchants couldn't help but take a swipe at their competitors in the city. "Oak Park merchants claim to have had a good holiday trade. They complain bitterly, however, of The Fair and the Boston Store, which are slowly, but surely, killing the retail business. The time will come when people will be forced to go to these cheap stores after their home merchants are driven out of business and, except for special sales, the purchasers pay a good price for an inferior article."

Because of the danger of fire Christmas trees were usually not brought into the house until Christmas Eve. And when the candles on these trees were finally lit, a pail of sand was always within reach to extinguish any fire that might erupt. The actual lighting of the candles on a decorated and highly flammable tree occurred only once or twice during the season.

BIBLIOGRAPHY

Brooke, Lee, *Yesterday When I Was Younger*, Oak Park and River Forest Oral History, (privately printed), 1989

Butters, George, *Early Ridgeland*, (typewritten and undated)

Cook, May Estelle, *Little Old Oak Park*, (privately printed), 1961

Danegger, Anne N., *Early Austin: From Its Beginning Until Annexation to Chicago in 1899*, Austin Friends of the Library, 1944

Financing An Empire: A History of Banking In Illinois, Vol. III, S. J. Clarke Publishing Co., 1926

Furbeck, Elizabeth Porter, *Personal Reminiscences of Pioneer Life*, (typewritten) Paper presented to the Society of the Pioneers of Chicago, May 25, 1898.

Gale, Charles Bolles, Editor, *A Report of the Committee of Early Residents of Oak Park and River Forest First Presented at the Annual Meeting of the Historical Society of Oak Park and River Forest*, (typewritten), May 21, 1971

Gale, Edwin O., *Reminiscences of Oak Park, Galewood and Vicinity*, (typewritten), 1898

Guarino, Jean, *Oak Park: A Pictorial History*, G. Bradley Publishing, Inc., 1988

Guarino, Jean, Docent Manual, Pleasant Home, May, 1987

Halley, William *Pictorial Oak Park*, (privately printed) 1898

Hausman, Harriet, *Reflections: A History of River Forest*, (privately printed), 1975

Hoagland, Gertrude Fox, ed., *Historical Survey of Oak Park, Illinois*, Federal Works Progress Administration Project #9516, Oak Park Public Library, 1937.

LeGacy, Arthur Evans, *Improvers and Preservers: A History of Oak Park, Illinois. 1833-1940*, PhD. Dissertation, University of Chicago, 1967

Miller, J. C, *Early Days in Oak Park*, Undated monograph compiled from histories written by William Halley and John Lewis

Nature's Choicest Spot: A Guide to Forest Home and German Waldheim Cemeteries, The Historical Society of Oak Park and River Forest, 1998

Oak Park and River Forest High School 1873-1976, Osla Graphics, Oak Park, 1976

Poplett, Carolyn O. with Mary Ann Porucznik, *The Gentle Force: A History of The Nineteenth Century Woman's Club of Oak Park*, A & H Lithoprint, 1988

Sanford, Marcelline Hemingway, *At the Hemingways*, University of Idaho Press, Centennial Edition, 1999.

Willard, Frances, *Glimpses of Fifty Years,* Woman's Temperance Publishing Association, 1889

NEWSPAPERS (various issues)

Oak Park Vindicator (1883-1885, 1890-1892, 1894-1901)

Oak Park Reporter (1887-1894), 1896-1897, 1899-1902)

Oak Park Argus (1900-1902)

Oak Park Reporter-Argus (1904-1906)

Oak Leaves (1902-1917)

INDEX